Vol. 97

No. 4

Bib
and Illuminator

FALL QUARTER **September, October, November 2025**

God Is "All" That

UNIT 1: God Is Always Present

UNIT 2: God Is All-Knowing

UNIT 3: God Is All-Powerful

Editor in Chief: James M. Leonard, Ph.D.
Managing Editor: Michelle Birtasevic
Edited and published quarterly by
LIFESTONE MINISTRIES
UNION GOSPEL PRESS
Rev. W. B. Musselman, Founder

ISBN 978-1-64495-795-0

LOOKING AHEAD

One of the greatest joys of studying the Scriptures is learning more about the character of God. This quarter will survey three of God's many attributes.

In the first unit, we see that God is always present. The best place to start is at the beginning, when God created the heavens and earth (lesson 1; Gen. 1:1-13). Then we move to a New Testament passage for information about Jesus' involvement at Creation (lesson 2; Col. 1:15-23). There, we also see that Jesus upholds all things by His power. Returning to the Old Testament in lesson 3, we go to Jeremiah 23:18-24, which helps us understand God's greatness in relation to His people. He is a God who is both far away and near to them. We complete the first unit with Psalm 139:1-16 (lesson 4), which shows how God knows and cares for us and is always with us.

In the second unit, we investigate four passages that reveal that God knows everything. God revealed to Pharaoh the future famine that would strike Egypt (lesson 5; Gen. 41:25-36). In Acts 4:32 through 5:11 (lesson 6), God's knowledge of Ananias and Sapphira's thoughts led to their undoing after they lied to God and the church.

Jesus exhibited the same knowledge as the Father in His encounter with Nathanael (lesson 7; John 1:43-51). Jesus again demonstrated His divine knowledge by revealing private information about the Samaritan woman (lesson 8; John 4:5-19, 28-29).

The third unit is dedicated to God's great power. In 1 Corinthians 2:6-16 (lesson 9), we see God's ability to provide spiritual wisdom to believers. Then we behold God's power to deliver His people through the Red Sea in Exodus 14:10-22 (lesson 10). Jesus showed the same power over nature as the Father when He calmed a raging storm (lesson 11; Mark 4:35-41).

God's power extends to cover more than natural events. In lesson 12, Jesus encountered a demon-possessed man (Mark 5:1-20). The man had tremendous strength, and no one could restrain him. But Jesus cast out the demons, and the man was restored to normal. In our final lesson, Isaiah 40:12-17, we find the answer to the rhetorical question, *Who is like God*? Through Isaiah's words, God provided comfort to His people by reminding them of His great power, knowledge, and sovereignty that He is willing to unleash on their behalf. We serve a mighty God!

—Glenn Weaver

PLEASE NOTE: Fundamental, sound doctrine is the objective of LifeStone Ministries, Union Gospel Press. The writers are prayerfully selected for their Bible knowledge and willingness to submit to the Spirit of Truth, each writing in his own style as enlightened by the Holy Spirit. At best we know in part only. "They received the word with all readiness of mind, and searched the scriptures daily, whether those things were so" (Acts 17:11).

EDITORIAL

GOD IS ALL-KNOWING

TOM GREENE

We can be amazed by mental feats. Alexander Alekhine, a world chess champion in the early twentieth century, once declared a forced checkmate in ten moves during a game he played *blindfolded.* The statistician Nate Silver rocketed briefly from obscurity into the spotlight in 2008 when he correctly predicted how all 538 electoral votes would be cast in the presidential election. Millions fill out brackets each March, hoping to be the first person to perfectly predict how the college basketball tournament will go, inevitably failing.

But God's knowledge makes all those achievements look laughably small. God is *omniscient,* meaning He is all-knowing. He not only knows everything about the events and thoughts of people in the present, He knows everything about the past. He knows everything about the future. He even knows everything that *would have happened* if things had gone differently!

God knows everything that has ever happened. In John 4, the Samaritan woman declared to her neighbors that Jesus told her everything she had ever done (John 4:29). He completely knew her past. The Lord's understanding is infinite (Ps. 147:5). Nothing is hidden from His sight (Heb. 4:13).

Not only does God know the past, but He also knows the future. In Genesis 41, God warned Pharaoh through a dream about a coming famine and sent Joseph to interpret it. Joseph was not able to do this because he had special magical abilities, but because God revealed it to him. Likewise, Daniel declared that he was able to interpret dreams, not because of his own natural ability—for no human has such ability—but because God reveals mysteries (Dan. 2:27-28).

God knows about future events such as famines because He is in control of the weather. He knows what we dream about because He is the one who oversees our dreams. His knowledge is not the result of careful observation and calculation of probabilities. It is the absolute certainty of One in charge of the world.

Not only does the Lord know about events taking place in the world, but He knows about the thoughts and emotions taking place inside us. Jesus knew about Nathanael's character when He first met him (John 1:43-51), and Ananias and Sapphira could not lie to God (Acts 4:32—5:11). Scripture is clear that God looks at our hearts and that He knows everything that comes into our minds (1 Sam. 16:7; Ezek. 11:5)! He knows all our ways and everything about us (Ps. 139:1-6).

Not only does He know everything about the past, present, and future; God knows what might have been! In Matthew 11, Jesus declared woe upon places where He had preached and said that if Tyre, Sidon, and Sodom had heard His preaching and seen His mighty works, they would have repented (vss. 20-22). Jesus knew not only what was, but what would have been! Likewise, God warned David what would happen if he remained in a certain city while Saul was pursuing him, and so David fled (1 Sam. 23:9-13). It is no wonder that the Bible says God knows everything (1 John 3:20). He not only knows what is, but what *would* be.

(Editorial continued on page 186)

SCRIPTURE LESSON TEXT

GEN. 1:1 In the beginning God created the heaven and the earth.

2 And the earth was without form, and void; and darkness *was* upon the face of the deep. And the Spirit of God moved upon the face of the waters.

3 And God said, Let there be light: and there was light.

4 And God saw the light, that *it was* good: and God divided the light from the darkness.

5 And God called the light Day, and the darkness he called Night. And the evening and the morning were the first day.

6 And God said, Let there be a firmament in the midst of the waters, and let it divide the waters from the waters.

7 And God made the firmament, and divided the waters which *were* under the firmament from the waters which *were* above the firmament: and it was so.

8 And God called the firmament Heaven. And the evening and the morning were the second day.

9 And God said, Let the waters under the heaven be gathered together unto one place, and let the dry *land* appear: and it was so.

10 And God called the dry *land* Earth; and the gathering together of the waters called he Seas: and God saw that *it was* good.

11 And God said, Let the earth bring forth grass, the herb yielding seed, *and* the fruit tree yielding fruit after his kind, whose seed *is* in itself, upon the earth: and it was so.

12 And the earth brought forth grass, *and* herb yielding seed after his kind, and the tree yielding fruit, whose seed *was* in itself, after his kind: and God saw that *it was* good.

13 And the evening and the morning were the third day.

NOTES

In the Beginning

Lesson Text: Genesis 1:1-13

Related Scriptures: Psalms 8:1-9; 104:24-30; Job 38:1-41; Isaiah 42:5-9; 2 Corinthians 4:6-7

TIME: unknown — PLACE: heaven and earth

GOLDEN TEXT—"And the earth was without form, and void; and darkness was upon the face of the deep. And the Spirit of God moved upon the face of the waters" (Genesis 1:2).

Introduction

This quarter's lessons will focus on some of the attributes of God. One of those attributes is that God is always present (sometimes called "omnipresence"). He is both present everywhere and present at all times throughout history. There has never been a time when God did not exist, and there will never be a time when God does not exist. He has no beginning point or birth and no endpoint. God has eternally existed in the three Persons of the Trinity: the Father, the Son, and the Holy Spirit.

Since God is always present, He is always near to His people. In all situations, believers can be confident that He both knows what is going on and is present with them. There is no problem they face that He does not know about or has not conquered before.

Our first lesson on God's omnipresence fittingly begins with Genesis 1, which records the beginning of all creation and presents God existing before the creation of the world and anything in it. We are not told what God did before that; we are simply told that He started everything at the beginning by creating the heaven and the earth.

LESSON OUTLINE

1. **GOD CREATES—Gen. 1:1-2**
2. **GOD SPEAKS—Gen. 1:3-13**

Exposition: Verse by Verse

GOD CREATES

GEN. 1:1 In the beginning God created the heaven and the earth.

2 And the earth was without form, and void; and darkness was upon the face of the deep. And the Spirit of God moved upon the face of the waters.

{Creating was the first action God performed in Genesis 1.}[Q1] That set the stage for what followed. God completely controlled the situation in this chapter, with every action verb attributed either to His direct act or to His command for His created entities to act.

{That is significant because it declares God as the Creator of all things.}[Q2] Adding to the effect, the text almost always explicitly lists God as the subject of a verb, rather than using a pronoun. For example, instead of the text saying, "He created," it explicitly says, "God created" (or performed some other action) in almost every instance.

Only the Creator deserves the worship and praise of humanity. With a constant refrain of God's actions, Moses let his ancient audience know that God, not the gods of the surrounding nations, created the world. Therefore, all allegiance is due to Him, not the false gods. Although the Israelites were subject to Egypt for a time, the Egyptian gods did not overthrow the one true God. Rather, He is the true Creator and Ruler, as demonstrated by His defeat of the Egyptian gods during the ten plagues (cf. Ex. 12:12).

After its initial creation, the earth was "without form, and void" (Gen. 1:2). {That phrase occurs only one other time in the Old Testament, referring to an inhospitable desert that is unproductive and therefore uninhabitable (Jer. 4:23).}[Q3] A similar phrase occurs in Isaiah 34:11, referring to a wasteland uninhabited by humans and fit only for wild animals. {In its beginning stage, the earth was empty, unproductive, and not a fit environment for life as we know it. God addressed that problem by forming the earth and filling it with vegetation and living creatures.}[Q4]

Before those creative acts, however, the Spirit was moving over the waters, preparing the earth for life. {That may not seem significant, but the Spirit's initial work over the waters sends a strong monotheistic message. God alone, from beginning to end, brought about the created world. No other gods contributed to the process.}[Q5]

GOD SPEAKS

3 And God said, Let there be light: and there was light.

4 And God saw the light, that it was good: and God divided the light from the darkness.

5 And God called the light Day, and the darkness he called Night. And the evening and the morning were the first day.

6 And God said, Let there be a firmament in the midst of the waters, and let it divide the waters from the waters.

7 And God made the firmament, and divided the waters which were under the firmament from the waters which were above the firmament: and it was so.

8 And God called the firmament Heaven. And the evening and the morning were the second day.

9 And God said, Let the waters under the heaven be gathered together unto one place, and let the dry land appear: and it was so.

10 And God called the dry land Earth; and the gathering together of the waters called he Seas: and God saw that it was good.

11 And God said, Let the earth bring forth grass, the herb yielding seed, and the fruit tree yielding fruit after his kind, whose seed is in itself, upon the earth: and it was so.

12 And the earth brought forth grass, and herb yielding seed after his kind, and the tree yielding fruit, whose seed was in itself, after his kind: and God saw that it was good.

13 And the evening and the morning were the third day.

God makes light (Gen. 1:3-5). It was in this initial, premature environment of creation that God spoke for the first time in recorded Scripture. That is the second action verb that God performed. He uttered a simple command, only two words in Hebrew—"Let there be light." Immediately, there was light. From the very beginning, creation listened to His voice. Would mankind, which He would soon create, do the same?

Verse 4 records the third and fourth verbs that God performed. He both saw and separated. After creating the light, God saw that it was good. {In Genesis 1, God's seeing is always followed immediately by calling something He made "good."}[Q6] The work of His good creation was truly glorious to behold.

God then divided, or separated, the light from the darkness. Dividing splits two things that were initially connected. God would again separate two entities on day 2, splitting the waters above and below to create the sky.

After separating light from darkness, God called the light "Day" and the darkness "Night" (vs. 5). *Calling* is the fifth different verb God performed in Genesis 1. This verb is slightly different from the verb "said." When the text uses "God said," it immediately follows with direct speech. Here no direct speech is recorded. The text simply reports that God called the light "Day" and the darkness "Night"; it does not record Him saying the words "Day" or "Night."

Now that light and darkness had been separated, there could be an evening and a morning. Day 1 of Creation concluded here. But day 1 hints at a pattern. If the passage of evening to morning marked one day, or the first day, then there would likely be further days. Indeed, as one continues to read Genesis 1, one immediately notices the pattern of different days of Creation. That pattern continues into the sixth day at the end of the chapter. The seventh day breaks the pattern as the text never records the statement "And the evening and the morning were the seventh day."

God makes the firmament (Gen. 1:6-8). The second day of Creation began like the rest of the days in chapter 1, with a command by God recorded in direct speech. If you were to look ahead at the beginning of each of the remaining Creation days in chapter 1, you would notice that they all begin with "and God said." That is another pattern. But notice something else. That phrase is followed by direct speech so that every day begins with a command by God. Every day has at least one speech, except the seventh day. {Yet again the seventh day breaks a pattern, indicating that it is the climax of the Creation week.}[Q7]

But there is something different about the speech on day 2 when compared with that of day 1. The speech on day 2 is much longer than the two-word speech on day 1. That demonstrates a further pattern. As the Creation week progresses, the speeches become longer, more numerous, or more complex. At first glance, it might seem that days 4 and 5 do not follow that pattern, so those days will be discussed further.

Day 4 records one speech containing twenty Hebrew words, while days 3 and 5 record two speeches. Day 3's first speech contains eight Hebrew words, and the second contains fourteen Hebrew words. Day 5's first speech contains eleven Hebrew words, and the second contains eight. Although the total number of words used on days 4 and 5 is less than that of day 3, both days 4 and 5 show further complexity over the previous days. Day 4's single speech is longer than either of the speeches on day 3.

Further, the speech on day 4 contains two explicit purpose statements, while none of the previous days contained any. The first purpose is that the created luminaries would be "for signs, and for seasons, and for days, and years" (vs. 14). The second is that the created luminaries would be for lighting the firmament or expanse in order to shed light on the earth (vs. 15).

In addition, although the two speeches on day 5 contain fewer combined words than those of day 3, day 5 uses a special introduction for its second speech. All the previous speeches in Genesis 1 begin the same way—"and God said." Day 5's second speech begins with "and God blessed them" (vs. 22). That difference indicates a heightening in the pattern. The heightening continues into day 6, which contains four speeches (including one introduced by "and God blessed them") and a purpose statement (vs. 29).

One might wonder, What is the point of the patterns and progressions? They point toward the seventh day, which breaks the pattern. On the seventh day, God rested from the work He accomplished on the previous days. The patterns and progressions also indicate that God was saving the best for last. His last act of Creation was human beings. Humans are the crown of God's creation.

Returning to day 2, we notice that after God's command to create the firmament or expanse by separating the waters, there is a narrative that records that this happened (vss. 6-7). The immediate recording of what God commanded is similar to day 1. God commanded the light to appear, and the narrative records that light appeared (vs. 3).

That pattern continues throughout the Creation week. Sometimes God's speech is followed by a lengthy narrative recording that God's command took place. At other times, God's command is followed by the statement "and it was so." Every speech in Genesis 1 is followed by an indication that what God commanded took place, except for the two blessings (cf. vss. 22, 28). That may be because the blessings are for God's creation to be fruitful and multiply. The normal means for procreation would take time. It would not be instantaneous as when God commanded His creative acts to take place. The reader has to wait and see whether God's creation would obey His voice by producing offspring, filling the earth, and, in the case of mankind, exercising dominion over the earth.

Day 2 records the sixth verb that God performed in Genesis 1. After commanding the waters to separate so that the expanse could appear, the narrative records that "God made the firmament" (vs. 7). He also separated the waters—using the same verb as in verse 4. When the waters separated, part went above the firmament, and the rest went below the firmament. God then called the firmament "Heaven," or sky, using the same verb as in verse 5.

The separation of the waters above and below recalls the creation myths of ancient Mesopotamia. In the Babylonian myth *Enuma Elish*, the god Marduk made the waters above and below from the carcass of the water monster Tiamat. God, however, did not do battle with the sea in Genesis 1. Instead, He spoke, made the firmament, and separated the waters. No battle was necessary, for nothing could oppose Him.

God makes the dry land (Gen 1:9-13). On day 3, God commanded the waters below the heaven to gather together and the dry land to appear. God called the dry land "Earth" and the waters "Seas." In His second speech on day 3, God commanded that the earth sprout vegetation and fruit trees and that these would produce according to their kind.

In the one speech on day 4, God commanded lights to appear and to separate the day from the night. {Since God created the day and night on the first day, days 1 and 4 are connected. On day 4, God created the lights to rule over what He created on day 1. Similarly, days 2 and 3 relate to days 5 and 6, respectively. On day 2, God created the firmament and the waters above and below. On day 5, God made water creatures and birds that filled the waters below and the sky. On day 3, God made the dry land and vegetation. On day 6, God created land animals and humans. They were to fill the earth, and humanity was supposed to rule over the rest of creation. The days of Creation recount how God both formed the earth and filled it so that the earth would be a proper habitation where life could exist.}[Q8] Through His speech, God brought life to the world and set up humanity to rule over the earth.

God created humanity as the pinnacle of Creation. As the Creation week progressed, the created beings became more complex and could accomplish more and more activity.

On the first day, God made day and night. On the second day, He made the sky, which separated the waters above and beneath. On the third day, God created the earth. He gave the earth the ability to sprout vegetation, including plants and trees that could reproduce after their kind. On the fourth day, God created lights that marked the seasons and years. He also made the great lights to rule the day and night, to shed light on the earth, and to separate the light and darkness. On the fifth day, God created water animals and birds and gave them the ability to reproduce and fill the earth. On the sixth day, God created land animals that could reproduce after their kind. As the last act of Creation, God made humans.

Unlike the previously created beings, God made humans in His image. He gave them the ability to reproduce and commanded them to subdue the earth. {As the pinnacle of Creation, humans could perform nearly all of the basic functions of the previously created beings and could rule over all the created world, including all of its inhabitants.}[Q9]

{Creating humans as the pinnacle of Creation is very different from other ancient creation stories at the time. In some of the Egyptian myths, humans were created by accident, and in the major Mesopotamian creation myth, the gods made humans to serve them and meet their needs. The Bible's account is much different; it gives dignity to humanity.}[Q10]

—James Frohlich

QUESTIONS

1. What was the first action God performed in Genesis 1?
2. Why is it significant that God either performed or commanded every action verb in Genesis 1?
3. In its only other occurrence in the Old Testament, what does the phrase "without form, and void" refer to?
4. What did God do to the earth so that it was no longer without form and void?
5. What is significant about the Spirit of God moving over the face of the waters?
6. In Genesis 1, what always immediately followed God seeing something?
7. What is significant about the seventh day breaking many of the patterns of the other days of the Creation week?
8. How did days 1, 2, and 3 of Creation relate to days 4, 5, and 6?
9. What benefits are given to humanity as the pinnacle of Creation?
10. How does the Bible's portrayal of the creation of humanity differ from that of other ancient stories of creation?

—James Frohlich

Preparing to Teach the Lesson

Christians agree that God created the universe. People might disagree on the details, but we affirm that He spoke everything into existence. Have you ever wondered what things were like *before* Genesis 1?

This new quarter is all about God. Who is He? What is He like? Why did He create us? Why does He love us? How is He different from us? Is there anything He cannot do?

TODAY'S AIM

Facts: to know that God has always existed and that He is the Creator.

Principle: to understand that God creates all things good and has all power.

Application: to live each day honoring Almighty God.

INTRODUCING THE LESSON

Many people have questions about God, but they try to find the answers in all the wrong places. Ask for examples of places where people find false or incorrect answers to their questions about God.

Our lesson today is from the first page of our Bibles. The central figure in Genesis 1 is our Creator God. History has always been *His story*.

DEVELOPING THE LESSON

1. God existed before everything (Gen. 1:1). God has always been God. He did not have a beginning and will never cease to be God. Before anything existed, God was God. The words "In the beginning" do not give us a date for creation, because time did not exist yet. Think about that! God is completely self-reliant and does not need anything to live. Before time, space, energy, and matter, God was the same God He is today. He is Lord over all creation not only because He existed before everything and everyone, but also because He created everything and everyone.

The reference to heaven and earth does not limit God's reach to those two places. This phrase means the entire universe and everything in it.

Most know the story of Job from the Bible. Do you remember when God rebuked Job for his attitude by asking Job where he was when the earth's foundation was laid and its dimensions established (Job 38)? The One who commands the ocean's waves is the one in charge, not us. All creation—including every one of us—must humble itself before the Creator King.

2. The earth used to be different (Gen. 1:2-8). With the first verse setting the stage with a firm, short statement, we read the description of what is almost indescribable. When we close our eyes and think of the planet Earth, we picture a blue globe with brown and green continents. We cannot draw a picture of the earth without any shape or form at all, but we believe it was once like that. Again, this shows the power of God to create something out of nothing. Light did not exist in verse 2, so there was darkness. But even when the earth had no form and there was no light, the Spirit of God was moving.

In verse 3, we read how God created the universe as we know it—He spoke it into existence. "God said, Let there be light: and there was light." The God we meet in Genesis 1 has all power. As we continue to read, we see Him divide the light from darkness and call the light day and the darkness night. Consider what the apostle Paul said about light in 2 Corinthians 4:6-7. The light shines out of the darkness and into our hearts "to give the light of the knowledge of the glory of God in the face of Jesus Christ." This was the first day.

On the second day, God created "the firmament." Some have described the firmament as an expanse, space, vault, or dome. As we read verses 6-8 together, we see a separation between the water on the earth and the water in the sky. This separation created the area where we live (in between the earth and its outer atmosphere). When we read about all this water, it may cause us to think about the story of Noah and the Flood that occurs just a few pages later.

God created the world in perfect harmony and balance. We have gone through droughts and seen the power of flooding water. Only God is creative enough to create the great, big, beautiful sky. Consider the words of Isaiah 42:5-9. God created everything and gave us breath. This same God wants us to love Him and live for Him. Amazing!

3. Everything we know was created by Him (Gen. 1:9-13). On the third day, God created the land and everything that grows on it. The Bible describes the creation of land as God gathering the water into large oceans so that the absence of water on the surface of the earth exposed the land. On day 3, God created grass, herbs, trees, and their seeds. In verse 11 we also see God creating the process of reproduction. Grass, herbs, and trees all make their own seeds, so more can be made naturally. This intelligent design is seen in most living things, including us. He does not have to come back down every spring to create new grass, herbs, and trees. He created living things to make more living things.

"After his kind" means we reproduce our kind. Grass creates grass seed, which makes more grass. Herbs come from herbs, trees from trees. When you step outside, take a few moments to look around at all the wonderful things God has made.

ILLUSTRATING THE LESSON

Genesis 1 teaches that before the first day, there was nothing. On the first day, God said, "Let there be light," and there was light! Only God can make anything and everything out of nothing.

CONCLUDING THE LESSON

Sometimes we pray small prayers hoping that things will work out. Instead of doubting, let us boldly call out to the One who existed before anything else. Our Heavenly Father created all that exists by speaking the words "Let there be." Since He did that, we know that He can do *anything* according to His will. We join with the psalmist by saying, "O Lord, how manifold are thy works! In wisdom hast thou made them all: the earth is full of thy riches" (Ps. 104:24).

ANTICIPATING THE NEXT LESSON

In our lesson today, we read about God the Father speaking the universe into existence and the Spirit moving upon the face of the waters. What about Jesus? Next week we will explore Colossians 1, which says God the Son made all things and is holding the universe together. Read John 1 and Colossians 1 as we prepare for this lesson.

—Adam Clagg

PRACTICAL POINTS

1. When tempted to doubt God's goodness or power, we can remember that He is the Creator of all things (Gen. 1:1).
2. The Holy Spirit prepared the earth for God's creative acts by moving over the face of the waters (vs. 2). The Holy Spirit also prepares our hearts to accept God's Word (cf. 1 Cor. 2:12-13).
3. Just as the creation immediately obeyed God when He spoke things into existence (Gen. 1:3), so should we when He guides us to do something.
4. We can take comfort in the fact that we are part of God's good creation (vss. 4-5; cf. vss. 26-31).
5. God limits His creation. He kept the waters in place and limited agricultural production to that which was "after [its] kind" (vss. 6-13).

—James Frohlich

RESEARCH AND DISCUSSION

1. According to the Bible, did anything exist before God began to create the world (cf. Gen. 1:1; Heb. 11:3)?
2. Which Persons of the Trinity were involved in creating the world (cf. Gen. 1:1-2; John 1:1-3)?
3. Why do you think the earth was initially created without form and void (Gen. 1:2)?
4. Why does Genesis 1 record God commanding something to be created and then contain a narrative stating that it happened (cf. vss. 3, 6-7, 9, 11-12)?
5. Is there any part of God's creation that you do not fully appreciate?

—James Frohlich

ILLUSTRATED HIGH POINTS

In the beginning God created (Gen. 1:1)

In the creation myth *Enuma Elish*, Marduk, one of the Babylonian gods, had to fight against the waters of chaos when creating the world. But God did not do so in Genesis 1, for nothing can resist God. He is the unrivaled Creator. The outcome is never in doubt when God participates.

When He spoke, all resistance ended. The waters fled to their place, and creation listened to the sound of His voice. Although the Bible and the ancient creation myths have plenty of differences, one thing they hold in common is that the creator deserves worship and obedience. If that held for the false gods of Egypt and Mesopotamia, how much more would it hold for the one true God, who actually created the world through the sound of His voice?

And it was so (vss. 7, 9, 11)

When the first humans rebelled against God through their sin, they acted inconsistently with their nature as created beings. When God created the firmament in the waters, it was just as He wanted, for "it was so." When God commanded the dry land to appear, "it was so." When God commanded that plants and trees be made, "it was so." Everything in creation obeyed God. The waters, the stars, the earth, the sea creatures, the land animals—everything followed His commands, except for the pinnacle of His creation. Mankind rebelled, bringing punishment and death. Sin's effects reversed creation. Sin led to death, whereas creation led to life. Even today, every time we sin, we go against the Creator and our state as created beings. May we obey His leading.

—James Frohlich

Golden Text Illuminated

"The earth was without form, and void; and darkness was on the face of the deep. And the Spirit of God moved upon the face of the waters" (Genesis 1:2).

Full of mystery and wonder, the Creation account of Genesis 1 has long been a subject of delight and debate. One thing that should never be forgotten, however, is that Genesis—and especially its opening chapter—was crucial for the nation of Israel. This chapter identified the God of Israel, explained the origins and purpose of the universe, and shaped Israel's mission as a nation. It defined their worldview.

After the breathtaking declaration in the opening verse about God's creation of the heavens and earth, we are given a glimpse of a tantalizing mystery: "The earth was without form, and void; and darkness was on the face of the deep. And the Spirit of God moved upon the face of the waters." What is being described here, and what life-changing implications does this intriguing verse hold for us today?

First, Moses tells us that after the initial making of the universe and planet Earth, the earth was "without form, and void." Theories abound as to the meaning of this phrase, but in the end, it means the earth had no definition, no order, no life. It was, as it were, a place that was unsuitable for life (cf. vss. 3-31).

Second, Moses informs us that "darkness was on the face of the deep." One need not speculate about any sinister presence here, for darkness in this context does not suggest sin or evil, but instead the absence of light and life.

Third, we find out at the end of verse 2 that God's Spirit was hovering over the waters. What a glorious mystery! For who is this "Spirit of God"? Although God is one (cf. Deut. 6:4), God is simultaneously more than one. Although He *alone* is God, He is clearly not alone, for this Spirit of God is with Him. We see that He "moved upon" the surface of the waters. What is the meaning of this theological riddle? The answer can only be found in progressive revelation—moving forward in the Bible and letting later revelation inform and teach us. What we discover is a "Who" and a "what."

The "Who" is, of course, the Holy Spirit Himself—the Third Person of the Trinity who is fully, equally, and eternally God. Possessing all the divine perfections that make Him equal to the Father and Son, the Spirit is distinguished only by His strategic role in the plan of salvation. This brings us to the "what."

The Spirit moving upon the waters suggests an abiding and sustaining presence that upholds, preserves, and protects. That is precisely what the Scriptures reveal about the Spirit. He abides in, sustains, upholds, preserves, protects, and empowers those who belong to Christ to grow in holiness and obey His Word.

Turning to the New Testament, we find that the Spirit is the One who regenerates, seals, comforts, sanctifies, and produces fruit in the lives of God's people. What does Genesis 1:2 do for us today then? It reminds us to worship the Spirit and to cling to the Spirit's sustaining, sanctifying power through His Word. This only makes sense as God's new creation in Christ (cf. 2 Cor. 5:17).

—Jerod A. Gilcher

Heart of the Lesson

Lights. Camera. Action! The Bible begins in Act I, Scene I (Gen. 1:1) with the wonder of Creation. In a split second, with a sheer act of His sovereign power, God brought the universe into existence out of nothing. Psalm 33:6 tells us, "By the word of the Lord were the heavens made; and all the host of them by the breath of his mouth." With a mere word, God caused space, matter, and time to exist, and the history of the world began.

Although it may be familiar, the account of Creation contains profound implications that have the power to transform our lives in significant ways.

1. The account of Creation is not only about creation itself but also about the eternal God who transcends His creation (Gen. 1:1-2). Before the beginning began, God was already there—and *had* been there forever. This is a God who needs nothing but Himself to be who He is or do what He does. Completely independent of His creation, He alone can (and *must*) be trusted as sovereign, supreme, and self-sufficient. The same God who made all things owns all things and rules all things.

For a brief time, however, the unformed and empty earth hung alone in a vast, silent universe, until suddenly, God spoke into the darkness.

2. The account of Creation reminds us that God is sovereign over creation (Gen. 1:3-5). The text then recounts to us the creation of light and the separation of day and night (vss. 3-5). The first day of Creation reminds us of the power and authority of God over all time and history.

The One who invented the means by which we measure time (days and nights) can be trusted to govern all that happens in those times with His perfect, infallible wisdom. God sees all things, knows all things, and, in a way unfathomable to us as finite beings, even *controls* all things for His glory and the advance of His plan.

3. God's Creation reminds us that God is generous, affectionate, and benevolent (Gen. 1:6-13). In verses 6-13 we see the creation of sky, water, land, and vegetation. This reminds us that God is not merely a Higher Power or an Intelligent Designer but also a generous and affectionate God who loves to provide for the people He created.

Paul declared to the people at Lystra that the God who made "heaven, and earth, and the sea, and all things that are therein . . . did good, and gave us rain from heaven, and fruitful seasons, filling our hearts with food and gladness" (Acts 14:15, 17). The God who created all things made those things to be enjoyed as a sample of His glory.

How should the church respond to this familiar Creation account? While there are many implications, we must remember that the God who created in the beginning is the same God who has already written the ending. Revelation 21:1 tells us that at the end of the age God will make a new heaven and earth. In between those two creations is the stunning drama of salvation unfolding in history.

At the center of history is Jesus Christ. He is the Star of the show and the One who not only made the entire universe (cf. John 1:3; Col. 1:16) but also makes new creatures out of the people who trust in Him (cf. 2 Cor. 5:17). The same Christ who made all things also rules all things and is in the business of making a new humanity by His grace.

—Jerod A. Gilcher

World Missions

The film *More than Dreams: The Story of Ali* (morethandreams.org) presents the testimony of Ali, a Muslim man from Turkey who came to faith as a result of an encounter with Jesus. In a flashback, he is depicted as a shepherd boy wondering about the beauty of a flower. Later on in the film, Ali has a discussion with a friend about flowers. He notes that they "grow in the dirt" and turn out beautiful when fertilized with manure. But then he asks, "So where does the smell come from? The beautiful fragrance? God uses filth to make beauty." Ali, who struggled with violence and alcoholism, nonetheless expressed a desire to know God.

Sometimes when we see the lives of people around us, perhaps we wonder how God could ever save and transform lives that are so tangled and bound up in sin. Some of us may wonder something similar about ourselves. Perhaps areas of our own lives need to be transformed by the power of God's Spirit.

In fits and starts, Ali began seeking God and eventually had an encounter with Jesus. Gradually, God's Spirit got hold of him, and he began to change so that the other women in the village where Ali lived with his family asked his wife if he could be an influence on their own husbands as well. Even as God brings the beautiful fragrance of flowers out of plants that are nourished in the dirt, so He can and does transform us. Through the Holy Spirit, God takes up residence in our lives and changes us.

The same Spirit of God that moved upon the face of the waters at Creation, filling the earth with beauty and wonder, also works transformation in God's people, drawing us to Himself and making us new. As Paul writes in 2 Corinthians 4:6, "For God, who commanded the light to shine out of darkness, hath shined in our hearts, to give the light of the knowledge of the glory of God in the face of Jesus Christ." God's Spirit does this in His people in North America, and the same Spirit, the very one who was active in the Creation event, also does so among believers in the Middle East, Asia, Latin America, Africa, Australia, and Europe!

Moreover, even as Ali marveled at how God could bring the beautiful fragrance of the flower out of the dirt, so Paul noted how "we have this treasure [of Christ's light] in earthen vessels, that the excellency of the power may be of God, and not of us" (vs. 7). The work of creation, from the making of soil and all kinds of plants emerging from it to the transforming work that God is doing within our own "earthen vessels," is all the work of the same Spirit.

Not only does God's Spirit create and transform God's people, but God's work of transformation is meant to lead to a Spirit-empowered, bold sharing of the good news of Jesus with people who have never heard. The same God who spoke light into existence also sent His Servant to be "a light to the Gentiles" for "salvation unto the end of the earth" (Isa. 49:6). Jesus, the great fulfillment of that prophecy, has invited His followers to become the "light of the world" as well, because He dwells in us through His Spirit (Matt. 5:14; cf. Phil. 2:15). Friends, the Spirit of God, who was present at Creation and even now transforms us, takes our hand and invites us to join Him in His work of mission among the nations! Let's join Him in this effort!

—Matthew Friedman

The Jewish Aspect

Moses likely wrote the book of Genesis about 1400 B.C. At that time, different myths ascribed the creation of the universe to the gods. Those myths were the anti-God influence of the day, and Moses wrote to combat them more than to answer modern cosmological questions. Some of the myths that Moses confronted were those of Egypt and Mesopotamia.

The Egyptians had several creation myths. The different myths related to various major cities and gods. Although those myths come from a variety of sources, time periods, and places throughout Egypt, together they parallel Genesis 1 in several important aspects, such as formlessness, darkness, wind, and deep waters at the beginning of Creation.

Other important parallels include wind moving over the waters and creating through speech. Due to these many similarities, Moses may have been directly refuting the Egyptian creation stories in his writing. Why would Moses do that? When he wrote, the Israelites had just come out of Egypt and would have been familiar with both the gods of Egypt and their creation myths. After being in Egyptian bondage, they could have been tempted to think that the Egyptian gods were stronger than the Lord. It is as if Moses was saying that the Egyptian gods did not create the world—the one true God did!

The major Babylonian creation myth was *Enuma Elish.* In that story, the god Marduk destroyed the sea goddess Tiamat and created the universe from her slain body. Her carcass became the waters above and below the earth. That provides an interesting similarity to Genesis 1, which also pictures waters above and below the earth. The differences, however, are many. For example, in the Babylonian account, humanity was made to serve the gods by doing the work that the gods no longer wanted to perform. Also, the waters do not strive against God in Genesis 1 as in the Babylonian myth. Rather, the waters offer no resistance to His divine commands.

The similarities between Genesis 1 and the ancient creation accounts let us know that Moses wrote partly to combat the cultural assumption that the gods created the physical world. The differences let Israel know that the one true God is superior to the false gods of Egypt and Mesopotamia and indeed everywhere else.

Genesis 1 is likely the best-known account of Creation in the Bible, but it is far from the Bible's only account. Every major genre of the Old Testament discusses Creation, including narrative, poetry, wisdom, and prophetic texts. Genesis 1's popularity probably derives from the fact that it is both the first and longest of the Creation accounts in the Bible.

The other Creation accounts show many similarities to Genesis 1 but also some distinctives. Similar to Genesis 1, some psalms depict no battle with the sea at Creation (Pss. 77; 104). Other psalms, however, picture God doing battle with the sea at Creation (Pss. 74; 89). These differences are likely due to the purposes of the different psalms. Psalms of praise (such as Psalms 77 and 104) extol God as the unrivaled Creator. The waters dare not even try to attack Him. Lament psalms (such as Psalms 74 and 89), however, use the sea as a metaphor for the trials God's people face. Since God vanquished the seas, He can also deliver His people from difficulty.

—James Frohlich

Guiding the Superintendent

What have you made of which you're most proud? A drawing? A poem? A cake? A spreadsheet? If someone encountered it, what would they know about you? Art bespeaks a creative maker. A poem bespeaks a beautiful mind. A spreadsheet bespeaks an ordered intellect. A cake bespeaks a hospitable soul. Today's text invites the same thought process: What attributes of God are seen in His creation of the heavens and the earth?

DEVOTIONAL OUTLINE

1. Introducing the Maker of heaven and earth (Gen. 1:1-2). The Hebrew word for *create* in Genesis 1:1 (Hebrew *bara*) refers to an action only God does. Humans can *form* (Hebrew *yatsar*; cf. Isa. 54:17) or *make* (Hebrew *asah*; cf. Ps. 115:8), but only God creates (cf. Ps. 51:10).

Genesis 1:2 described the earth as "without form, and void." The meaning of that phrase is clarified by its use in Jeremiah 4:23 to describe the effects of God's judgment on Jerusalem: disarray and chaos. In the first three days of Creation, God addressed the lack of form. The next three days addressed the empty void.

2. The Maker of heaven and earth's powerful word (Gen. 1:3-13). Students may notice the repetition of "And God said" (vss. 3, 6, 9, 11). God created, but since He is immaterial (cf. John 4:24), He created by His powerful word rather than with physical hands (cf. John 1:1-3).

God evaluated His creative work as "good" (Gen. 1:4, 10, 12). The goodness of creation remained even after the Fall (cf. 1 Tim. 4:4-5), and that goodness tells us something about the Maker (cf. Rom. 1:20). God is good, so His omnipresence is beneficial. When sin entered creation, however, God's presence became intimidating (Gen. 3:8) and spelled judgment for sinners (cf. Mic. 1:3). Thankfully, by grace through faith in His saving promises, God has made His omnipresence good news again for all who will trust in Him.

Ask teachers and students to consider the disorder, chaos, formlessness, or unrest in their own lives. They cannot bring order and goodness into these situations themselves, but the omnipresent God of Genesis 1 can and will for those who trust and behold His glory in Jesus Christ (cf. 2 Cor. 3:18). Order is a benefit of God's presence that is demonstrated throughout the Bible (cf. Mark 5:15; Col. 2:5).

CHILDREN'S CORNER

Children marvel at God's amazing creation. Whether they see a glossy green frog, a brightly colored leaf with serrated edges, or cotton candy clouds against a blue sky, they gaze at creation with awe and wonder. God wants us to be like children as we are caught up in wonder at the Creator and His creation.

Jesus took a little child and told His listeners that if they welcomed a little child in His name, they welcomed the child's Creator, the Lord Jesus (Mark 9:36-37).

As you teach this lesson to the children in your class, without any materials, ask the students to make a tree, a flower, an animal, or a person. Generate a conversation about creation and how God created the entire world, including humans, by spoken words. Reiterate how God formed and filled everything. Then give the children playdough or modeling clay, so they can make something. Explain the difference between creating something from nothing as God did and making something from materials available around us.

—Matthew Swale

SCRIPTURE LESSON TEXT

COL. 1:15 Who is the image of the invisible God, the firstborn of every creature:

16 For by him were all things created, that are in heaven, and that are in earth, visible and invisible, whether *they be* thrones, or dominions, or principalities, or powers: all things were created by him, and for him:

17 And he is before all things, and by him all things consist.

18 And he is the head of the body, the church: who is the beginning, the firstborn from the dead; that in all *things* he might have the preeminence.

19 For it pleased *the Father* that in him should all fulness dwell;

20 And, having made peace through the blood of his cross, by him to reconcile all things unto himself; by him, *I say*, whether *they be* things in earth, or things in heaven.

21 And you, that were sometime alienated and enemies in *your* mind by wicked works, yet now hath he reconciled

22 In the body of his flesh through death, to present you holy and unblameable and unreproveable in his sight:

23 If ye continue in the faith grounded and settled, and *be* not moved away from the hope of the gospel, which ye have heard, and which *was* preached to every creature which is under heaven; whereof I Paul am made a minister.

NOTES

Before All Things

Lesson Text: Colossians 1:15-23

Related Scriptures: 1 Kings 8:12-19, 27-30; Psalm 89:19-29;
John 1:1-3, 14-18; Ephesians 2:11-22; Hebrews 2:5-10

TIME: between A.D. 60 and 62 — PLACE: from Rome

GOLDEN TEXT—"[The Son] is before all things, and by him all things consist" (Colossians 1:17).

Introduction

Last week we began our study of God's omnipresence with His existence before creation. This week we study a passage that includes an emphasis on Jesus' preexistence as the Son of God.

In Colossians 1:14-23, Paul focused exclusively on the Son. In fact, apart from verse 15, Paul seemed to deliberately avoid direct reference to God the Father in those verses. Why would he do that?

The Colossian believers were under attack from false teachers who urged them to engage in practices not required of Christ's disciples (cf. 2:16-23). Those teachers likely used fear of powerful spiritual entities as motivation.

In that context, the Colossians needed to know they could cling to their "Head," Jesus Christ, without fear (cf. vs. 19). Paul emphasized that Jesus is equal with God the Father in every way to show that His worldwide rule and redemption are completely trustworthy.

LESSON OUTLINE

1. **CHRIST'S PREEMINENCE OVER ALL CREATION—Col. 1:15-17**
2. **CHRIST'S PREEMINENCE IN THE NEW CREATION—Col. 1:18-20**
3. **APPLYING CHRIST'S PREEMINENCE TO BELIEVERS—Col. 1:21-23**

Exposition: Verse by Verse

CHRIST'S PREEMINENCE OVER ALL CREATION

COL. 1:15 Who is the image of the invisible God, the firstborn of every creature:

16 For by him were all things created, that are in heaven, and that are in earth, visible and invisible, whether they be thrones, or dominions, or principalities, or powers: all things were created by him, and for him:

17 And he is before all things, and by him all things consist.

Christ's identity in creation (Col. 1:15). Paul began his praise of the Son of God by calling Him the "image of the invisible God." When the Son of God became a man, it became possible for human beings, in a sense, to *see* the unseeable God. {As the Father's image, the enfleshed Son visibly and perfectly revealed the Father to a world that otherwise groped after Him in darkness (cf. John 1:18; 14:7-9).}[Q1]

Paul then referred to Christ as the "firstborn of every creature" (Col. 1:15). We usually associate "firstborn" with physical birth order, which might lead us to wonder whether Paul was teaching that Christ was merely the first created being. The very next verse, however, dismisses that interpretation by declaring that all things without exception were created through Christ.

Instead, we need to understand the term "firstborn" in light of its Old Testament background. Because a firstborn son held rights to the best part of his father's inheritance, "firstborn" came to refer to privilege in addition to birth order. Numerous times in the Old Testament, God called Israel His "son" (cf. Ex. 4:23; Hos. 11:1). When He put to death all the firstborn sons of Egypt, He redeemed His own firstborn son Israel. He then required His people to redeem all their firstborn sons by a sacrifice as a symbol of His redemption of Israel (Ex. 13:2, 13). In Psalm 89:27, God referred to King David as His "firstborn" because of David's place as the highest king in all the world.

{In the Old Testament, therefore, "firstborn" referred theologically to the status of God's chosen and preeminent person or nation. By calling Christ the "firstborn of all creatures," Paul acknowledged Him as the highest Being in all the universe.}[Q2]

Reasons for Christ's identity in creation (Col. 1:16-17). To prove his claim that Christ occupies that highest position, Paul further explained Christ's relationship with creation. He is not merely the greatest *in* the universe; He rules *over* the universe as its all-powerful Creator. Nothing in all creation was made apart from Christ.

Speaking into the Colossians' specific context, Paul added that Christ even created "thrones," "dominions," "principalities," and "powers" (vs. 16). {Based on the use of those terms elsewhere in Paul and in contemporary Jewish writings, Paul was almost certainly referring to categories of powerful spiritual beings, not human entities or governments.}[Q3] The culture in Colossae emphasized fear and worship of such beings. Paul understood that demonic entities were behind the worship of those false gods and posed a real threat to anyone coming in contact with them (cf. 1 Cor. 10:20-22).

Implicit in Colossians 1:16 was an argument frequently employed by the Old Testament prophets: the idols of the nations consist of materials that owe their very existence to the Creator. Therefore, they and the people that worship them have as much chance of disrupting God's plans as a grasshopper has of disrupting the plans of a powerful king (cf. Isa. 40:17-24). Paul encountered similar idolatry in Asia Minor (cf. Acts 19:23-41), but he understood that even the most powerful gods worshipped there were impotent in their Creator's presence. And Jesus Christ is that Creator!

The spiritual powers, along with everything else in the universe, were created not only *through* Jesus Christ, but also *for* Him. Both humans and spiritual powers may pursue their own selfish ends for a time, but in doing so, they wrest the creation from its intended goal, Jesus Christ. That is something the Son of God will not allow to continue indefinitely, so we can be confident that the distorted goals of our fallen world will all fall away, and only those things that were done *for Christ* will endure (cf. 1 Cor. 3:10-15; 15:58).

Since Christ is the Creator, His existence is not dependent on any part of creation; rather, all creation is dependent on Him. Notice that Paul does not say Christ *was* before all things, which we would expect if Paul was merely speaking about Jesus' chronological existence before creation. Instead, he says that Christ *is* before all things (Col. 1:17). That statement echoes what Jesus said to the Jews in John 8:58: "Before Abraham was, I am." Paul was speaking not only of Christ's preexistence but also of His self-existence above and apart from creation.

The flip side of Christ's independent existence is creation's moment-by-moment dependence on Him. Christ did not create the world as a watchmaker creates a watch, putting every detail in place and then letting it tick away. Rather, Christ must be actively involved in every part of creation at every moment, because "by him all things consist" (Col. 1:17). His power holds all things together.

CHRIST'S PREEMINENCE IN THE NEW CREATION

18 And he is the head of the body, the church: who is the beginning, the firstborn from the dead; that in all things he might have the preeminence.

19 For it pleased the Father that in him should all fulness dwell;

20 And, having made peace through the blood of his cross, by him to reconcile all things unto himself; by him, I say, whether they be things in earth, or things in heaven.

Christ's identity in the new creation (Col. 1:18). It is worth noting at this point that most biblical scholars believe verses 15-20 were originally part of an early Christian hymn that Paul adapted for his letter, perhaps with a few modifications to fit the Colossians' context. The first half of the hymn, which extols Christ for His creating work (vss. 15-17), is remarkably paralleled by the second half, which extols Him for His reconciling work (vss. 18-20).

In relation to Christ's creating work, Paul identified Christ as the image of God and the firstborn of creation (vs. 15). Now, in relation to His reconciling work, Paul identified Christ as "the head of the body, the church" and "the beginning, the firstborn from the dead" (vs. 18).

{By calling Christ the "beginning" in relation to His reconciling work, Paul implied that Christ's resurrection was the start of a new creation just as glorious as the original one. In this context, "firstborn from the dead" likely relates to both time and prominence. Not only was Christ the first chronologically to receive a resurrection body, but His resurrection also opened the way for every one of His followers to receive a similar resurrection body (cf. 1 Cor. 15:20-23).}[Q4]

Reasons for Christ's identity in the new creation (Col. 1:19-20). Paul defended Christ's preeminence in the new creation with language similar to his defense of Christ's preeminence in creation. In verse 16, Paul wrote, "*By him* were all things created . . . all things were created *by him* and *for him*" (emphasis added). Using the same prepositions in verses 19-20 (though the English translation differs), Paul wrote, "It pleased the Father that *in him* should all fulness dwell; and . . . *by him* to reconcile all things *unto himself*" (emphasis added).

At first glance, we might assume that last prepositional phrase, "unto himself," refers to the reconciliation of all things to God the Father. In other letters, Paul makes that exact point (cf. 1 Cor. 15:24). Here, however, the phrase cannot grammatically refer to anyone other than the Son (Fee, *Pauline Christology*, Hendrickson). {By speaking of the Son's role in reconciliation in such similar terms to the Father's role, Paul accomplished His goal of presenting Christ as equal with the Father in every way. As Christ is both the source and the goal of creation (cf. vs. 16), so He is both the source and the goal of the new creation.}[Q5]

Perhaps that exclusive focus on the Son in these verses is also behind Paul's decision to refer to God as the "fulness" in verse 19 rather than explicitly naming Him. (The Greek lacks "the Father," which is why those words are italicized in this lesson's Scripture block.) We know from the similar wording in 2:9, however, that this is indeed a reference to God Himself dwelling in Jesus.

{The language of 1:19-20 revolves around Old Testament temple imagery. Just as the temple was the temporary dwelling place of God, so Christ is the permanent dwelling place of God. And just as people came to the temple to sacrifice animals and obtain peace with God, so people can now come to Christ, who shed His own blood to obtain peace with God.}[Q6]

Notice, however, that Christ reconciled more than just people through His death and resurrection; He reconciled the whole creation! To emphasize the all-encompassing nature of Christ's reconciliation, Paul once again repeated language from the first half of the hymn. {As Christ is the Creator of heaven and earth, so He is the Reconciler of heaven and earth, restoring the whole creation to its original purpose of existing for His sake.}[Q7]

APPLYING CHRIST'S PREEMINENCE TO BELIEVERS

21 And you, that were sometime alienated and enemies in your mind by wicked works, yet now hath he reconciled

22 In the body of his flesh through death, to present you holy and unblameable and unreproveable in his sight:

23 If ye continue in the faith grounded and settled, and be not moved away from the hope of the gospel, which ye have heard, and which was preached to every creature which is under heaven; whereof I Paul am made a minister.

All throughout verses 15-20, Paul's sole focus was Christ and His preeminence in every aspect of creation and reconciliation. Now, with a decisive "and you" (vs. 21), he turned to address the Colossian believers and how all this affected them. Paul reminded the Colossians that they were once as far away from reconciliation as they could get. They had been aligned with the hostile forces of darkness and, therefore, "alienated" from Christ.

Paul's abrupt interjection "yet now" mirrored the reality of Christ's abrupt interjection in the lives of the Colossian believers. Using yet another series of three prepositions, Paul directly applied to the Colossians the truths just declared about Christ: they were reconciled "*in* the body of his flesh *through* death" to be presented "*in his sight*" (vs. 22; emphasis added).

The language of being presented before Christ as holy and blameless reflects wedding imagery used elsewhere in Paul's letters. In 2 Corinthians 11:2, Paul described himself as one who arranged for the church's marriage to Christ so they could be presented to Him as a bride adorned for a wedding. Likewise, in Ephesians 5:25-27, Paul described the church as pure and spotless, cleansed by Christ's blood so they could be presented as His bride. {That pure relationship as His spiritual bride is the goal of Christ's reconciliation of the church.}Q8

In Colossians 1:23, Paul gave a condition for reconciliation: continuing in the faith. Their faith in Christ was to be "grounded and settled." Throughout the rest of the letter, Paul described the firmness of the Colossians' faith (1:4; 2:5, 7, 12), so 1:23 was not meant to inspire fear but to encourage the Colossians to maintain what was already true about them. Still, we should not overlook Scripture's urgency that believers must endure to the end. {As Paul explained to the Colossians, one of the main ways to remain "grounded and settled" in faith is to set our hope on the gospel we have heard (1:23)—including the very truths about Jesus that Paul expounded in the preceding verses.}Q9

The end of verse 23 serves as a transition into Paul's next line of thought. Verses 15-23 spelled out the content of the gospel, and now Paul was going to defend his role as a minister of that gospel to the Colossians (1:24—2:5).

{It might seem like an exaggeration for Paul to say the gospel had been preached "to every creature," but this was similar to the way Luke (one of Paul's fellow missionaries) portrayed the situation at the end of Acts. There Luke implied that Paul's ministry in Rome, the epicenter of first-century culture and commerce, fulfilled the book's thesis statement that the gospel needed to reach "the uttermost part of the earth" (1:8). Since Paul wrote Colossians from Rome, he was likely reflecting that same theology in Colossians 1:23. By referring to all creation, Paul may have been emphasizing the cosmic impact of the gospel that he had already expressed in verse 20.}Q10

—Matthew Robinson

QUESTIONS

1. How does Christ's identity as the "image of the invisible God" affect humanity (Col. 1:15)?
2. How does the Old Testament help us understand what Paul meant by calling Christ the "firstborn of every creature" (vs. 15)?
3. What are the "thrones," "dominions," "principalities," and "powers" Christ created (vs. 16)?
4. How does Christ's resurrection relate to His identity as the Head of the church?
5. Why might Paul have emphasized creation's reconciliation to Christ rather than to the Father?
6. How do verses 19-20 reflect Old Testament temple imagery?
7. How does the reference to heaven and earth in verse 20 connect Christ's reconciling work to His creating work?
8. What does the wedding imagery in verse 22 tell us about the goal of Christ's reconciliation?
9. What must believers do to ensure their faith is "grounded and settled" (vs. 23)?
10. Why was it not an exaggeration for Paul to say the gospel had been preached in all creation?

—Matthew Robinson

Preparing to Teach the Lesson

The Bible declares, "Jesus Christ [is] the same yesterday, and to day, and for ever" (Heb. 13:8). It emphatically declares that the eternal Son of God who created all things is Lord of all.

We do not fully understand the Trinity, but every time God spoke in the Old Testament, Jesus spoke with Him. When God performed a miracle, He did so in concert with Jesus, God the Son. Our lesson will help us see one God in three Persons throughout history reaching out to us with love.

TODAY'S AIM

Facts: to know that God has always existed as Father, Son, and Holy Spirit.

Principle: to understand that God revealed Himself in Jesus Christ.

Application: to live each day knowing that the Savior of our souls is also the God of all the universe.

INTRODUCING THE LESSON

When we were younger, we often thought that older people "just don't understand." Now that we are older, we want to help young people because we remember what life was like at that age. We try to warn them of the dangers of life, but many times they do not listen.

Jesus is able to understand us, for He became one of us. Imagine the thirty-three years Jesus lived on the earth as one of us. He preached with authority because all authority is His. Even though He was born in a manger, He is the Creator of all.

DEVELOPING THE LESSON

Colossians 1 powerfully reveals Jesus as God the Son. He is so much more than merely a good teacher or prophet. He is not just the founder of one of the great religions of the world. Jesus Christ is, was, and always will be God. He is God in the flesh, the God who created the universe, and the God who saves our souls. Hebrews 2:5-10 reveals the plan of God for Christ to be born as one of us ("a little lower than the angels") so He could suffer and experience death. The One who is crowned with glory and honor is the One who created all things.

1. He is (Col. 1:15-18). Jesus is the "image of the invisible God." As we read the Bible, we see many occasions when God appeared to someone (from a burning bush, from a whirlwind, as the Angel of the Lord, and more). Each of those appearances had a temporary function. In Colossians, we read that Jesus *is* the "image of the invisible God." He is also the firstborn of all creation. The term "firstborn" is a designation of honor. This is not referring to the manger or teaching that Jesus was created. He has always been God the Son. In Psalm 89:27, King David is described as the "firstborn, higher than the kings of the earth," even though he had older brothers. The term does not mean he is the first one born.

Colossians 1:16-17 explains what the original readers of Genesis 1 did not fully understand. All things were created by God the Son. All means *all*. He created everything in the universe and all living things (including angelic beings). Everything was created not only *by* Him but also *for* Him.

"He is before all things" (vs. 17) reflects the Genesis 1 account. Since He existed before there was even a universe, He is chronologically before all. The phrase "by Him all things consist" gives us a powerful truth regarding how the world works. The power of Christ holds the universe together. That includes all things physical or spiritual. Jesus Christ has the whole world in His hands.

Jesus has a resurrected body, but He also views us (the church) as His body, and He is the Head (vs. 18). The verse continues by saying that He is the beginning. That should prompt us to think about Genesis 1 or John 1. We may also think of Revelation 22:13, where Jesus says, "I am Alpha and Omega, the beginning and the end, the first and the last."

Colossians 1:18 continues by proclaiming the Son is "the firstborn from the dead." We see that term "firstborn" again, but this time it is explained as a term of honor and distinction to highlight His "preeminence." Of all the billions who have lived and died, the Son of God is ruler of them all.

2. He was (Col. 1:19-21). The apostle Paul continued his inspiring teaching about the Son of God by describing His atoning sacrifice on the cross. When the Son came to live on earth as Jesus Christ of Nazareth, He remained fully God. As fully God and fully man, He was the only person who could offer the world peace with God. Verse 20 says He made that peace "through the blood of his cross." His death on the cross offered reconciliation, so believers are no longer enemies of God.

Sometimes we forget how lost we were before Jesus saved our souls. Ephesians 2 describes us in our past condition as "strangers from the covenants of promise, having no hope, and without God in the world" (vs. 12). But in Christ Jesus we are no longer far from God (vss. 13, 17). The One who is peace (vs. 14) made peace (vs. 15) by preaching peace (vs. 17). We used to be strangers, but now are part of God's family (vs. 19)!

3. He will (Col. 1:22-23). Because the almighty Creator made us righteous through His death on the cross, He will present us as holy, blameless, and unreproveable. When the end comes, it is Jesus who will present you as holy before Him. You will be free from any accusation.

Our last verse declares that all this is available to the believer. God has brought reconciliation. Now we must continue in the faith and never depart from the hope of the gospel.

ILLUSTRATING THE LESSON

Jesus shows us exactly who God is. All things were created through Him, and by Him we are saved. Jesus is, was, and will always be.

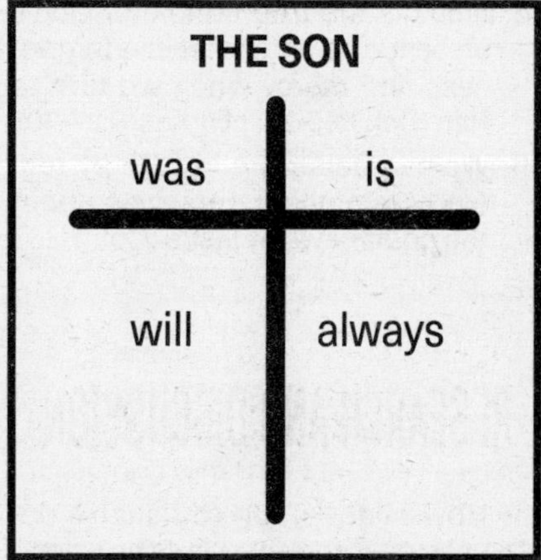

CONCLUDING THE LESSON

God is so amazing that the great temple Solomon built could not contain Him (1 Kgs. 8:27). Yet, the omnipresent God was made flesh and lived among us. John 1:14 says He is "full of grace and truth." Verse 17 reminds us that Moses gave the law, "but grace and truth came by Jesus Christ."

ANTICIPATING THE NEXT LESSON

Next week we will look at the pervasiveness of God's presence. He is everywhere at the same time, making Him a God who is close at hand and far away at the same time.

—Adam Clagg

PRACTICAL POINTS

1. If we want to know what God is like, all we have to do is look at Jesus, His perfect image (Col. 1:15).
2. We do not need to fear anything in the universe, because Jesus has power over it all (vs. 16).
3. Even on our worst days, the continuing existence of the world is proof of God's goodness toward us (vs. 17).
4. The life of the church comes from Jesus Christ, the Head of the body (vs. 18).
5. Jesus is the true temple of God's presence, so we can receive forgiveness and mercy when we turn to Him (Col. 1:19-22; cf. 1 Kgs. 8:27-30).
6. We can persevere in faith by regularly reminding ourselves about the good news of Jesus (Col. 1:23).

—Matthew Robinson

RESEARCH AND DISCUSSION

1. How might a non-Christian's despair over current events be a good launching pad for sharing the gospel based on Colossians 1:15-23?
2. In what ways have you felt pressure from today's culture to worship or fear something other than Christ? How can Christ's preeminence over creation help you withstand that pressure?
3. What truths in Colossians 1:15-23 can motivate us to move away from a self-centered approach to our faith and toward a Christ-centered approach?
4. What habits can you begin (or continue) that will help you treat your relationship with Jesus as the goal of your life?

—Matthew Robinson

ILLUSTRATED HIGH POINTS

Image of the invisible God (Col. 1:15)

Off the coast of New York stands the Statue of Liberty. The tablet she holds reads "July 4, 1776" in Roman numerals, representing the independence of the United States. Broken chains lie at her feet, representing the abolishment of slavery. In these ways, the statue is an image of the invisible ideals of freedom and hope.

In a similar way, Jesus Christ is the image of the invisible God. Unlike Lady Liberty, however, Jesus is a living person who reveals God in much greater ways than through His physical appearance. He represents God by speaking His words and embodying His holy rule in a way Adam and Eve were meant to do in Eden but failed (cf. Gen. 1:26-28).

For him (Col. 1:16)

The way we approach everyday life depends on the goals we have for ourselves. For example, a person's eating habits will be significantly different when trying to lose weight than when trying to gain muscle (or when pursuing no health goals at all!).

Verses 15-23 teach that the goal of everything in all creation is Jesus Christ, and the goal of His death and resurrection is to give us a reconciled relationship with Him.

Reconciled (vs. 21)

Imagine if a bride and groom said their wedding vows but then never talked to each other again. That would be foolish, because the point of two people getting married is to spend the rest of their lives together. But we are just as foolish if we profess faith in Christ and then fail to develop that relationship throughout the rest of our lives.

—Matthew Robinson

Golden Text Illuminated

"[The Son] is before all things, and by him all things consist" (Colossians 1:17).

This text is found in the middle of a series of staggering assertions about the supremacy of Christ. In Paul's letter to the Colossians, the need was urgent to display Christ as matchless and supreme, against a false teaching that threatened the church at Colossae. Secular philosophies, claims about mystical experiences, legalistic tendencies, and false views of Christ were poisoning this local church. In response, Paul wrote a letter to display the worth and matchless supremacy of Jesus Christ.

The verse in focus here (vs. 17) highlights two features of Christ that are necessary to know and understand to both worship Him rightly and trust Him deeply.

First, Paul wrote that Christ is "before all things." This was now the third time since verse 15 that Paul mentioned "all things." By "all things," Paul meant "all things" in the universe without exception. In verse 16, Paul declared twice that Christ made "all things" as the Creator, and here in verse 17, he proclaimed that Christ is "before all things." This is the eternal preexistence of Jesus Christ. Paul ruled out the possibility that Christ could be a created being. As the One who is "before" all things, He is the One who shares with the Father absolute eternality. There never was a time when Jesus Christ was not. He is the "I AM" (Ex. 3:14), the self-existent One and the One who is "the same yesterday, and to day, and for ever" (Heb. 13:8).

Second, Paul declared that Christ also is the One in whom "all things consist." What does it mean that all things "consist" in Christ? It means that in Him all things hold together. That is, He upholds "all things by the word of his power" (Heb. 1:3). Should He cease His continuous sustaining activity, "all things" would disintegrate. What a stunning thought! Who would have guessed that the blue-collar Nazarene, the carpenter's son, born in a dirty stable, who, in the eyes of the world, died an unfortunate death in the clutches of His enemies, is actually the One who holds the entire universe and maintains its existence? Jesus Christ has all authority in heaven and on earth (cf. Matt. 28:18); He is "far above all principality, and power, and might, and dominion, and every name" (Eph. 1:21). One day, every knee will bow before Him, and every tongue will confess that He is Lord (cf. Phil. 2:10-11).

These are indeed lofty thoughts—in fact, they are among the loftiest thoughts a human can think. And these are the very thoughts Paul wanted the Colossians to think. Why? What is gained by such lofty theology? What is achieved with such theological precision? The answer is clear: lofty thoughts of Christ produce deeper worship and deeper trust. You cannot truly worship what you are not exhilarated by. You cannot truly trust a Savior who is not supreme. In Christ, we find a Savior who is infinite, eternal, uncaused, uncreated, self-existent, and sovereign. What trial in life is not dwarfed by His majesty? What earthly treasure is not made dim by comparison to His beauty? What threat in life is not tamed by His supremacy? Therefore, let us trust and treasure the Christ who is before all things and upholds all things.

—Jerod A. Gilcher

Heart of the Lesson

The mission of Christ to save sinners is more complex and beautiful than most Christians realize. Yes, Christ came to earth to reconcile sinners to God through His death, but He also came to do more than that. His bloody death on the cross not only makes peace between God and people but also between God and *the entire universe*!

When Adam unleashed the virus of sin in the beginning, he set off a chain reaction of destruction that resulted in the ruin of the entire cosmos. Paul tells us in Romans 8:19-23 that all creation groans in agony from the curse of sin, longing to be set free. The all-sufficient solution, therefore, to a curse-filled creation is a divine Savior who became man and reconciled both sinners *and* creation back to God.

That is one of the great realities found in Paul's magisterial praise of Christ in Colossians 1:15-23. Here we see the divine Savior whose incarnation and sacrificial death repairs all that Adam broke and regains all that Adam lost. Although full of deep theology, this passage also contains surprisingly practical insights that shape and transform our lives.

1. Christ's preeminence in creation (Col. 1:15-17). As the "image of the invisible God" (vs. 15), Jesus Christ is the fully human, fully divine Savior who can not only sympathize with the full range of human experience but also save human beings by His sovereign power.

"The firstborn of every creature" (vs. 15) is a term of dignity and rank. In other words, Christ is the Heir, the rightful Owner of all creation who is "higher than the kings of the earth" (cf. Ps. 89:27). That is true because all things in heaven and on earth were created by Him (Col. 1:16). Jesus Christ is the divine Creator and rightful Owner of the cosmos.

In order to truly trust and treasure Christ as we ought, we need to understand His eternal preexistence and His infinite power with which He sustains the universe. As the One who is "before all things" and the One in whom "all things consist" (vs. 17), Christ is eternally trustworthy to uphold all things.

2. Christ's preeminence in the church (Col. 1:18). The eternal, divine King of creation is also the Head and Ruler of the church. Despite any concerns we may have over the state of the church today, the great "firstborn from the dead" will ensure that the body of Christ is protected by His power and presented as holy and blameless before God (cf. vs. 22).

3. Christ's work of reconciliation (Col. 1:19-22). Jesus Christ reconciles not only sinners but even "all things unto Himself" (vs. 20). The day will come in the future when all the universe will be in subjection to Jesus Christ, who through the blood of His cross will bring peace to all things, both on earth and in heaven.

4. Our response (Col. 1:23). How should believers live in light of the absolute supremacy of Jesus Christ? Paul supplies a clear application for our lives: we must continue in the faith. We must persevere, firm and steadfast, and never waver from the hope of the gospel. That means that we must saturate our minds with the gospel and cling tenaciously to our hope, knowing that our supreme Savior, who upholds all things by the Word of His power, is upholding us as well.

—Jerod A. Gilcher

World Missions

I grew up in a Jewish family, and though we did not observe many Jewish practices, one of the baseline elements that we did believe was monotheism. We were very strong in our understanding that God is one, and we regularly recited the *Shema* prayer (based on Deuteronomy 6:4): "Hear O Israel, the Lord our God; the Lord is One." Indeed, I still regularly recite that statement today, and Jesus Himself used the language of Deuteronomy 6:4 when asked about the greatest commandment (Mark 12:29-30).

For many Jewish people, the idea that Jesus is God, that He is within God's very Self, is challenging to grasp. I found that to be similarly true for the Muslim people among whom I worked in South Asia for many years. The greatest difficulty for them was in grasping the reality of the incarnation. Yet I also observed that when people truly grasped that reality, everything else began to fall into place. I used to notice that principle at work specifically in regard to Jewish and Muslim people. Over the years, however, I have realized it is true for *everyone*, because the incarnation, the reality that the uncreated God entered and joined himself with His creation and humanity in the person of Jesus, is central to the gospel itself.

In our previous lesson, we focused on the Creation account in Genesis. The prologue of John's Gospel mirrors the account in Genesis by placing the "Word" in the beginning with God (John 1:1-3), but it also describes the incarnate Christ as "full of grace and truth" (vs. 14), mirroring God's self-description in Exodus 34:6-7 and elsewhere (Bauckham, *Jesus and the God of Israel*, Eerdmans). In Colossians 1:15-18, Paul reiterated the reality that Jesus is within God's very Self but then took it to the next level. He made it clear that we and all creation are reconciled to God because the incarnate God also died and rose again to bring everything back into a right relationship with Him.

Some years ago, I was involved in discipling a Muslim gentleman who had put his faith in Jesus. "Ahmed" (a pseudonym) had received a vision of Jesus, and not long after, he came to faith in Jesus. He and I were reading together through John 14, and we came to verse 6, in which Jesus famously states, "I am the way, the truth, and the life: no man cometh unto the Father, but by me." I noted to Ahmed that when Jesus refers to Himself as "Way," "Truth," and "Life," He is quite intentionally naming Himself with attributes of God, something that would not have been lost on His disciples or on early readers of John's Gospel. Ahmed's face lit up, and he exclaimed, "Not only that, but He also tells Martha in John 11:25, 'I am the resurrection and the life,' naming himself not only as 'life' but, with the word 'resurrection,' naming himself as the One who will oversee Judgment Day!"

That brings us back to our Colossians passage. Demonstrating the reality of the incarnation is not merely an important element of apologetics; it touches on the very foundation of everything we believe as Christians, as well as everything else in life. We are redeemed by the sacrifice of Jesus, who is within God's very Self, on the cross of Calvary. He has removed not only our guilt but also our relational alienation from God. That is an eternal truth for people from *all* nations.

—*Matthew Friedman*

The Jewish Aspect

Colossae was a breeding ground for spirituality—but not in a good way. The Colossians, like many in first-century Asia Minor, both worshipped and dreaded a plethora of gods and goddesses, and they associated many natural phenomena, such as constellations, with spiritual beings. Such beliefs often resulted in great fear. Many of the spirits were considered malevolent, and archaeologists have found numerous curse tablets in Asia Minor that were apparently used to call on spiritual beings to hurt one's enemies (Arnold, "Colossians," *Zondervan Illustrated Bible Background Commentary*, vol. 3, Zondervan).

Paul showed an awareness of that spirit-oriented background throughout Ephesians and Colossians, both of which he wrote to churches of Asia Minor, while also connecting that background with a Jewish understanding of spiritual entities. In Colossians 2, he urged his readers to dispel the influence of "the rudiments of the world" (vss. 8, 20), likely a reference to certain gods of their culture (Arnold, 384).

Similarly, numerous times in both Ephesians and Colossians, Paul identified "principalities," "powers," and "dominions" as the enemies of Christ and His followers (cf. Eph. 3:10; 6:12; Col. 1:16; 2:15). Twenty-first-century readers might naturally associate such terms with government authorities. Paul's audience, however, would have understood these as references to spiritual entities, not only because of their cultural background but also because the terms bore that sense in numerous contemporary Jewish writings (Arnold, 380). Ephesians 3:10 confirms that interpretation by locating the rulers and powers in "heavenly places" (cf. 6:12).

Although the terms can be used in other ways depending on the context, Paul used them in the sense of spiritual entities in all but one instance in his letters to churches in Asia Minor. (The term for "ruler" is used in its alternate sense, "beginning," in Colossians 1:18.)

Interestingly, in his other letters, Paul frequently used the terms for "power" and "principality" in different ways (see especially Titus 3:1, where they clearly refer to earthly institutions). That distinction between usage in Asia Minor letters and other letters strengthens the likelihood that Asia Minor's worship and fear of spiritual beings was acutely affecting the churches there.

In Colossians 1:16, Paul listed "dominions," "principalities," and "powers," along with "thrones," as specific examples of entities that Christ created. By identifying them as created beings rather than as non-entities, Paul interpreted the Colossians' pagan culture through a Jewish lens. Elsewhere, Paul taught that a person who worshipped a pagan god came under the influence of a demon associated with that god (1 Cor. 10:20)—a teaching that reflected several Old Testament texts (cf. Deut. 32:17; Ps. 106:37). That meant that participation in pagan worship was more dangerous than some disciples supposed (cf. 1 Cor. 10:21-22), but it also meant that the pagan culture's so-called gods were under Christ's authority.

What an encouragement Paul's words would have been to the Colossian believers! The beings their culture feared most were mere creations of Christ and, therefore, were subject to His power and rule. As members of Christ's kingdom, the Colossian believers were no longer under the Satanic "power of darkness" (Col. 1:13), so they had nothing to fear from demonic entities.

—Matthew Robinson

Guiding the Superintendent

To help learners see this text not as a random list of attributes but an intentionally crafted statement about Christ, encourage them to (1) note the elements of the text that relate to the unit topic, omnipresence; (2) highlight repeated terms to track Paul's intended focal points; and (3) watch for the thematic progression of the text.

Each section of the passage conveys Christ's omnipresence. The text moves from Christ's preeminence in creation (vss. 15-17) to His preeminence in the church (vss. 18-20) to His preeminence for every individual believer (vss. 21-23). Therefore, Christ's omnipresence benefits creation, Christians collectively, and believers individually.

DEVOTIONAL OUTLINE

1. Creation is by, through, and for Christ (Col. 1:15-17). The climactic statement in the first section asserts that "by him all things consist" (vs. 17). This means that He *holds together* all things, including "all things . . . visible and invisible" (vs. 16). The Son must be present with all things to hold them together (cf. Heb. 1:3).

2. The church is by, through, and for Christ (Col. 1:18-20). The next section conveys the omnipresence of Christ by teaching that "he is the head of the body, the church" (vs. 18). Just as one's head is always present with one's body, so Christ is present with His global body, the church, such that helping, ignoring, or persecuting individual Christians constitutes helping, ignoring, or persecuting Jesus Himself (cf. Matt. 25:40, 45; Acts 9:4-5).

3. Salvation is by, through, and for Christ (Col. 1:21-23). The final section contributes to a book-wide theme in Colossians. Reconciliation with God occurs "in the body of his flesh through [his] death" (vs. 22). The preposition "in" functions in Colossians to convey each believer's union with Christ (cf. 1:2, 14), which is how His omnipresence spiritually benefits Christians.

Students may notice several repeated terms that unite the passage's sections and convey Christ's omnipresence. The phrase "all things" recurs six times, conveying the completeness of Christ's work in creation (vs. 16), kingship (vss. 17-18), sustenance (vs. 18), and reconciliation (vs. 20). Similarly, the word "heaven" is repeated three times to emphasize the scope of the Son's work in creation (vs. 16), redemption (vs. 20), and calling sinners to salvation (vs. 23). Finally, Christ is the "firstborn of every creature" (vs. 15) and "firstborn from the dead" (vs. 18), indicating His supremacy over and in the universe.

CHILDREN'S CORNER

Every child needs to know Jesus as God the Creator. He created the entire world and everything in it, including every person, both children and adults. Because we are all created by Christ, it is only right to get to know the One who made us! Children also need to know that Jesus holds them and all things together. No matter how difficult a situation seems, children must learn that Jesus holds them together. He is like the super glue of life. Children also need to see Christ as the Head of the church. Make sure children understand that people are the church, and they go to a building. As the Head of the church, Christ must be in charge. Everything that is done on this earth and in this life exists to bring Him honor and glory and praise. Teach your students that their lives are to honor Christ.

—*Matthew Swale*

SCRIPTURE LESSON TEXT

JER. 23:18 For who hath stood in the counsel of the LORD and hath perceived and heard his word? who hath marked his word, and heard *it*?

19 Behold, a whirlwind of the LORD is gone forth in fury, even a grievous whirlwind: it shall fall grievously upon the head of the wicked.

20 The anger of the LORD shall not return, until he have executed, and till he have performed the thoughts of his heart: in the latter days ye shall consider it perfectly.

21 I have not sent these prophets, yet they ran: I have not spoken to them, yet they prophesied.

22 But if they had stood in my counsel, and had caused my people to hear my words, then they should have turned them from their evil way, and from the evil of their doings.

23 *Am* I a God at hand, saith the LORD, and not a God afar off?

24 Can any hide himself in secret places, that I shall not see him? saith the LORD. Do not I fill heaven and earth? saith the LORD.

NOTES

In Heaven and Earth

Lesson Text: Jeremiah 23:18-24

Related Scriptures: Deuteronomy 31:24-29; Jeremiah 23:9-15; Isaiah 57:15-21; Ezekiel 13:1-16; Acts 17:24-31

TIME: probably between 597 and 586 B.C. PLACE: Jerusalem

GOLDEN TEXT—"Can any hide himself in secret places that I shall not see him? saith the Lord. Do not I fill heaven and earth? saith the Lord" (Jeremiah 23:24).

Introduction

Jeremiah 23 wrestles with a theological question that pervades the whole book of Jeremiah: What is truth?

Truth is an attribute of God's character (cf. Ex. 34:6). That is why living a life of obedience to God is called walking in truth (Ps. 86:11). It was because God is true that Abraham rightly trusted Him, even when all other objective evidence would make such an act illogical (Gen. 15:6). But faith is not baseless or unreasonable. It instead recognizes God as the only perfect truth and therefore as perfectly trustworthy. Any attempt to interpret reality apart from Him is fundamentally, irreparably flawed.

Prophets in Jeremiah's day were not walking in or speaking God's truth. How was Jeremiah to respond? One angle he took was to emphasize God's omnipresence. No false prophet can hide from His presence, and that means no false prophet will ultimately succeed.

LESSON OUTLINE

1. **COUNTERFEIT CREDENTIALS—Jer. 23:18-20**
2. **PROFITLESS PROPHETS—Jer. 23:21-22**
3. **RADICAL REALITY—Jer. 23:23-24**

Exposition: Verse by Verse

COUNTERFEIT CREDENTIALS

JER. 23:18 For who hath stood in the counsel of the Lord and hath perceived and heard his word? who hath marked his word, and heard it?

19 Behold, a whirlwind of the Lord is gone forth in fury, even a grievous whirlwind: it shall fall grievously upon the head of the wicked.

20 The anger of the Lord shall not return, until he have executed, and till he have performed the thoughts of his heart: in the latter days ye shall consider it perfectly.

The divine council (Jer. 23:18). There are generally four main components to ancient prophecies: the divine source, the prophets themselves, the divine message, and the human recipient of the message. The source of Jeremiah's conflict with the other prophets would seem primarily to be a conflict of message. After all, both he and the other prophets were speaking to the people of Judah. And both claimed to be speaking for God. Yet their messages were as different as night and day. Surely resolving the conflict was simply a matter of analyzing the message to see which one seemed truer.

That was not the path Jeremiah chose to take. {Rather, he claimed that the reason there was a conflict between him and the other prophets was that they had not actually heard from God.}[Q1] Their message was as detached from the mouth of the Lord as the messages supposedly coming from the prophets of Baal (cf. vs. 13). It was not just the prophecies that were false. The prophets were false.

Clearly, that was a very bold claim. To our modern ears, it also seems like a claim impossible to defend. How can a person prove that someone did not hear from God?

However, Jeremiah's targeted attack made perfect sense in light of the cultural understanding of a prophet's role. To hear directly from God as a prophet involved standing in the "counsel [or council] of the Lord" (vs. 18), which was an experience both unusual and verifiable. For us to fully appreciate the gravity of the false prophets' deception, we need to examine the biblical understanding of the divine council and how the role of a prophet fit into it.

The phrase may not be familiar for modern readers, but it is a concept present throughout the Bible. The Psalms frequently described God ruling from the midst of a collective of beings (cf. 82:1; 89:5-7), and the prophetic visions of God's throne portrayed Him surrounded by powerful, supernatural entities (Isa. 6:1-3; Rev. 4:4-11). Taken alone, these texts might be interpreted as merely describing a vibrant fan base of angelic beings who praise God nonstop for eternity. But the divine council is a more complex concept than that.

{The idea of a god as part of a collective was common in many ancient cultures. Even today, we are familiar with the gods of Greek or Norse mythology, such as Thor, Athena, Loki, or Aphrodite. Such pantheons were likewise found in the mythology of Egypt, Assyria, Babylon, and various Canaanite peoples. Every pantheon presented different gods who ruled over various aspects of the physical world, from the forces of nature to the inner workings of empires. Although the identities of those gods changed depending on the culture, the underlying principle remained the same: the universe was run by a team of divine beings, usually overseen by one being who had proven to be more worthy than the others.}[Q2]

{The biblical concept of the divine council bears some similarities but is fundamentally different. Whereas in all other religions the gods would frequently challenge one another for rank and supremacy, in the Bible there is no question who the King of kings, Lord of lords, and God of "gods" is (Deut. 10:17; cf. Rev. 19:16).}[Q3] There should be no mistake, even in the spiritual world among powerful spiritual beings: there is none like God. He is the Creator of all, the only uncaused Cause, the One from whom all things derive their existence (cf. Col. 1:15-17).

Although the identity of the supreme Ruler over the biblical divine council is clear, the roles and ranks of its other members are speculative. The cherubim and seraphim are rarely depicted outside of the throne room (cf. Ezek.

10), meaning that their position on the flowchart of authority is probably high, much like the advisers in ancient human courts. Meanwhile, the angels carrying messages between God and His creation likely fill a lower position on the chart.

Even though our knowledge of such a flowchart is extremely limited, understanding its existence is important for seeing how the prophet relates to the divine council. For a supernatural being, the angelic role as messenger between God and people is likely one of the lower positions. But when that role is given to a human, it is an elevation of status. A human welcomed into the throne room of God is transformed by the experience (cf. Isa. 6:1-7).

{Only those humans who are chosen and changed are capable of truly seeing the spiritual realm coexisting around them (cf. 2 Kgs. 6:17). That transformation is necessary so the prophet can clearly communicate what he sees and hears.}[Q4] The prophet stands as a divinely appointed ambassador who can do nothing other than speak the word God has given to him.

The incoming storm (Jer. 23:19-20). The other prophets were proclaiming messages that appealed to the masses, but as Jeremiah proved in verse 19, he was the only one among them who had truly been granted the role of prophet. {He could see what those other prophets could not. He had a clear view of the impending doom that was coming for God's people.}[Q5]

The visual description of God's wrath as a "whirlwind" (Jer. 23:19), likely best imagined here as a tornado, is a common prophetic symbol (cf. Ezek. 13:13; Amos 1:14). In the Psalms, storms are described as God's "chariot" (104:3), His weapon of choice (18:13-14), and the manifestation of His power (29:3-10). Storms remain a powerful symbol to this day to depict ferocious strength.

The whirlwind took on an even deeper meaning in the prophetic message. {As elaborated later in Jeremiah, the incoming storm was more than just a meteorological event. It was a metaphor for the impending invasion and conquest by the Babylonian Empire (cf. Jer. 25:15-32; Isa. 30:30).}[Q6] Like an unstoppable tornado, the destructive armies from the east would decimate the Judean landscape and lay waste to Jerusalem. God would especially focus their terrible energy toward those who stood guilty before Him, including the very false prophets who claimed to speak on His behalf.

That outpouring of wrath would lead to an ironic conclusion. The prophets would finally see the truth about God. They would recognize Jeremiah's message as authentic. They would have an eye-opening experience of God's incredible power. But it would not launch them into a prophetic ministry. It would be the end of their days.

PROFITLESS PROPHETS

21 I have not sent these prophets, yet they ran: I have not spoken to them, yet they prophesied.

22 But if they had stood in my counsel, and had caused my people to hear my words, then they should have turned them from their evil way, and from the evil of their doings.

Absent authority (Jer. 23:21). The prophets came under a different level of scrutiny in verses 21-22. They no longer faced the criticisms of Jeremiah alone. God Himself raised His voice against them, and His accusation was decimating. He did not send those prophets. He did not give them His divine message. They did not speak for Him.

By voicing this accusation, God was defending Himself in a sense. {The disastrous results of the false prophets' messages could open the door for people to point accusing fingers at God. Once the calamity did come on the people of Israel, people might claim that He had not told the people the truth about what was coming.}[Q7] Therefore, God wanted His people to know in advance that He planned to send them into exile. He was innocent of treachery, because He had told them well ahead of time what He was doing and how He would accomplish it.

God readily acknowledged that He was a God of justice and wrath. What He would not tolerate was any misrepresentation of His character. Anyone presenting a message that diminished Him in any way, even though it might make Him seem more acceptable to the masses by promising peace, was seen as an act of slander.

Disappointing discourse (Jer. 23:22). It was one thing for God to simply say that these prophets did not speak for Him. But He went on to demonstrate it with irrefutable proof.

According to God, if these prophets, who claimed to have stood (like Jeremiah) in His inner council and heard His words, were telling the truth, their message would have generated action. The people would have responded by repenting and turning from sin—case closed.

But is that true? Jeremiah was a true prophet, stood in the council of God, and proclaimed God's words. Yet the people did not repent. So did God's "proof" actually prove anything?

{God's evidence actually hearkened back to the prophetic criteria given in Deuteronomy 18:21-22. A prophet's message was tested by comparing what they claimed would happen (the content) against what actually did happen (the outcome). God told Jeremiah that his message would not be well received (cf. Jer. 1:8, 18-19). He warned Jeremiah that the people would refuse to listen to him (7:27). Therefore, their negative reaction to Jeremiah's message was, ironically, proof that his message was valid.}[Q8]

Meanwhile, other prophets claimed God would deliver the people from the day of destruction and give them peace (14:13; 28:1-17). That did not happen. God did not speak to these prophets, and that would be proven when their message of peace did not come to fruition.

RADICAL REALITY

23 Am I a God at hand, saith the Lord, and not a God afar off?

24 Can any hide himself in secret places, that I shall not see him? saith the Lord. Do not I fill heaven and earth? saith the Lord.

God followed His accusation against the prophets with three rhetorical questions that exposed how little they actually knew Him. These questions would also teach His people an important lesson about reality.

God's reach (Jer. 23:23). The first question asked whether God is only God when people are close to Him. {One reason people were confident that God would not send His people into exile was that the temple stood in Jerusalem. Why would He send them away from His temple, the place where His presence dwelled? Surely He wanted them close enough that He could keep an eye on them, speak to them, correct them, and bless them.}[Q9]

That line of thinking was common in the ancient world. People carried their household idols with them when they traveled to ensure their gods stayed nearby. Every community had their own local gods, which they thought held power over a certain limited area. That was one reason why the Assyrian and Babylonian practice of removing people from their homelands was so terrifying. It meant separation from the watchful eyes of their gods and ancestors. It meant being cut off not only physically but also spiritually.

But through His rhetorical question, God reminded the people that He is not so confined. There is no place outside of His reach. Even if His people were taken from His temple, they were not taken from His presence. He can and will interact with His people, no matter where they may be.

God's rule (Jer. 23:24*a*). God next asked whether there is a place anyone can hide from His view, presumably to do something in secret without God's knowledge or to somehow escape God's punishment. That was something another prophet, Jonah, had tried to do when he fled in the opposite direction of where God called him to go. Jonah, of course, found that to be an exercise in futility.

Coupled with the last question, we see a targeted attack against the delusions of the false prophets. It was ridiculous for them to falsely claim they had experienced God's presence and received God's authority and message while they remained under God's eyes and within God's reach.

God's realm (Jer. 23:24*b*). Finally, God presented the truth that the false prophets had totally failed to grasp. He fills heaven and the earth. This idea has one of two connotations, both of which are true. First, God makes the universe full. As the Creator of space, time, planets, and living things, He actively gives substance and shape to every living thing. If something is there, it is because God put it there.

Second, and perhaps more incredibly, God's presence fills the universe. He is not confined to national or geographic boundaries. He is literally everywhere, across all of space, time, and invisible realms. There is not a micrometer of reality outside of His presence.

{Ultimately, the prophets' fatal flaw was that they had too small a view of God.}[Q10] They could not conceive of how the God of love and blessing could also be the God of wrath and judgment. They could not grasp how the God of peace could use war and violence for His purpose. They were afraid that going through exile from the Promised Land would mean being exiled from God Himself. Their fear pushed them to false prophecy.

—Isaiah Campbell

QUESTIONS

1. What did Jeremiah say was wrong with the false prophets?
2. What was the divine council like according to the mythology of ancient nations outside of Israel?
3. How is the biblical idea of a divine council different?
4. What was the relationship between the divine council and Old Testament prophets?
5. What did Jeremiah understand about Israel's future that none of the false prophets did?
6. What was the "whirlwind" Jeremiah prophesied about (Jer. 23:19)?
7. What false claims about God might have been made if He did not defend Himself against the false prophets?
8. How did the people's lack of repentance serve as proof that Jeremiah was a true prophet and the others were not?
9. What misconception about His presence did God address in verse 23?
10. What was the false prophets' fatal flaw?

—Matthew Robinson

Preparing to Teach the Lesson

Some qualities of God make Him completely different than everyone and everything else in the universe. You and I can only be in one place at once. But God exists everywhere at the same time.

This characteristic of God is called omnipresence. Jeremiah 23:24 says, "Can any hide himself in secret places that I shall not see him? saith the Lord. Do I not fill heaven and earth? saith the Lord." Our lesson this week will show us that He is both near and far at the same time. God is everywhere.

TODAY'S AIM

Facts: to know that God always exists in heaven and on earth.

Principle: to understand that no one can hide from the Lord.

Application: to live each day knowing God is everywhere at the same time.

INTRODUCING THE LESSON

There are times in life when we wonder whether God is with us. We question His presence during difficult days. We see tragedy in the news and wonder, Where is God?

Scripture reveals that God is omnipresent. He is everywhere. No one else shares this quality with God, not even Satan. Only the Lord Almighty fills heaven and earth.

DEVELOPING THE LESSON

1. God's wrathful presence (Jer. 23:18-22). Jeremiah 23:18-22 shares the Lord's disdain for false prophets. The latter verses of today's lesson need to be understood in that context. God's omnipresence in this passage was not primarily meant to inspire comfort; it was primarily meant to inspire confidence in God's judgment. The false prophets would not be able to escape His judgment in heaven or on earth. Since He is everywhere, He can deliver His wrath anywhere.

2. God's presence near and far (Jer. 23:23). In verse 23, we see the Lord use an interesting two-part question to reveal more about Himself to us. "Am I a God at hand, saith the Lord, and not a God afar off?" Regarding the first part of the question: is He a God at hand? The answer is yes! He is near, here, at hand, nearby. God is immanent.

What about the second part of the question? Is He far away? Yes. He exists on the other side of the street, the city, the country, the world, and the universe. In the same moment in time, God is both here and there, because He is everywhere.

In the New Testament, the apostle Paul appealed to this characteristic of God's presence as he preached in Athens. As an educated man, Paul used logic and reason to help the highly educated Greeks see how foolish it was to believe they could create a god with their hands or buy one at the market. The final verses of Acts 17 record Paul's attempt to persuade his listeners to turn from fake gods of their own design to the one true God who cannot be contained.

In verse 24, Paul explained that the God who created the world is Lord of the entire universe. He does not live in any particular temple. He lives everywhere! Not only is He omnipresent, but He is self-reliant. Many false gods demanded food, drink, and sacrifices, but the Lord does not need anything. Instead, He gives us "life, and breath, and all things" (vs. 25).

Verse 28 is interesting because it includes quotes from Greek philosophers. Even unbelievers can be correct sometimes.

Paul again appealed to their logic. As the offspring of Almighty God, we cannot create a god using gold, silver, or stone.

Paul's testimony of the omnipresent God had similar results to what we see today: some mocked, others said they might listen another day (vs. 32), and some believed (vs. 34).

3. God's presence in heaven and on earth (Jer. 23:24). Verse 24 continues with two other questions to help solidify the truth of God's omnipresence and to express the practical application. The second question in this verse asks, "Do not I fill heaven and earth?" Since the answer is yes, the first question is terrifying to the false prophets: "Can any hide himself in secret places that I shall not see him?" The false prophets may be able to deceive those who listen, but they cannot hide from the omnipresent God (cf. Ezek. 13:1-16).

References to God's dominion over heaven and earth abound in the Old Testament. Deuteronomy 31, for example, records Moses finishing writing God's law before his death. After all the words of the law were written, Moses expressed his desire to speak the words of the law aloud in order to call heaven and earth to testify against the elders and officials.

The fact that heaven and earth serve as witnesses for the Lord shows that God has dominion over them. His presence everywhere implies His dominion everywhere. We see in Moses' statement not only that God dwells in both heaven and earth but also that His words are divine law in heaven and earth.

Even the format of the law reflected God's dominion over both heaven and earth. The first four commandments focus on our relationship with God. The other six commandments teach us how to treat one another. We see that the law has a heavenly focus and an earthly focus. The God of heaven and earth made an eternal covenant with the people of earth who are also citizens of heaven. He makes laws that pertain to every sphere of life because His ruling presence is everywhere.

ILLUSTRATING THE LESSON

Our perfect God is both near to us and far away because He is everywhere all at once. Nothing can contain the almighty God.

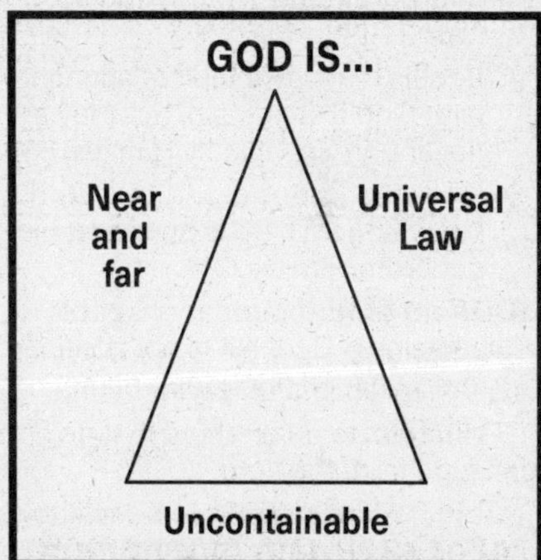

CONCLUDING THE LESSON

The God of heaven and earth rules both. He lives everywhere. His law is universal. The God of heaven came to earth to show us the way. We still live on earth, but everyone who believes becomes a citizen of heaven. This is not just true of the afterlife. Even now, we are seated with Christ in the heavenly realm. He walks with us in the valley of the shadow of death. God is everywhere, so we are never alone. Remember that God lives "in the high and holy place," but He also lives here with us to revive our spirits and hearts (Isa. 57:15).

ANTICIPATING THE NEXT LESSON

Next week we will learn that nothing is hidden from God. Since He is everywhere and knows everything, we cannot hide our sins or ourselves.

—Adam Clagg

PRACTICAL POINTS

1. For a message from God to be authentic, the messenger must have a relationship with Him (Jer. 23:18).
2. The test of truth is time. Lies are always exposed eventually (vss. 19-20).
3. Ignoring the reality of God's justice misrepresents Him to the world (vss. 21-22).
4. People may sever their relationship with God through sin, but they are never unreachable by Him (vs. 23).
5. Nothing is done without God's knowledge. There is no secret hidden from Him (vs. 24).
6. There is no boundary capable of containing God. He is not confined to any nation, kingdom, planet, or galaxy.

—Isaiah Campbell

RESEARCH AND DISCUSSION

1. If the Bible says the Lord is the "God of gods" (Deut. 10:17), does that mean other gods exist (cf. 1 Chr. 16:24-26)?
2. How did God prepare Israel for the rise of false prophets (cf. Deut. 18:18-22)?
3. How does God's act of punishing sin illustrate His faithfulness to His covenant (cf. 28:15-37)?
4. How can believers be sure that they are not deceived by false messages (cf. Col. 2:6-10)?
5. What are some ways that confronting people about deception can build up the church (cf. Eph. 4:13-16)?
6. Why might a person think God is "afar off" from him or her? How might you encourage that person from Scripture (cf. Rom. 8:35-39)?

—Isaiah Campbell

ILLUSTRATED HIGH POINTS

Stood in the counsel of the Lord (Jer. 23:18)

Imagine walking into the throne room of a powerful, wise king. Of course, before you could even walk in, you would have to be permitted by the armed guards standing in the doorway. You would probably face interrogation by one of the king's administrators to assess whether or not you warrant face time with the monarch. Then, as you walk across the ornately decorated throne room, you might take in all the activity around you. Perhaps there would be musicians and dancers performing in the background. The king's chef might be serving tasty food and beverages to those scattered around the room. The king himself would be flanked by advisers, officials, and guards.

This is the kind of image the biblical authors had in mind when they described the "counsel of the Lord." Coming into God's presence was like entering the throne room of a king.

Can any hide himself (vs. 24)

Playing hide-and-seek with a child is not nearly as fun for the adult as it is for the child. When kids are very little, they often have the flawed belief that they can only be seen by people they themselves can see. For them, playing hide-and-seek is simply a matter of closing their eyes. That means the act of finding them is about as challenging as trying to find the ground beneath your feet.

When kids get older, however, they can become quite good at playing hide-and-seek. That spells trouble for their parents, who almost inevitably begin to panic as they search high and low.

Thankfully, God always wins at hide-and-seek. It is really not even worth playing against Him.

—Isaiah Campbell

Golden Text Illuminated

"Can any hide himself in secret places that I shall not see him? saith the Lord. Do not I fill heaven and earth? saith the Lord" (Jeremiah 23:24).

No one is better at asking questions than God Himself. And yet, the questions God asks are never to acquire information *for* Himself, but instead to give information *about* Himself. In Jeremiah 23:24, the Lord asks two questions that reveal something profound about His infinite character, namely, His omniscience and omnipresence. God's omniscience is His exhaustive, eternal knowledge of all things with absolute perfection. His omnipresence means that God is everywhere at once in the totality of His being.

The Lord's questions in this chapter were given at a time when false prophets filled the land of Judah. Sinister and presumptuous, these false prophets exacerbated an already disastrous spiritual climate and hastened the people's doom as Babylonian armies prepared to invade in the near future. In this context, the Lord used rhetorical questions to reveal His divine attributes of omniscience and omnipresence. We will examine these questions, the doctrines they reveal, and some implications for our lives.

Question 1: "Can any hide himself in secret places that I shall not see him?" Here, the Lord does not need information from us but instead is providing us information about Himself. There are significant changes He wishes to bring about in our lives through this reflection upon His character. Clearly, the doctrine He intends us to see is His divine omniscience: His perfect, infinite, simultaneous knowledge of all things. God knows all because He sees all. The Lord weighs the motives of human beings (cf. Prov. 16:2), and He "knoweth the secrets of the heart" (Ps. 44:21). That is a powerful incentive for authentic holiness. God is not content with mere external conformity to a code of ethics, but instead the Lord looks at the heart (cf. 1 Sam. 16:7). The Lord's question here in Jeremiah leads to careful and conscientious obedience in even our most private, secret moments, for we know that God Himself can see and hear us in the secret places.

Question 2: "Do not I fill heaven and earth?" The question is rhetorical. The Lord does indeed fill heaven and earth. That is His attribute of omnipresence. Yet to "fill heaven and earth" does not mean God is like a physical substance or gas, but that there is no place in the universe where He is not. He is present in every inch of His creation in the totality of His being.

That means that we are always standing on holy ground, because *God* is there. The doctrine of God's omnipresence reminds us that there is no such thing as a secular or private moment, for God sees all and knows all. And He sees it not through the secondhand reporting of an angel, but rather by His own personal, eyewitness knowledge. It is a great help against temptation and sin to know that God is always near and ready to intervene and deliver His people from temptation. "In him we live, and move, and have our being" (Acts 17:28). God's all-filling presence is a reminder to us that He is always near, especially in and through His Word, to give us the grace we need to put His glory on display.

—Jerod A. Gilcher

Heart of the Lesson

Our relationship with God determines whether we see His attributes as beautiful or as dreadful. If someone is God's enemy, His attributes of holiness, sovereignty, and power are not a source of comfort; they are instead a source of dread and terror. On the other hand, if someone is reconciled to God through Christ, those attributes of God are a source of delight and hope. That is the issue that arises in Jeremiah 23:18-24.

1. Warnings from God (Jer. 23:18-22). Sinister and presumptuous false prophets filled the land of Judah during the days of the prophet Jeremiah. Their deceptions aggravated an already disastrous spiritual climate of apostasy and sin.

In that context, the Lord spoke of some of His divine attributes that should cause false prophets then and now to tremble and repent of their sin. In verses 18-22, God warned of His anger and declared His disapproval of false prophets. He declared that He had not spoken to these prophets, but they dared to speak on His behalf. He had not invited them into His council, but they claimed to know His will.

2. Questions from God (Jer. 23:23-24). The Lord then asked a series of powerful questions about His glorious character.

God's first question, "Am I a God at hand, . . . and not a God afar off?" (vs. 23), was pointed and rhetorical. There was no debate in the matter: He *is* a God far off and not merely a God "at hand." God's meaning, of course, was not that He is distant or unaware of things. Rather, the sense is that God is no small local deity from whom one might hide, but a God who rules all things from heaven and therefore sees all things, both near and far.

God's first question, then, points to His perfections of transcendence and omniscience. God transcends His creation and sees all that happens in His creation. Those attributes warn the wicked that nothing escapes His notice, but they simultaneously comfort the believer with God's all-seeing sovereignty.

God then asked, "Can any hide himself in secret places that I shall not see him?" (vs. 24). Here God asked a question to draw attention to His perfections of omnipresence and omniscience. God is everywhere all at once and knows all things perfectly. The answer to His question is obvious: there is no location in the universe where a person may hide from God's all-seeing vision. David declared in Psalm 139:7: "Whither shall I go from thy spirit? or whither shall I flee from thy presence?" Indeed, God even knows the secrets of the heart (cf. 44:21).

Unbelievers cannot hide from God, and believers know that God is always near them, ready to comfort and strengthen their souls, for "in him we live, and move, and have our being" (Acts 17:28).

Finally, God asked, "Do not I fill heaven and earth?" (Jer. 23:24). Again, the question was designed to draw attention to the Lord's omnipresent nature. As God, He is present everywhere. He is not spread out like a tapestry; rather, He inhabits every place in the universe with the totality of His being. His fullness is in space. His fullness is in the very room in which you sit. That makes every space and place holy ground. That reality is either ignored by or disturbing to His enemies, but for those reconciled to Him through His Son, it is one of the greatest comforts in the world.

—Jerod A. Gilcher

World Missions

It was a lively youth fellowship in the early 1980s, meeting every week in a high school classroom for an evening of worship and Bible teaching. The musical style of the worship was a mix of contemporary rock and folk, often including several women and men on guitars, sometimes with one or two on hand drums. The participants were from a variety of churches in the area. Baptists, Methodists, Reformed, and Pentecostals met together and often headed off to a diner after the fellowship concluded for further late-night conversations.

On this one evening, not long after the worship began, three people no one in the fellowship knew came in together and sat close to the center of the gathering. As was often the case, the worship faded into a contemplative quiet after several songs of praise. Suddenly, a voice was raised, and as people looked up, they saw it was a young lady who seemed to be the leader of the three newcomers. From the manner in which she spoke, it seemed that her words were meant to be understood as some sort of prophetic speech, and she spoke about accessing "power for abundant living." Some of those present, however, had questions concerning these visitors and the nature of what was spoken. Though it was clearly meant to be taken as spontaneous, there was a rehearsed quality to it. The three departed as soon as the meeting was over.

Some inquiries later revealed that the young visitors were from a new religious movement called The Way International, a group that presented itself as a kind of Pentecostal fellowship but denied the deity of Christ—that Jesus is within God's very Self, eternal and uncreated. Alarmingly, it also turned out that they were at the time engaged in a program of infiltrating genuinely Christian groups.

That anecdote provides us with a bit of a warning concerning groups that might seek to bring confusion to the church. Jeremiah 23:21 warned about other false prophets that God did not send and "yet they ran." He had "not spoken to them, yet they prophesied." Nonetheless, we can be grateful that when people arise who seek to distort the Scriptures or to provide "prophecies" that cannot legitimately claim to have been revealed by the Holy Spirit, God sees all these things and will provide guidance on how to bring counsel to any who have been confused. As God declared in verse 24, "Can any hide himself in secret places that I shall not see him? . . . Do not I fill heaven and earth?" In the case of the youth fellowship, local teachers with wisdom and discernment were able to provide counsel to those who were confused, and teaching was arranged for the fellowship as a whole.

The lessons learned through that experience proved to be valuable in the future ministry of many of those young people as they heard and obeyed a call from God to head to the mission field. For example, some years ago, a discussion ensued among workers with a focus on helping communities of discipled believers emerge in Muslim contexts. One of those in the conversation argued that it should be acceptable for leaders in such communities to reject the deity of Christ as they "worked out their theology." Reflecting on the incident in that long-ago youth fellowship, one of the workers was able to raise important questions to counter teaching that would have had dangerous consequences.

—Matthew Friedman

The Jewish Aspect

Prophets proliferated cultures across the ancient world, particularly in the regions around ancient Israel. From Egypt to Babylon, prophets were key to a society's ability to function. They were essential for running an effective government and a profitable economy. Most important, prophets were considered the key agents in maintaining healthy foreign relations. The foreign relationship in question, of course, was between the nation and the gods.

In our day, many people do not believe any kind of spiritual realm even exists. In ancient cultures, however, the existence of the spiritual world was never in question. They anxiously sought ways to integrate the spiritual realm into their physical realities. Of primary importance was finding ways to communicate with those who inhabited the spiritual realm, from dead ancestors to gods. People skilled in divination, like astrologers and fortune tellers, were in high demand. However, the group we classify as "prophets" were prized far above the others. This special group claimed to hear from a god directly. They were the gods' mouthpieces, their messengers, and their ambassadors.

For the most part, Israel's prophets fit perfectly into the role as displayed in other ancient cultures. They represented a significant segment of the population (cf. 1 Sam. 10:10-12; 2 Kgs. 2:3-7), were sought out for counsel (cf. 1 Sam. 28:6; 2 Kgs. 3:11-13), and were often given prominent roles in the courts of the kings (cf. 1 Kgs. 1:22-23). However, Israel's prophets were unlike any other prophets on earth because of the One for whom they claimed to speak. These prophets spoke for the Lord, the God of Israel.

The audience to whom God's prophets spoke was also unique. Certainly, God's prophets spoke to powerful people like kings and priests, just as prophets in other nations did. However, they also spoke directly to the people of Israel, even the poor and the oppressed. In so doing, God's prophets represented His heart for all the people. The God of Israel made it clear that the entire nation, not just an elite class, was worthy of His message.

The other unique characteristic of God's prophets was the content of their messages. While prophets-for-hire typically tailored their messages to please whoever was paying for their services, God's true prophets sought only to please Him. Therefore, when the nations of Israel and Judah descended into sin and debauchery, God's prophets spoke messages of rebuke, judgment, and doom. Because of that, God's prophets were often on the run, hunted by angry monarchs, never sure if they would live to prophesy another day (cf. 18:4).

A century before Jeremiah's time, the prophet Isaiah proclaimed Israel's destruction by the formidable Assyrian army. Now Jeremiah warned the Southern Kingdom, Judah, about their own impending day of judgment, this time at the hands of the Babylonians. Needless to say, this was not a message people in Judah wanted to hear.

But Jeremiah faced a challenge far more sinister than threats to his life and livelihood. There were other prophets at the time who claimed to speak for God, yet they spoke messages more palatable to the masses. The question that therefore needed to be answered was simple: Who actually spoke for God?

—Isaiah Campbell

Guiding the Superintendent

Today's text juxtaposes the storm-like judgment of God with His friend-like counsel. Teachers may want to ask students which of those most resonates with their immediate association with the word "God," and why. When is God like a storm, and when is God like a friend?

Jeremiah spoke to people in the years, months, and even weeks leading up to Jerusalem's destruction in 586 B.C. at the hands of Babylon. In Jeremiah 23:18-24 we find the prophet urging the people to yield to the omnipresent Lord before disaster overtakes them.

DEVOTIONAL OUTLINE

1. The storm of the Lord (Jer. 23:18-22). Jeremiah used a storm metaphor several times to depict the fierceness of God's judgment. Some of those texts, including 23:18-24, aim the terrifying storm of judgment at unrepentant Judah. Others, such as 30:23-24, aim the terrifying storm of judgment at Judah's enemies. Both of those texts refer to "the thoughts" (23:20) or "the intents" (30:24) of the Lord's "heart." What does a terrifying storm have to do with the Lord's heart? J. Michael Thigpen explains that the two texts reveal God's "willingness to cause his people grief because his heart's desire is to bring his people back into relationship with him" ("The Storm of YHWH: Jeremiah's Theology of God's Heart and Motives," *Bibliotheca Sacra* 176). Though fierce, the storm that drove Judah to repentance was driven by the fury of God's kind heart (cf. Rom. 2:4).

False prophecy is a book-wide theme in Jeremiah. Jeremiah proclaimed that the false prophets did not rely on the Lord (2:8; 23:13) or His Word (5:13; 23:21), did not align their lifestyle with the ethical demands of His Word (6:13; 23:11), did not treat true prophets justly (20:2; 26:8), and most importantly, did not call the people to repent of sin (23:14). Instead of calling for repentance, they gave false hope that Judah would not be conquered by Babylon (27:9) but would enjoy peace (14:13-15) or, at worst, endure only two years of exile (28:11).

Jeremiah testified that true prophets call for repentance (Jer. 35:15) based on previous Scripture (6:16). Unrepentant devotees of false prophets should fear that the Lord is "a God at hand" (23:23).

2. The secret of the Lord (Jer. 23:23-24). The "whirlwind" (Jer. 23:19), or storm, of the Lord is another pervasive theme in Jeremiah. Those who refuse to repent and trust God's Word cannot hide from the omnipresent Judge. God asks, "Do not I fill heaven and earth?" (vs. 24). This is great news for the repentant believer but not for those who play at church without hating their sin and clinging to the cross. God is against the false prophets who steal His words.

The intimate secret of God is quite a contrast to His intimidating storm, but herein lies the mystery of divine omnipresence. Those who refuse to repent cannot hide from the omnipresent God, but those who do repent and believe the word of the gospel enjoy the fellowship of the omnipresent Counselor.

CHILDREN'S CORNER

Children and youth can be especially susceptible to false teaching because they are in the process of learning how to think for themselves. Ask children in your classes who they go to when they need advice. How do they know they can trust those people? Emphasize to children that the best way to know whose advice to trust is to see who gives advice based on the truths of God's Word and who does not.

—*Matthew Swale*

SCRIPTURE LESSON TEXT

PS. 139:1 O LORD, thou hast searched me, and known *me*.

2 Thou knowest my downsitting and mine uprising, thou understandest my thought afar off.

3 Thou compassest my path and my lying down, and art acquainted *with* all my ways.

4 For *there is* not a word in my tongue, *but*, lo, O LORD, thou knowest it altogether.

5 Thou hast beset me behind and before, and laid thine hand upon me.

6 *Such* knowledge *is* too wonderful for me; it is high, I cannot *attain* unto it.

7 Whither shall I go from thy spirit? or whither shall I flee from thy presence?

8 If I ascend up into heaven, thou *art* there: if I make my bed in hell, behold, thou *art there*.

9 *If* I take the wings of the morning, *and* dwell in the uttermost parts of the sea;

10 Even there shall thy hand lead me, and thy right hand shall hold me.

11 If I say, Surely the darkness shall cover me; even the night shall be light about me.

12 Yea, the darkness hideth not from thee; but the night shineth as the day: the darkness and the light *are* both alike *to thee*.

13 For thou hast possessed my reins: thou hast covered me in my mother's womb.

14 I will praise thee; for I am fearfully *and* wonderfully made: marvellous *are* thy works; and *that* my soul knoweth right well.

15 My substance was not hid from thee, when I was made in secret, *and* curiously wrought in the lowest parts of the earth.

16 Thine eyes did see my substance, yet being unperfect; and in thy book all *my members* were written, *which* in continuance were fashioned, when *as yet there was* none of them.

NOTES

Nothing Is Hidden from God

Lesson Text: Psalm 139:1-16

Related Scriptures: Job 42:1-6; Psalm 121:1-8; Matthew 6:5-8; Romans 11:33-36; Hebrews 4:12-13

TIME: between 1011 and 971 B.C. PLACE: Israel

GOLDEN TEXT—"Whither shall I go from thy spirit? or whither shall I flee from thy presence?" (Psalm 139:7).

Introduction

The life of the mind and the life of the heart come together beautifully in Psalm 139. Each of the three sections noted below (vss. 1-6, 7-12, 13-16) contain a similar alternating movement—a reflection about God and then an awe-filled response. In the first two sections, the response is more of a hushed awe than praise. In the third section, David's wonder spills over into praise.

There are different types of psalms, sometimes called genres. There are psalms that praise, give thanks, lament, teach, and reflect. Psalm 139, however, shows the limits of genre-based interpretation. Is it a praise psalm (cf. vs. 14)? Is it a lament psalm (cf. vss. 19-22)? Is it a penitential psalm (cf. vss. 23-24)? Is it a wisdom (teaching) psalm (cf. vss. 1-6)? It depends on which verses one emphasizes! One thing is certain: the complexity adds to the psalm's poetic beauty.

LESSON OUTLINE

1. **THE INESCAPABLE GOD KNOWS US—Ps. 139:1-6**
2. **THE INESCAPABLE GOD PURSUES US—Ps. 139:7-12**
3. **THE INESCAPABLE GOD FASHIONED US—Ps. 139:13-16**

Exposition: Verse by Verse

THE INESCAPABLE GOD KNOWS US

PS. 139:1 O Lord, thou hast searched me, and known *me.*

2 Thou knowest my downsitting and mine uprising, thou understandest my thought afar off.

3 Thou compassest my path and my lying down, and art acquainted *with* all my ways.

4 For *there is* not a word in my tongue, *but*, lo, O Lord thou knowest it altogether.

5 Thou hast beset me behind and before, and laid thine hand upon me.

6 *Such* knowledge *is* too wonderful for me; it is high, I cannot *attain* unto it.

Verses 1-4 reflect on the personal nature of God's knowledge. Verses 5-6 respond by declaring how wonderful God's knowledge is. David reflected on the reality that God searched his heart. Before David spoke a word, God knew it (vs. 4). God even knew his thoughts (vs. 2)!

God's knowledge (Ps. 139:1-4). God knew David's every movement and word. God has personal and intimate knowledge of everything every person does. God knows our mundane movements, thoughts, ways, and words. He knows every thought *you* have and every word *you* speak! Nothing is secret from Him.

While God could have used His knowledge of David's life to judge him, David knew that God's knowledge of him was both relational and loving (cf. Ps. 51). David was so convinced of God's mercy that he mentioned the same concept of God searching and knowing him at the end of the psalm to ask God to reveal unconfessed sin in his life so he could walk more faithfully.

{Whether God's intimate knowledge of a person's sins is happy news or haunting news depends on whether that person is walking in repentant faith.}[Q1] In David's life, there were times when God's knowledge was a source of comfort and vindication (cf. 41:12). There were also times when God's knowledge of David's actions and words was a source of extreme spiritual discomfort and unrest (cf. 32:3-4). The difference between God's omniscience being happy or haunting is not whether a person has been good enough but whether the person humbly admits a need for God's mercy, forgiveness, and grace (cf. 51:1-4).

David's response (Ps. 139:5-6). {As David moved from reflection on divine omniscience to his response, it becomes clear that he was happy and not haunted when he wrote Psalm 139 (cf. vss. 5-6).}[Q2] In verse 5, David considered what God did with His knowledge of him. David used a Hebrew term that usually refers to an army besieging a city (cf. 2 Kgs. 6:24). Being besieged by God would be terrifying for an unrepentant sinner. But a repentant sinner like David would draw comfort from the besieging nearness of God.

David's praise started in Psalm 139:5-6 with his dazzled bewilderment of God's merciful knowledge of his entire life. {David mentioned God's knowledge of him three times in verse 6. First, David utilized a concept often used to describe the miraculous. God knowing and still loving sinners who believe His promises is a miracle. It is wonderful! Second, David used a Hebrew word that can mean high and exalted (cf. Isa. 12:4) but can also describe the kind of high ground used as a military defense (cf. Deut. 2:36). David was safeguarded and fortified in knowing that He was fully known and yet fully loved by the Lord. Third, David could not wrap his mind around the extent of God's knowledge.}[Q3] Even what little David knew about how much God knows revealed how little David knew. It is incomprehensible!

THE INESCAPABLE GOD PURSUES US

7 Whither shall I go from thy spirit? or whither shall I flee from thy presence?

8 If I ascend up into heaven, thou *art* there: if I make my bed in hell, behold, thou *art there*.

9 *If* I take the wings of the morning, *and* dwell in the uttermost parts of the sea;

10 Even there shall thy hand lead me, and thy right hand shall hold me.

11 If I say, Surely the darkness

shall cover me; even the night shall be light about me.

12 Yea, the darkness hideth not from thee; but the night shineth as the day: the darkness and the light *are* both alike *to thee*.

Sometimes theology and doctrine get a bad reputation for being passionless or cold. Psalm 139 presents a beautiful alternative, reflecting on complex and deep truths related to the omnipresent (everywhere-present) and omniscient (all-knowing) nature of God in a passionate, worshipful way. Meditating on God's omniscience leads to wonder (vs. 6). Ruminating on God's omnipresence leads to recognizing God's light (vs. 12). Mulling over God's creative power in the womb leads to praise (vs. 14). Theologians call the nearness of God His immanence.

Human imagination might assume that lofty attributes like omniscience, omnipresence, and omnipotence would imply a God uninterested in the dust and bustle of human life. Psalm 139 counters with glorious truths. He is almighty, and He is near! Both are true, and this leads David to awe and worship.

Verses 7-10 reflect on God's presence with and pursuit of His people. Verses 11-12 respond by declaring the illuminating light that comes from God's presence *and* pursuit of His people. {David toured the cosmos in verses 8-10. Whether he was in the heights, the depths, or the farthest reaches of the known world, God was there.}[Q4]

Although the New Testament speaks more clearly about the Holy Spirit than the Old Testament does, He is mentioned throughout the Old Testament, including as early as Genesis 1:2. He is mentioned here in Psalm 139:7 as well. The Trinity is not a late invention of the New Testament church; it is a firm, biblical truth.

God's presence everywhere (Ps. 139:7-10). Verse 7 uses two words for movement. The first refers to any basic travel, but the second refers to running and fleeing. {The second word is also used in Jonah 1:10, when the prophet fled from God's presence. Whether or not David was traveling or running from God, as Jonah later would, he knew the presence of God's Spirit was there regardless. The last line in verse 8 carries the meaning of "Behold, there You are!" It was as if David were saying to himself or anyone who would run from God, "Surprise! You can't outrun God!"}[Q5]

The Hebrew word *Sheol* is used in Psalm 139:8 and is here translated "hell," though the word has a variety of uses. {In the Psalms, Sheol can refer broadly to the place of the dead (cf. 6:5) or danger that threatens death (cf. 30:3; 116:3).}[Q6] The psalmists seem to imply that both believers and unbelievers go there (cf. 6:5; 9:17). This word may refer broadly to the place of the dead, not just hell as we understand it today.

The concept is an example of progressive revelation. Old Testament saints had accurate knowledge about life after death but did not know as much as would eventually be revealed in the completed Scriptures. Like New Testament believers, Old Testament believers saw life after death as being in God's hands (cf. 16:10-11). They did not know, however, the specifics of heaven and hell that were revealed in the New Testament. The concept of Sheol reminds New Testament believers that even though Jesus defeated death, death is still not good. Stunningly, Psalm 139:8 says that God would be with David even in Sheol.

God's interaction with David progresses and personalizes in this section. In verse 8, God was there. In verse 10, God did two things. The first thing God did was guide. Where David went, God led and guided. The second thing God did was expressed using a Hebrew word that often describes grabbing hold of someone forcefully (cf. Judg. 12:6). Perhaps this matches the word "flee" in Psalm 139:7. When David ran, God held him tight.

David's response (Ps. 139:11-12). {Verse 11 imagines circumstances in which darkness surrounded David. Sometimes the Psalms use darkness to indicate despair (88:6), danger (143:3), or judgment (107:10-12). Herein lies the beauty of God's presence and pursuit—God's presence is a light even in the darkness. Some people only feel God's presence when their mood or circumstances are light, but Psalm 139:12 declares that He is in our darkness too.}[Q7]

Unlike other ancient people who assumed that gods had limited, local influence (cf. 2 Kgs. 17:26), David knew that the one true God was everywhere. This would have been reassuring to Israelites living centuries after David's lifetime who experienced exile.

Ancient Near Eastern people assumed that when one army defeated another army, the victors' gods defeated the gods of the defeated army (cf. Isa. 37:12). God's people in exile would likely have wondered whether the Babylonian gods defeated the Lord, whether the Lord was with them in exile, and whether they ought to go ahead and appease the gods of their captors (cf. Dan. 3:1-30). Praying God's words through David in Psalm 139 would have answered those questions with the glorious truth that God remains in control, and He is with His people no matter where they go or what happens to them.

THE INESCAPABLE GOD FASHIONED US

13 For thou hast possessed my reins: thou hast covered me in my mother's womb.

14 I will praise thee; for I am fearfully *and* wonderfully made: marvellous *are* thy works; and *that* my soul knoweth right well.

15 My substance was not hid from thee, when I was made in secret, *and* curiously wrought in the lowest parts of the earth.

16 Thine eyes did see my substance, yet being unperfect; and in thy book all *my members* were written, *which* in continuance were fashioned, when *as yet there was* none of them.

{Verses 13-16 reflect on the personal nature of God's creation of each person. Psalm 139 has long assisted Christians in pursuit of biblical self-worth. If God carefully made all people, then each human matters greatly. Every person we meet at work, at church, or walking down the street matters and is worthy of dignity and respect, because every human is personally made by God in His image.}[Q8]

Embedded within these verses is David's response of praise (vs. 14). Verse 13 offers a reason for the personal knowledge, presence, and pursuit described up until this point in the psalm. Why does God, who knows everything about His sinful people, still give them His light? Because He created them.

David's tour of the cosmos in verses 7-12 zooms in on the womb. This is not the only time David focused on the womb. In Psalm 51, when David lamented his sin and asked for God's restoring grace, he talked about the womb in order to show how deep the sin problem is. He knew that his sin began before his first breath (vs. 5). His point is connected here. {God's personal knowledge, interest, and presence with David stretched back before his first breath. That is how pervasive His presence is. God was caring for David before and during his earliest development.}[Q9]

{Regarding God's presence with him in his mother's womb, David reflected on four truths (not necessarily in the text's order here). First, God made his internal organs (vs. 13), which is the sense of the phrase "possessed my reins." David used a term often translated as "kidneys," but sometimes it simply refers to one's inner parts.

Second, God made his "substance" (vs. 15). David used a rare word here that seems to refer to the structuring frame of one's body, or one's bones. Notice that in verse 13, the first line refers to internal organs, then the second line uses the word "me." In verse 15, the first phrase refers to bones, then the second phrase uses the word "I." David was equating his physical body with himself. Some people today assume that their immaterial soul is their real self and that the physical body is less important to God. David would disagree, for he referred to his material body as the careful handiwork of God. Elsewhere, God commands worship not just from human souls but from human bodies (cf. Rom. 12:1-2), and one day He will resurrect physical human bodies (1 Cor. 15:40-44).

Third, God's formation of David's body is described as a knitting or weaving project (Ps. 139:13, 15). Both verses 13 and 15 compare God making human bodies to careful needlework. Knitters will appreciate the precision and care that this image involves. David was amazed at how personally involved God has always been with his existence. Master weavers or quilters do not knit without a plan for their handiwork.

Fourth, David reflected on God's omniscient plan for his life (vs. 16). God forming, assessing, pursuing, and seeing David would not make sense unless there was a plan for the handiwork.}Q10 God knew all of David's days before they unfolded, and this truth made the future less daunting. This omniscient plan was presented in terms of a book containing all of David's days. A good author does not write without purpose, and neither does God have His people's lives written in His book without a good plan.

David's response culminated in praise (vs. 14), although it interrupted His reflection rather than concluding it. The basis of David's praise is twofold. First, the forming and weaving from verse 13 is described as fearful and wonderful. Second, David said the activity or work of God in making him was wonderful. Both reasons for David's praise use a Hebrew word related to the one used in verse 6 that often describes miracles. David knew on a deep level that the way God makes humans is miraculous. The proper response to God is praise! Let us join David in this and praise God!

—Matthew Swale

QUESTIONS

1. What determines whether God's thorough knowledge of us is comforting or disquieting?
2. How did David feel about God's thorough knowledge of him when he wrote Psalm 139?
3. How did David describe God's knowledge of him?
4. What is the main point of verses 8-10?
5. What did David say to anyone trying to escape God?
6. What can the Hebrew word *Sheol* sometimes mean?
7. What might David have been implying when he said that God is a light in the darkness?
8. What is one reason that every human life is precious?
9. When did David say God began caring for him?
10. What four truths did David reflect on regarding God's presence with him in his mother's womb?

—Tom Greene

Preparing to Teach the Lesson

In this last lesson of unit 1, we will continue to explore the omnipresent nature of God. God is everywhere at the same time. Since He is everywhere, we cannot hide anything from Him. This week's key theme is the Lord's knowledge of our life and world. God knows our hopes and dreams, our failures and shame. We cannot hide our sins from the God who never leaves us.

TODAY'S AIM

Facts: to see that nothing is hidden from God.

Principle: to grasp that God sees all and knows all.

Application: to realize the futility of trying to hide from God.

INTRODUCING THE LESSON

Hide-and-seek is a popular children's game. Some people are better at hiding than others. Some are excellent at finding people. Can you imagine playing hide-and-seek with God? Of course not! Since God is everywhere, we cannot hide from Him.

DEVELOPING THE LESSON

1. God knows our thoughts (Ps. 139:1-6). In this beautiful poem, King David expresses a wonderful aspect of God being always present. Nothing is hidden from the Lord who searches us and knows us fully. We can hide from others but not from God. The psalmist says God knows what we do all day—sitting, rising, going out, lying down (vss. 2-3). God even knows what we are going to say before we say it (vs. 4). Verse 5 continues with a comforting aspect of this: since God is always with us, we know His arms are wrapped around us and His hand is on us. This truth about God is wonderful (vs. 6)!

Since God is everywhere, He is even in our minds and hearts. Job 42:1-6 contains one of Job's speeches to the Lord. He acknowledged that God can do all things, but then he added that no thought can be kept from God's sight. Isn't that amazing? Even if we think about hiding a thought from the Lord, we cannot. That is humbling.

In Romans 11:33-36, Paul said similar things about the knowledge of God: "O the depth and riches both of the wisdom and knowledge of God" (vs. 33)! Verse 34 is a quote from Isaiah 40:1. Is there anyone who gives God advice? Does He even need counsel? Of course not!

Hebrews 4:12-13 goes even further to help us apply this truth. If God knows everything, including our thoughts and what is in our hearts, then He can judge even our thoughts and the intent of our hearts. Not only does He judge what we say and do, but He already knows the attitude of our hearts. Nothing can be hidden from Him! That is one of the beautiful things about the gospel. God calls everyone to repent. He already knows our sin, but repenting brings our sin to light so that we may be washed in His blood and forgiven. When God washes away our sins, they are erased forever by the power and love of Jesus Christ.

Of course, if God knows our minds and hearts, then He knows the things we think about, including our prayers. In Matthew 6:5-8, Jesus taught about prayer. He scolded hypocrites who prayed openly and loudly. The attention they received from others was their reward. Instead, He instructs us to go into a private place to pray. Our Father who sees our secret prayers will reward us openly. How is God able to do those things? He can do them because He is everywhere and because nothing is hidden from Him. God hears your silent prayers because He is everywhere. He can reward you publicly because He is everywhere. You can trust Him with your most secret thoughts because He is everywhere.

2. Where can I hide? (Ps. 139:7-12). Verse 7 is our golden text for this week: "Whither shall I go from thy spirit? or whither shall I flee from thy presence?" Of course, the answer to these questions is "nowhere." These rhetorical questions lead to some extreme examples of a God who is everywhere. Is God in heaven, hell, the wings of the morning, and the uttermost parts of the sea? Yes, He is everywhere! Then the psalmist gets very practical: wherever we are, God will lead us with His hand, and He will hold us fast.

3. The blessing of God's omnipresence (Ps. 139:13-16). In verse 13, the psalmist turns our attention to the privacy of a mother's womb. With today's technology, we have images and videos of a forming child. But for most of human history, no one could see the baby except for God. Verses 13-16 beautifully illustrate the creative care of the Lord when He is preparing our bodies for a life of serving Him. The Lord not only sees and is present as a child is growing; He is also involved.

Most of us can relate to this psalm. When we cry out for help, we look up and call out to God. When we need help, we cry to the One who made everything and is everywhere. He is the one who can provide the help we need.

He will not let our feet slip. The Lord never sleeps. He constantly watches over us. He is the shade on a hot day and will protect us at night. He can keep us from all harm and watch over our lives.

ILLUSTRATING THE LESSON

God knows us inside and out. He is the very reason for our existence. God, who gives life, was even involved with our growth as babies in our mothers' womb. He is the only One who knows us completely. Not only does God fully know us, but there is nowhere we can hide from God's gaze. He sees everything, including the places we go, the thoughts we think, the words we say, and the things we do. God is always with us, and there is nothing we can hide from Him.

CONCLUDING THE LESSON

This lesson is a natural progression in the unit. Since God is everywhere, it is logical that nothing can be hidden from Him. Thankfully, the Lord does not just leave us to figure things out. He lays out the truth clearly in His Word.

ANTICIPATING THE NEXT LESSON

Next week, we will begin the next unit in this quarter: God's omniscience. In the four weeks of lessons, we won't just study the doctrine of God knowing everything. Each week, we will study a different time in history when God revealed what He knows to someone. We will explore the stories of Pharaoh, Ananias and Sapphira, Nathanael, and a Samaritan woman.

—Adam Clagg

PRACTICAL POINTS

1. We can take comfort in the fact that God knows us completely (Ps. 139:1-6).
2. We can take comfort in knowing that God is with us wherever we go (vss. 7-10).
3. Even the darkest circumstances are not difficult for God (vss. 11-12).
4. Life begins at conception and should be celebrated (vs. 13).
5. No matter our physical features, we can praise God for carefully and wonderfully designing us. We should not mock people for their physical appearance (vss. 14-15).
6. We can take comfort in knowing that God has a plan for our lives (vs. 16).

—Tom Greene

RESEARCH AND DISCUSSION

1. If God knows all our thoughts before we speak, why pray?
2. If God is everywhere, why does He sometimes feel distant?
3. How should we respond to the fact that God knows everything? Is that how you typically respond?
4. How are these verses comforting in times of difficulty?
5. What are the practical implications of God knitting us together in our mother's womb (vs. 13)?
6. If all God's works are wonderful (vs. 14), how should that impact the way we view people we consider exceptionally sinful?
7. What practical implications should knowing that God has a plan (vs. 16) have on our daily lives?

—Tom Greene

ILLUSTRATED HIGH POINTS

Thou hast beset me behind and before (Ps. 139:5)

Imagine being on the run from fierce enemies. Cold, alone, and afraid, it might be hard to sleep at night, knowing that your pursuers could be getting closer. But now imagine that you are surrounded by the world's largest and best-trained army while sleeping in a luxury hotel. You would be able to sleep comfortably and worry-free! God surrounds and protects His people far better than any human army could.

The uttermost parts of the sea (vs. 9)

In 1973, two workers were laying a transatlantic telephone cable when an accident trapped them over fifteen hundred feet below sea level. After spending over eighty-four hours underwater, they were finally rescued with roughly twelve minutes of oxygen remaining. That was the deepest submarine rescue in history!

Even more miraculous was God's deliverance of Jonah in the belly of a fish! Whether God's people travel far across the sea to distant lands or are trapped *beneath* the sea, God is always present and able to deliver them.

In thy book all my members were written (vs. 16)

Some authors start writing without knowing where the story will go. Others, like J.R.R. Tolkien, take tremendous pains to prepare and outline before writing. Tolkien developed the entire Elvish language before writing his famous *The Lord of the Rings* series!

God is not a directionless author waiting to see what happens. He has a carefully prepared plan. When difficulty strikes, we can trust that He has a plan, even if we cannot recognize it.

—Tom Greene

Golden Text Illuminated

"Whither shall I go from thy spirit? or whither shall I flee from thy presence?" (Psalm 139:7).

There is no hide-and-seek with the God of the universe. No one can hide from Him, and He never needs to seek anyone. By virtue of His *omnipresence* (God's presence everywhere in the totality of His being) and His *omniscience* (perfect, infinite knowledge of all things), there is nothing and no one God does not see. Hebrews 4:13 tells us that no creature is hidden from God's sight, but "all things are naked and opened unto the eyes of him with whom we have to do."

This is precisely the truth that brought David such comfort in his afflictions in Psalm 139. In the midst of wicked men and murderous enemies who sought his life and blasphemed his God, David found solace in deep contemplation of the attributes of God. God's attributes of omnipresence and omniscience brought particular comfort to his anxious soul.

David asked this question of God in verse 7: "Whither shall I go from thy spirit? or whiter shall I flee from thy presence?" One gets the sense that this question was less for God than it was for David himself. He marveled at such a God whose Spirit and presence were in every single part of the universe. There was no escape from God. There is nowhere He cannot see and nowhere He is not present. In verse 6, David declared: "Such knowledge is too wonderful for me; it is high, I cannot attain unto it." David thus models for us how a robust theology of God's character soothes the soul in troubled times. Let us turn to a brief exposition of verse 7, accompanied by some practical insights for life-change.

First, the question. David asked one question in two different ways. "Whither" and "whither" ask the same thing from overlapping perspectives. More importantly, however, David addressed these questions to God Himself ("thy Spirit" and "thy presence"). Clearly, David was not seeking information from God; instead, he expressed astonishment about the character of God *to* God. This was worship. As David considered the staggering reality that God is everywhere at once, he exclaimed back to God the glory of His own immensity. He could ascend into the stratosphere, and God is there; he could descend into the depths of the earth, and God is there too (vs. 8). Were he to sail to the farthest shore of the ocean, God would lead him there (vs. 10). There is no escape from the presence of God, and *that* is among the greatest comforts for a believer.

Second, the comfort. God's "presence" and "spirit" are parallel. Indeed, they are one and the same. David's comfort was knowing that God was not observing his plight from a distance or sending transmissions of His power from another galaxy. Rather, God's personal presence through His Spirit was in David's midst. God was present to bless, strengthen, comfort, and satisfy David's deepest longings. God not only sees all things; He is present in every space and moment and reigning over all things.

These realities supply the believer assurance amidst the deepest fears, comfort amidst the greatest trials, and fellowship amidst painful loneliness. There is no hide-and-seek from God, and that satisfies our souls.

—Jerod A. Gilcher

Heart of the Lesson

We are daily beset with things we cannot control or predict. That has the potential to send us into depression, fear, worry, and concern. What is the cure for such feelings?

Scripture provides what may seem a surprising secret for those nagging maladies of the soul. Many assume that the cure for fear and anxiety lies in a change of circumstances. While that may be desirable, the Word of God provides a deeper, more pervasive power over fear and anxiety: deep contemplation of the attributes of God.

In Psalm 139 David found himself amid wicked men and enemies who sought his life and blasphemed his God. David asked at the end of the psalm for God to know his "thoughts" (vs. 23). In Hebrew these are literally "anxieties" or "anxious thoughts." Despite his fear and anxiety, in Psalm 139:1-16 David acknowledged three realities that conquer fear, worry, and anxiety: God's omniscience, omnipresence, and sovereignty.

1. The omniscience of God (Ps. 139:1-6). David knew that God was aware of every moment of his existence. His heart, desires, and thoughts were all understood by God with divine perfection. God was "acquainted with all [his] ways" (vs. 3). Not only that, but God also knew his words before he even spoke them (vs. 4). As David contemplated that glorious reality, he declared with astonishment that such knowledge was too wonderful for him (vs. 6).

David's response of wonder to God's omniscience is instructive for us. The way to combat worry and fear is careful and even rigorous contemplation of the God who sees all things and knows all things. To put it another way, the cure for worry in the soul is to wonder at the majesty of God.

2. The omnipresence of God (Ps. 139:7-12). God is present everywhere in the fullness of His being. Even if David could ascend into the stratosphere, God is there. If he could descend into the depths of the earth, God is there too. Were he to even plunge himself into the deepest part of the ocean, it would be God Himself who led him there. Darkness impairs our sight, but David declared that to God, "the night shineth as the day" and "the darkness and the light are both alike to [Him]" (vs. 12).

That truth supplies our souls with courage to trust in the ever-present God, whose all-sufficient presence is found in every square inch of the universe.

3. The sovereignty of God (Ps. 139:13-16). This is a mighty anchor for the soul! What crushes faithless fear and cultivates fearless faith more than the conviction that God not only made us but designed us before time began? David declared in verse 13 that God shaped him in his mother's womb. He further proclaimed that all of his days (even the dangerous, fear-filled days he experienced at the time of writing the psalm) were designed by God "when as yet there was none of them" (vs. 16). Thus, the all-governing sovereignty of God not only sustained David's soul in danger but moved his soul to joyful worship: "How precious also are thy thoughts unto me, O God! how great is the sum of them!" (vs. 17).

David models for us that the way to live in the midst of fear is to reflect on our all-knowing, ever-present, and sovereign God who moves us to worship.

—Jerod A. Gilcher

World Missions

A number of years ago, in an unnamed nation that required "creative access" for foreign missionaries, a team leader received a former colleague with whom he had previously worked for many years. That former colleague was staying in the home of a local family that was away for an extended period of time. One evening, the team leader had arranged to meet with his former colleague at the house where he was staying. From there the two of them were to walk over to the team's ministry center, where they planned to meet with a gentleman from a Muslim family background who had come to faith in Jesus and had recently been baptized.

Throughout the day, the leader repeatedly called the phone in the local family's house, but no one answered. While phone service in that country could sometimes be erratic, the lack of response seemed unusual, and the leader began to sense that something was amiss. Nonetheless, as evening approached, he boarded a bus and began making his way to meet with his old friend.

As the leader prayed all along the way during the bus ride, a sense of alarm began to grow within him that something had gone awry that day and that, rather than going to meet his old friend, he should just go directly to their ministry center to meet with the new disciple. He rationalized, however, and became concerned about disappointing his friend and appearing neglectful, so he continued on to the house where his friend was staying.

The alarm grew more insistent as he approached his bus stop and as he got off the bus and began to walk in the direction of the house. Finally, as he turned the final corner en route to his destination, this thought crossed his mind: "What will you do if, when you arrive, you find the door ajar and your friend inside, surrounded by the police?" He brushed aside that final thought as paranoid.

When he walked down the alley toward the door, however, he was surprised to find it ajar, and as he pushed it open, he was shocked to see that his friend was indeed surrounded by policemen, who were interrogating him and searching the house. The policemen turned to the door, and one of them immediately pointed to the leader standing at the door, likely with his mouth agape, and asked who he was!

While the visiting friend was ultimately able to return to his country and the leader faced no long-term consequences, the experience provided an opportunity to reflect on the guidance of the Holy Spirit in ministry and in times of crisis. As the psalmist writes, "Whither shall I go from thy spirit? or whither shall I flee from thy presence?" (Ps. 139:7) and "The Lord shall preserve thee from all evil: he shall preserve thy soul. The Lord shall preserve thy going out and thy coming in from this time forth, and even for evermore" (121:7-8).

God knows all and sees all. He knows the end from the beginning. He sees over the horizon and knows the big picture of all that is happening, and thus we should learn to trust the guidance of His Spirit, which is always in agreement, of course, with the written Word of God.

The leader realized that God had sought to guide him in the midst of his crisis, and he was reminded that God is never surprised by anything, never caught off guard by any development. He realized, too, that even amid his own missteps, God had protected him.

—Matthew Friedman

The Jewish Aspect

The book of Psalms developed alongside the whole Old Testament. Psalm 90 was written in Moses' lifetime. The latest psalms, like Psalm 107, were written after the return from exile. As the rest of the Old Testament books were being written, so too was its hymnbook. As such, Psalms broadly reflects the story of Israel.

Books 1 through 2 of Psalms are mostly written by David and end in a baton-passing psalm written by (or perhaps about) his son Solomon. Books 1 through 2 loosely follow the spiritual height of Israel's monarchy. Book 3's darkness reflects the disintegration and eventual fall of Israel and Judah (cf. 80:16) and ends without a human king (cf. 89:49). Book 4 responds to the empty human throne by looking to God as Israel's King (cf. Ps. 99) and asking for restoration to the land (cf. 106:47). Book 5 begins with the return to the land (107:2-3) and ends with a preview of unending heavenly praise (cf. Pss. 146—150). Psalm 139 is in book 5—a strange place for a psalm by David since Psalm 72:20 saw him exiting the limelight. The logic of hearkening back to David's words, however, shows how Psalm 139 fits into the Old Testament storyline: just as God never stopped pursuing David, God would never stop pursuing Israel and Judah as they returned from exile.

Music buffs like to learn about the circumstances giving rise to their favorite lyrics. Some of David's psalms make that easy by containing a historical title explaining the circumstances of writing (cf. Ps. 51), but Psalm 139 is not one of them. There are faint clues in the psalm, but readers cannot be certain. For example, David talked about enemies (vss. 19-22) but did not appear to sense an imminent threat the way he did when Saul (Ps. 57) or Absalom (Ps. 3) pursued him. Additionally, David mentioned his sin but asked God to point it out to him (139:23-24), which rules out times after great blunders of his life when he knew how he had sinned (cf. 2 Sam. 11; 24). Perhaps David wrote this later in his reign when he could look back on times when he ran from God (Ps. 139:7).

Why was David so vague in Psalm 139? It seems that David sometimes kept his psalms vague so that God's people could more readily utilize a generalized prayer throughout the ages. Modern songwriters often do this too, refraining from using the names of the people songs are written about so that fans can sing the song and map the lyrics onto their own lives. The priest or scribe who arranged the Psalms in their present order probably understood this because Psalm 139 comes shortly after Psalm 137's reflection on life in the Babylonian Exile. David knew that God was with him wherever he went, and Psalm 139 would remind the Israelites in Babylon that God is always with His people.

The claim of divine omnipresence was somewhat revolutionary in David's day. The common assumption among ancient Near Eastern people was that the gods operated in a limited area. When traveling to a new place, people assumed that they would need to learn how to appease the local gods (cf. 2 Kgs. 17:26). By contrast, David knew that the God of Israel demonstrated supremacy in Egypt, the wilderness, and the Promised Land. God is with His people regardless of their location, and He alone deserves their allegiance.

—Matthew Swale

Guiding the Superintendent

Poetry and theology inform our grasp of Psalm 139. Whereas sounds rhyme in English poetry, concepts rhyme in Hebrew poetry. The second line often informs the first line.

The psalm reflects on God's omniscience (vss. 1-6) and omnipresence (vss. 7-12, 15). Psalm 139 helps us keep these truths personal. David asked for guidance because of God's omniscience (vss. 1, 23-24). David wanted his community and his personal life (vss. 19, 24) to reflect God's attributes. God is omniscient, omnipresent, and omnipotent, but His knowledge of us is personal (vss. 1-4), His pursuit of us is personal (vss. 7-10), and His creation of us is personal (vss. 13-14).

Here are a few questions teachers might ask: When have you run from God? How did He bring you back? How did you realize God was with you?

DEVOTIONAL OUTLINE

1. The inescapable God knows David (Ps. 139:1-6). God's knowledge is personal (vv. 1-4). He knows everything, but He is also personal and cares about the details of our lives. David says that God's knowledge is wonderful (vv. 5-6). The all-knowing God knows you intimately and still loves you. Do you live realizing you are hemmed in and protected by the ever-present, all-knowing King?

2. The inescapable God pursues David (Ps. 139:7-12). God's pursuit is personal. David could not flee from God's presence, because the omnipresent God was pursuing him. God's presence illuminates even the darkest nights as if it were daytime. David said God's hand would lead and hold him. What does it mean to you that you cannot escape God's presence (vs. 7)? How should you live knowing that God is pursuing you? Do you allow God's nature to inform the way you live?

3. The inescapable God fashioned David (Ps. 139:13-16). What does it mean to you that you were personally crafted by God in your mother's womb (vs. 13)? If God forms and cares for children in their mother's womb, then what should our responsibility be to little ones in the womb?

David grounded his self-worth in God's creation (vs. 13). Do you seek validation in people and accomplishments or in the God who formed you? David recognized that God's creation is praiseworthy (vss. 15-16). Once David personalized God's attributes, he praised (vss. 6, 14, 17) and petitioned (vss. 19, 23) God. Do you praise God for His characteristics, or do your prayers only consist of requests?

CHILDREN'S CORNER

Children need to learn that God knows everything about them because He created them. God knows them better than anyone else, and He loves them. He fashioned them in their mother's womb. They were taken care of even before they were born. No one is born as an accident or a mistake.

Not only does God know them; He is also everywhere. If they climb the highest mountain or dive into the deepest sea, God will find them. Children love hide-and-seek, but Psalm 139 tells us that no one can hide from God.

Teach children that they should never compare themselves with others. They are each beautiful in their own unique way. In this digital age it is easy to compare ourselves with others. But we are all fearfully and wonderfully crafted by the Master Designer, and His Word states we have great value. We are all His masterpieces.

—Matthew Swale

SCRIPTURE LESSON TEXT

GEN. 41:25 And Joseph said unto Pharaoh, The dream of Pharaoh *is* one: God hath shewed Pharaoh what he *is* about to do.

26 The seven good kine *are* seven years; and the seven good ears *are* seven years: the dream *is* one.

27 And the seven thin and ill favoured kine that came up after them *are* seven years; and the seven empty ears blasted with the east wind shall be seven years of famine.

28 This *is* the thing which I have spoken unto Pharaoh: What God *is* about to do he sheweth unto Pharaoh.

29 Behold, there come seven years of great plenty throughout all the land of Egypt:

30 And there shall arise after them seven years of famine; and all the plenty shall be forgotten in the land of Egypt; and the famine shall consume the land;

31 And the plenty shall not be known in the land by reason of that famine following; for it *shall be* very grievous.

32 And for that the dream was doubled unto Pharaoh twice; *it is* because the thing *is* established by God, and God will shortly bring it to pass.

33 Now therefore let Pharaoh look out a man discreet and wise, and set him over the land of Egypt.

34 Let Pharaoh do *this*, and let him appoint officers over the land, and take up the fifth part of the land of Egypt in the seven plenteous years.

35 And let them gather all the food of those good years that come, and lay up corn under the hand of Pharaoh, and let them keep food in the cities.

36 And that food shall be for store to the land against the seven years of famine, which shall be in the land of Egypt; that the land perish not through the famine.

NOTES

God Warns Pharaoh through Dreams

Lesson Text: Genesis 41:25-36

Related Scriptures: Genesis 40:1—41:24, 37-57; 50:15-21; Psalm 105:16-22; Daniel 2:17-49

TIME: 1886 B.C. PLACE: Egypt

GOLDEN TEXT—"This is the thing which I have spoken unto Pharaoh: What God is about to do he sheweth unto Pharaoh" (Genesis 41:28).

Introduction

As soon as Adam and Eve sinned in the Garden of Eden, God set His redemptive plan into motion. First, He promised that one of Eve's descendants would crush the head of the deceiving serpent (Gen. 3:15). Then He narrowed the focus of that plan to one family. The restoration of God's blessing to humanity would come through Abraham and Sarah (12:1-3; cf. 17:19).

By the time of Genesis 41, God's chosen family consisted of Abraham's grandson Jacob (Israel) and his children. Jacob's favorite son, Joseph, had provoked his eleven brothers to jealousy by recounting two dreams that prophesied that he would rule over them, and they had responded by selling him into slavery.

As Joseph would later explain, God intended from the start to bring him to Egypt through his brothers' wicked plot (50:20). The reason for that becomes evident in chapter 41, which recounts a famine that endangered not only Egypt but also the entire Mesopotamian world, including Jacob and his family.

LESSON OUTLINE

1. **GOD'S REVELATION— Gen. 41:25-32**
2. **JOSEPH'S WISDOM— Gen. 41:33-36**

Exposition: Verse by Verse

While in Egypt, Joseph was thrown into prison because of a false accusation. In prison, he met two fellow prisoners—Pharaoh's baker and cupbearer. Both of them had disturbing dreams one night, and Joseph interpreted the dreams for them. In return, Joseph requested that the cupbearer, whom he accurately prophesied would return to Pharaoh's service, remember him when he was restored (chap. 40). The cupbearer, however, forgot all about Joseph until Pharaoh had two troubling dreams of his own.

{Ancient Egyptians believed that dreams were one of the primary ways their gods communicated with them. Not every dream was considered significant, but as we see in Joseph's story, when people sensed a supernatural element in a dream, they sought its meaning. Dream interpretation was such a big deal that the Egyptians compiled books for deciphering the meaning of each dream component.}[Q1]

The clearest evidence we have of Egyptian dream interpretation is found in an ancient document called Papyrus Chester Beatty III, dated to the thirteenth century B.C. but possibly copied from an earlier time period. The document contains a list of dream components, labeling each one as "good" or "bad" along with suggested meanings (Currid, *Against the Gods*, Crossway).

In Genesis 41, however, the best of Pharaoh's advisers had no idea how to interpret his dreams (vss. 8, 24). That is when the cupbearer remembered Joseph.

GOD'S REVELATION

GEN. 41:25 And Joseph said unto Pharaoh, The dream of Pharaoh *is* one: God hath shewed Pharaoh what he *is* about to do.

26 The seven good kine *are* seven years; and the seven good ears *are* seven years: the dream *is* one.

27 And the seven thin and ill favoured kine that came up after them *are* seven years; and the seven empty ears blasted with the east wind shall be seven years of famine.

28 This *is* the thing which I have spoken unto Pharaoh: What God *is* about to do he sheweth unto Pharaoh.

29 Behold, there come seven years of great plenty throughout all the land of Egypt:

30 And there shall arise after them seven years of famine; and all the plenty shall be forgotten in the land of Egypt; and the famine shall consume the land;

31 And the plenty shall not be known in the land by reason of that famine following; for it *shall be* very grievous.

32 And for that the dream was doubled unto Pharaoh twice; *it is* because the thing *is* established by God, and God will shortly bring it to pass.

Famine foretold (Gen. 41:25-27). Joseph made it clear to Pharaoh that his dream had not come from one of the Egyptian gods but from the one and only God. Further, the two dreams were really one dream because they had the same meaning, and God had sent it to reveal something significant to Pharaoh about His plans for Egypt's immediate future. In the Hebrew word order, "what [God] is about to do" is at the beginning of the sentence (vs. 25), thus placing the emphasis less on the fact that God revealed something to Pharaoh and more on the impending act of God that the dream revealed.

Pharaoh's dream involved two sets of seven "kine" (cows) and two sets of seven ears of wheat. In each case, the first set was plump and the second set thin, and the second set consumed the first without getting any plumper. {Pharaoh called the plump ears of wheat "good" (vs. 22) and the thin cows "poor" (vs. 19; literally "bad" or "evil").

In light of the ancient Egyptian tendency to label different elements of dreams either "good" or "bad," these descriptions may indicate that Pharaoh recognized the first sets as good omens and the second sets as bad omens.}[Q2] But beyond that, he did not know what they meant.

{Joseph explained first that the sets of seven each represented seven years. Since the two dreams were really one doubled dream, that meant the cows and wheat ears represented the same two seven-year stretches. The good sets of cows and wheat represented seven productive years for the land. The bad sets represented seven years of famine.}[Q3]

Although Pharaoh and his wise men had been unable to arrive at this interpretation, the interpretation undoubtedly would have made sense to them. Cows and wheat were two of their most important resources, and a famine would certainly result in similar-looking cows and wheat as what Pharaoh saw in his dream.

Famine foretold a second time (Gen. 41:28-31). Joseph then repeated the interpretation to Pharaoh, using nearly identical language as in verse 25 to reemphasize that God had revealed to Pharaoh something *He* was going to do very soon in Egypt (vs. 28). The famine would not result from the Egyptian fertility gods withdrawing their favor, as Pharaoh might otherwise have presumed. It would result from God's intervention.

{In the second telling of the interpretation, Joseph provided more detail. First, he revealed the geographical extent of the years of plenty. It would extend across the entire land of Egypt (vs. 29). Second, he revealed the extent of the famine's devastation (vss. 30-31).}[Q4] We can imagine Pharaoh's shoulders slumping more and more under the weight of the impending catastrophe as Joseph added detail after detail. The famine would bring such devastation that the prior years of plenty would be forgotten. It would "consume," or destroy, the land (vs. 30). It would make the years of plenty unknown, removing every shred of evidence that the land had ever produced abundantly. And it would be "very grievous" (vs. 31; literally, "very heavy").

Notice the emphasis Joseph placed on the "land" in this second telling of the interpretation, repeating the term four times in three verses (vss. 29-31). Perhaps we would expect him to emphasize the danger of starvation for the people, but instead he emphasized the destruction of the land. Why would that be?

{"Land" (sometimes translated as "earth" or "ground," depending on context) is a prominent theme in Genesis. God created and filled the earth (1:1-31), commissioned Adam and Eve to have dominion over the earth (vs. 26), but then cursed the ground (different word, but similar concept) because of Adam's sin (3:17) and had to destroy the earth because of rampant wickedness (6:11-13).

Throughout Genesis, we see God's plan unfold to restore the land to its original purpose. He promised never again to destroy the whole earth by water (9:11) and promised to give Abraham's descendants a land that would become the focal point of His redemptive work (12:7). Receiving abundance from the earth was a sign of God's blessing (27:28), and receiving little from the earth was a sign of the removal of God's blessing (cf. vs. 39). Even though the land in view in chapter 41 is primarily Egypt, not the Promised Land, Pharaoh's dream highlighted the land's continuing struggle to survive and produce under sin's curse.}[Q5]

Doubling down (Gen. 41:32). A lot of things occur in pairs in Genesis 41. Two years passed between the prisoners' dreams and Pharaoh's dreams (vs. 1), Pharaoh had two dreams (vs. 5), Pharaoh's dream was recounted twice (vss. 1-7, 17-24), and Joseph gave its interpretation twice (vss. 25-27, 28-31). Even within Joseph's interpretation, two key phrases occur twice: "The dream [of Pharaoh] is one" (vss. 25, 26) and "What God is about to do he sheweth unto Pharaoh" (vs. 28; cf. vs. 25).

{All of this doubling culminates in verse 32, where Joseph revealed that the doubling of Pharaoh's dream indicated both the certainty and the immediacy of what God was about to do.}Q6 By doubling his interpretation and the two key phrases mentioned above, Joseph mirrored Pharaoh's doubled dream. In this way, he implicitly expressed the urgency of the situation to Pharaoh even before he spoke explicitly about it in verse 32. Joseph was helping Pharaoh see that drastic action needed to be taken. That would prepare Pharaoh for the drastic suggestion Joseph was about to make for how to address the problem.

JOSEPH'S WISDOM

33 Now therefore let Pharaoh look out a man discreet and wise, and set him over the land of Egypt.

34 Let Pharaoh do *this*, and let him appoint officers over the land, and take up the fifth part of the land of Egypt in the seven plenteous years.

35 And let them gather all the food of those good years that come, and lay up corn under the hand of Pharaoh, and let them keep food in the cities.

36 And that food shall be for store to the land against the seven years of famine, which shall be in the land of Egypt; that the land perish not through the famine.

Overseers for the land (Gen. 41:33-34*a*). In verses 33-36, the theme of "land" continues, with the term occurring six times in those four verses. Now, however, instead of issuing a warning, Joseph proposed a plan that would spare the land from its coming devastation. That proposal involved two steps.

First, Pharaoh would need to appoint numerous overseers, including a right-hand man he could "set . . . over the land of Egypt" (vs. 33). The responsibilities of the right-hand man sound much like the descriptions of viziers from a later Egyptian dynasty (1550-1295 B.C.). Those viziers took on most of the governing responsibilities for Egypt but were second in command to Pharaoh. Similarly, Joseph suggested that Pharaoh appoint a second-in-command to carry out the rest of the plan he was about to propose.

To qualify for such vast responsibility, the second-in-command would need to be "discreet and wise." {There may be a hint of irony here, as Pharaoh's leading advisers were called "wise" in Genesis 41:8, but they could not even tell Pharaoh the meaning of his dream, let alone come up with its solution.}Q7 Joseph, on the other hand, had already demonstrated his wisdom and discretion and was clearly the most qualified person for the job. Pharaoh would quickly recognize that and appoint Joseph as his second-in-command, explaining that no one could be found who would be as "discreet and wise" as Joseph was (vs. 39).

Pharaoh's immediate recognition of Joseph as superior to his own trusted advisers demonstrates God's ability to show His strength through human weakness (cf. 1 Cor. 1:27). Imagine the president of a country inviting a federal prisoner into a presidential advisers' meeting. The prisoner gives such good advice that the president decides to make him his chief adviser. That sounds like a preposterous situation. Yet it is not far from what actually happened for Joseph. God displayed His strength and wisdom through Joseph's weak and impossible circumstances.

Preservation of the land (Gen. 41:34*b*-36). Joseph recommended that Pharaoh appoint "officers," or overseers, throughout the land of Egypt. The overseers' job would be to collect a portion of the land's abundance in the first seven years, store it away, and guard it until the seven years of famine came.

The phrase "take up the fifth part of the land" (vs. 34) requires further explanation. Some think this means that the overseers would take one fifth of the land's grain as a tax during the seven abundant years, while others think it is an idiom that refers more generally to organizing the land's crops. These different interpretations arise because the verb translated as "take up the fifth part" is the verbal form of the number five, but it is also sometimes used in military contexts to refer generally to the organization of ranks.

The difficulty with the first interpretation is that it seems unlikely one fifth of the grain from the first seven years would be enough to feed both Egypt and all the surrounding nations for the next seven years (cf. vss. 56-57). It also seems to conflict with the directive to collect "all the food" of the good years in verse 35 (possibly meaning all the food that was not needed to feed the people during those years). The difficulty with the second interpretation is that Genesis 41 is not a military context.

{Although arguments could be made for either interpretation, a possible solution to the dilemma is that here the term means not to take one fifth but to divide into five parts, which would fit with the meanings sometimes associated with verbal forms of other numbers (cf. Deut. 19:3) (Hamilton, *The Book of Genesis: Chapters 18-50*, Eerdmans). In that case, the verse may indicate that whatever grain the overseers gathered would be divided between five locations, or store cities (cf. Gen. 41:35).}[Q8]

Store cities were common in the ancient world. Sometime after Joseph's death, the enslaved Israelites built two store cities for Pharaoh (Ex. 1:11). Several kings of Israel and Judah kept store cities as well (cf. 2 Chr. 8:4-6; 16:4). Those cities were designated for storage of government property.

{Joseph emphasized that the goal was for the land not to "perish" (literally, be "cut off") due to the famine.}[Q9] Normally, the Old Testament speaks of individuals being cut off from their land or people, usually as a result of unfaithfulness to a covenant with God (cf. Gen. 17:14; Zech. 13:8), but here it was the land itself in danger of being cut off.

{Joseph's wise response would not merely alleviate the problem for the people of Egypt; it would save the nation and, through it, people from all the surrounding nations as well. That included Joseph's own family in Canaan. Through Joseph's enslavement and imprisonment in Egypt, God had prepared a way for His chosen family, and thus the lineage of the coming Savior, to survive.}[Q10]

—*Matthew Robinson*

QUESTIONS

1. Why were dreams important to the ancient Egyptians?
2. How did Pharaoh describe the cows and wheat in his dream, and why might that explain how worried he was about its interpretation?
3. What did the fourteen cows and fourteen ears of wheat in Pharaoh's dream represent?
4. How did Joseph's second telling of the dream's interpretation differ from the first?
5. How does Joseph's emphasis on the "land" relate the famine to the wider narrative in Genesis?
6. What did the doubling of Pharaoh's dream signify?
7. What was ironic about Joseph's recommendation that Pharaoh find a "wise" man as his second-in-command?
8. What did it mean that the overseers would "take up the fifth part of the land" (Gen. 41:35)?
9. What was the goal of Joseph's suggested plan?
10. How did deliverance from the famine impact the larger redemptive story of Scripture?

—*Matthew Robinson*

Preparing to Teach the Lesson

This lesson begins the second unit of the quarter. The theme is God's omniscience—He knows everything. He knows anything that can be known. Nothing takes God by surprise.

Today's lesson focuses on the story of Joseph in Genesis and how God knew both the smallest details of His life and the details of a future famine. God warned Pharaoh, the king of Egypt, through his dreams and then gave knowledge to Joseph to interpret those dreams.

TODAY'S AIM

Facts: to see how God used knowledge of future events.

Principle: to understand that God knows everything and can share that knowledge with people.

Application: to encourage students to trust God's care.

INTRODUCING THE LESSON

Is there anything God does not know? Over and over in the Bible, we see the One who always knows all things. This characteristic is called *omniscience*.

DEVELOPING THE LESSON

1. God sends Pharaoh dreams (Gen. 41:25). The events in chapter 40 prepared Pharaoh, his officials, and Joseph for the dramatic event in chapter 41.

Joseph was in prison, along with two of Pharaoh's officials. God worked through their dreams and gave Joseph the correct interpretation.

The two officials were the king's chief butler and chief baker. The captain of the king's guard instructed Joseph to serve them. One night they both had strange dreams. Since there was no one to explain their dreams to them, they were sad. (Perhaps, in their previous occupations in the palace, they had access to the royal magicians.) Joseph did something that we should do when people are sad: he encouraged them to turn to God. Joseph trusted God to give him the interpretation. This is similar to what God did in the lives of Daniel, Hananiah, Mishael, and Azariah many years later (cf. Dan. 2:17-49).

The chief butler shared his dream of a vine with three branches. When it budded, it immediately blossomed, and he saw ripened grapes. Pharaoh's cup was in his hand, so he squeezed the grapes and handed the cup to Pharaoh.

After Joseph heard the dream, God enabled him to interpret it, since God knows the minds of all people. Joseph told the butler that the three branches represented three days. In three days, Pharaoh would restore him to his previous position.

The chief baker was watching and listening to this great interpretation, so he also told Joseph his dream. The baker dreamed of three baskets of bread on his head. The top basket had wonderful baked goods for the king to enjoy, but birds ate the bread out of the basket. God also gave Joseph this interpretation, but it was not good news. Joseph told the baker that the three baskets represented three days. Within three days, Pharaoh would lift off the baker's head and hang his body on a tree. The birds would eat his flesh.

After three days, on Pharaoh's birthday, both interpretations were fulfilled. Even though Joseph asked the butler to help him, the butler forgot about Joseph until Pharaoh had his two mysterious dreams two years later.

Our lesson text picks up in the middle of that story. Genesis 41:25-36 contains the interpretation of Pharaoh's dreams from the beginning of the chapter.

2. God interprets Pharaoh's dreams (Gen. 41:26-32). In these verses, we see God's omniscience in two ways. First, He revealed the interpretation of Pharaoh's dreams to Joseph. Second, God revealed the future through Pharaoh's dreams. These two dreams were one message from God.

The seven good cows and seven good heads of grain both foretold seven good years. The seven thin cows and seven empty heads of grain blasted by the east wind foretold seven years of famine. Take note of the golden text in verse 28. This is more than a prophet or psychic can do! Only an omniscient God can say and show these things. We see God working in the minds of Pharaoh and Joseph, using a dream that revealed something about to happen. God's knowledge is eternal.

Joseph continued to explain Pharaoh's dreams in detail. Seven years of great plenty were coming, but seven years of severe famine would follow. God gave the double dream because He had established these events, and they would certainly come to pass.

3. God blesses Joseph and His chosen family (Gen. 41:33-36). We see God's prosperous plan for Joseph's life in the last part of our text. Joseph told Pharaoh to look for a wise man to oversee the land of Egypt. God had a plan for Joseph and a plan for the people. Joseph said Pharaoh should appoint officials to gather one fifth of the grain during the years of plenty. Those officials would store the grain during the years of plenty so the people would not starve during the famine.

Years later, all that God had revealed in the dreams and interpretations had come to pass. During the famine, Joseph's brothers came to Egypt seeking food. There was a great reunion, and God provided for the descendants of Abraham, Issac, and Jacob. In Genesis 50, we see Joseph's brothers lying to him again, but he used the wisdom that our omniscient God gave him. We see Abraham's family line saved and preserved. Psalm 105:16-22 recalls this event and reminds us that all these things were done by God.

ILLUSTRATING THE LESSON

Pharaoh is the title of the king of Egypt. When we think of Egypt, what symbol comes to mind? A pyramid. This represents Egypt and Pharaoh. Our lesson today teaches us that God knows all.

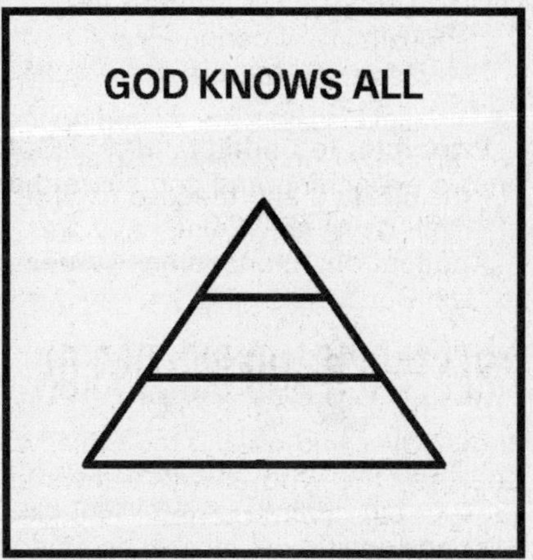

CONCLUDING THE LESSON

We see the hand of God working in Egypt and its governing leaders. We read of God speaking to multiple people through visions and Joseph's interpretations. The God of heaven knows everything happening in the world and directs events so that He receives the glory.

ANTICIPATING THE NEXT LESSON

Our lesson next week will be in Acts. We will study the story of Ananias and Sapphira to understand that God knows everything in our minds and hearts.

—Adam Clagg

PRACTICAL POINTS

1. God prepares for the protection of His people (Gen. 41:25-27).
2. Natural disasters like famines show that the earth still suffers under the curse of sin (Gen. 41:28-31; cf. Gen. 3:17; Rom. 8:20-22).
3. When God determines to do something, it will certainly happen (Gen. 41:32).
4. Amid trials, God expects us not only to trust Him but also to use practical wisdom (vss. 33-36).
5. God has given humans the responsibility of caring for the earth (41:33-36; cf. 1:26).
6. Natural disasters are a good opportunity for Christians to display both the wisdom and the love of Christ (Gen. 41:33-36; cf. Acts 11:27-30).

—Matthew Robinson

RESEARCH AND DISCUSSION

1. Does God still speak to people through dreams today? What cautions should we take when someone claims to hear a message directly from God (cf. Deut. 13:1-5; Acts 17:11; 1 Cor. 14:29)?
2. Why would the Bible portray God as bringing about something as destructive as a famine (Gen. 41:25, 28)? What other Scripture passages might help us understand this (cf. 3:17-19)?
3. Why did God send Joseph to prepare for the famine rather than prevent the famine altogether?
4. What can we do to respond wisely and compassionately during crises (Gen. 41:33-36; cf. Acts 11:27-30)?

—Matthew Robinson

ILLUSTRATED HIGH POINTS

The dream was doubled (Gen. 41:32)

When good public speakers come to a key sentence in their speech, they often repeat it for emphasis, perhaps even saying it slower the second time so that the audience doesn't fail to miss it. Hearing repetition like that is similar to coming across a bolded or italicized sentence in a book. That is what God did for Pharaoh by doubling his dream.

Set him over the land (vs. 33)

The second-in-command role Joseph suggested sounds a lot like what came to be known as a vizier in later Egyptian periods. Although viziers were not first in command, they had similar power to Pharaoh and actually did a lot more active ruling than Pharaoh did.

Today, one of the closest parallels to a vizier is the role of prime minister or chancellor. For example, in Germany, the president is considered the head of state and has veto power, but the chancellor holds most of the government responsibilities.

That the land perish not (vs. 36)

God expects us to show Christ's love to others by preparing for moments of crisis and responding wisely to them.

One Christian organization that has consistently put that principle into practice emphasizes that local churches are often in the best position to offer help and relief in the wake of natural disasters or other crises.

Individual churches can have a different kind of impact on their local community than a centralized relief program ever could. Their outreach can be more personal, and it can also open up opportunities to share the gospel as people see God's love in action through His church.

—Matthew Robinson

Golden Text Illuminated

"This is the thing which I have spoken unto Pharaoh: What God is about to do he sheweth unto Pharaoh" (Genesis 41:28).

God reveals Himself and loves to make His plans known to His people. One example of this is found in Genesis 41. God reveals Himself in multiple ways: 1) through the dreams of Pharaoh; 2) through the interpretation of Joseph; and 3) through His own sovereign control of life and history.

First, God communicated through the dreams of Pharaoh. God communicated through dreams, however, and He communicated the future. Later, Joseph revealed to Pharaoh that his two dreams were one and the same, and both revealed a devastating famine soon to break upon the land. God's sovereign freedom is on full display here as He (a) reveals himself to a pagan king; (b) controls the content of Pharaoh's dreams; and (c) reveals the future through these dreams.

Second, God communicated through Joseph. Joseph made clear that none of his powers were from himself but granted to him by God: "It is not in me: God shall give Pharaoh an answer of peace" (vs. 16). He then declared to Pharaoh in verse 28: "What God is about to do he sheweth unto Pharaoh." Joseph was merely the agent—a messenger. God was the sovereign source of that message.

Third, God communicated through His own sovereign control of life and history. Again, Joseph declared twice to Pharaoh: "God hath shewed Pharaoh what he is about to do" (vs. 25). "What God is about to do he sheweth unto Pharaoh" (vs. 28). Joseph explained to Pharaoh that God was more than merely *aware* of what would happen, He *controlled* what would happen. God was the great Doer, Actor, and Lord—not just over the land of Israel, but over the kingdom of Egypt as well. Thus, through the dreams and the interpretation, God revealed Himself as absolutely sovereign over all events that transpire in history.

What implications may we glean from this for our lives today?

1) God does more than just know the future, He controls the future. God showed Pharaoh what He was about to *do*—not what He had merely *seen* unfolding in the future. God does not just predict the future, He predestines it. God knows the future because He ordained what the future will be. He "worketh all things after the counsel of his own will" (Eph. 1:11). However, we must also remember He does not tempt people to sin (Jas. 1:13).

2) God reveals and communicates His plans that He may be worshipped rightly. God is not truly treasured unless He is treasured as the God who has absolute dominion over life and history. Without His sovereignty, God's love and compassion would be powerless. Without His sovereignty, even His omniscience would only be a hollow comfort. But it is a great comfort in the soul of the believer that the God who has spoken is the God who is sovereign. This is what helps us see that God can be trusted and that all fear is illogical in light of His sovereignty. The God who has revealed Himself also manages the world with flawless perfection. Therefore, come feast or famine, war or peace, we take great comfort knowing that God has already shown to us what He is going to do.

—Jerod A. Gilcher

Heart of the Lesson

From a human perspective, it is often hard to see the sovereignty of God. In other words, it does not *appear* that God is in control of history. Many things seem random, chaotic, and out of control. Yet the Word of God assures us that God remains at the helm of all events in history. One vivid display of God's providence came in the life of Joseph. From Genesis 37 through 50, God revealed that He can use all events—including people's sin and evil—for good.

In Genesis 41 specifically, we see God's control of a massive famine that affected Egypt and the surrounding countries. God revealed that future famine to Pharaoh through dreams that He later interpreted through Joseph.

In both Joseph's interpretation and the context of Joseph's life, we find three principles of God's control that give us unconquerable hope.

1. God's control over history is intimate and personal (Gen. 41:25-28). In this passage, God displayed His *providence*, which refers to His working in and through every moment of life to accomplish His desired ends. God is not distant, remote, and indifferent; He is actively working all things for His glory. We see this in the repeated declaration of Joseph to Pharaoh, "God hath shewed Pharaoh what He is about to do" (vs. 25; cf. vs. 28).

It is crucial to pay attention to Joseph's precise language: the famine was something *God* would bring about. Sovereignty is not a spectator sport, and God is not passive. He actively rules and guides all things by His power for His glory and for our everlasting good. Oh what comfort and strength that supplies in our struggles and fears!

2. God's control over the events of history is specific and expansive (Gen. 41:29-36). We see this in the details of the famine. It would be a famine of seven years. Not more, not less—seven. God both "called for a famine upon the land" (Ps. 105:16) and determined its exact duration.

So it is with all history. God numbers the stars and knows them by name (Ps. 147:4; Is. 40:26); God determines the life span of the sparrow (Matt. 10:29); God superintends the paths of arrows (cf. 1 Kgs. 22:34), every roll of the dice (Prov. 16:33), and even who would be involved in the death of His Son (Acts 4:27-28). This is our Father's world, and He has authority over all of it.

3. God's control over history is centered on His Son whom He sent. The sovereignty of God is not the mere brute force control of history for its own sake. God's control relates to His Son. We see this in the ripple effects of Joseph's life: God sent the famine upon Egypt, which would lead to the preservation of Israel *in* Egypt (cf. Gen. 50:20). That would lead to the exodus over four hundred years later, the conquest of Canaan, the establishment of Israel as a nation, the eventual arrival of the Messiah, His death and resurrection, and finally His triumphant return and global kingdom.

The events of Joseph's life were part of God's larger plan for history, culminating in Christ. That is true of our lives as well. The details of our lives are all part of God's global plan for history. That gives great courage and comfort, since we know that God is leading us to a future kingdom and eternal bliss to come.

—Jerod A. Gilcher

World Missions

The young South Indian lady was in her mid-twenties and was becoming increasingly recognized within her mission organization as an effective leader with an emphasis on spiritual maturity. In her late teens, with the support of her parents and pastor, she had traveled a long distance from her small hometown—a three-day journey by train and bus—for her mission training outside a large city in a different part of India.

After that initial training, she had spent a year on a ladies' evangelism team before being reassigned as staff in the training program itself. She was eventually asked to lead the program. In that role she counseled students in the discipleship program and often went to different parts of the country to lead teams from the school for outreach. She was known to teach and counsel students concerning the importance of receiving the guidance of the Holy Spirit, subject to the written Word of God, especially when facing major decisions.

On her occasional visits home to her family, she was often presented with marriage proposals. On one or two occasions, she got the sense that both her parents and pastoral leadership thought she should accept a proposal and get married, especially because she was at the expected age of marriage for a young lady in that culture. She knew, however, that she needed to put the principles she had been teaching others into practice in her own life, and as she sought God's will in each case, God made it clear that she was not to respond in the affirmative.

But now she was at a crossroads. She had a number of choices before her but did not know how she should decide between them. One option was to commit herself to two more years of leading the training program, which she had been asked to do. Another was to join a team that would pioneer the same discipleship training program in her home state and in her native language.

She had continued to pray for weeks, seeking the guidance of the Holy Spirit, but found herself facing only silence. She tried to figure out why she was not hearing anything from God, tried to confess any sins that might have been lurking under the surface, but still: silence. Why was God not giving her clear guidance, as He had in the past?

And now, another choice: a young man from another country, a colleague who had been working in the same organization and in the same city (but in a different ministry), gave her a marriage proposal. She responded to that proposal as she had to all the others: she would have to pray about it.

That evening, God finally gave the guidance she sought. Through a radical dream, He made it clear to her that the next step she was meant to take in her ministry and in her life was marriage. Even as God showed Pharaoh what He was about to do on a national level, saying through Joseph that "what God is about to do he sheweth unto Pharaoh" (Gen. 41:28), so the very same God spoke to this young lady in a dream about what she was supposed to do on a personal level, guiding the next step for her life.

The young man who proposed to her had sought God's guidance too, but in his case, God spoke through different means. As he had been reading devotionally through the book of Ruth, especially focusing on the cross-cultural marriage of Boaz and Ruth, he felt certain that God was leading him to make this young lady his wife.

—Matthew Friedman

The Jewish Aspect

One major Old Testament theme, especially prevalent in Genesis and Exodus, is God's protection of the "seed," or offspring, of Eve, whom God promised would crush the head of the deceiving serpent (Gen. 3:15). That promise ultimately referred to the Messiah, but it also referred to all those connected with the Messiah (cf. Rom. 16:20).

In the Old Testament, the "seed" under God's protection primarily consisted of the nation of Israel, from which the Messiah would be born. Throughout the Old Testament, we see Israel almost constantly facing either spiritual temptation (cf. Num. 25:1-9) or physical annihilation (cf. Ex. 1:15-16), both of which threatened to thwart God's plan of redemption. But God extended His protection every time.

In Genesis 41, we see one such threat. A famine like the one Joseph foretold had the power to wipe out entire nations. People in the ancient world depended heavily on their crops, and those crops were at the mercy of geography and weather patterns more so than they are today. (For example, a person could not just turn on a hose during a drought.) When the crops of a region failed, the best-case scenario was for the people of that region to travel to a different country and live there until their own country's famine ended (cf. Gen. 12:10; 26:1).

Ancient Egypt was known for its fertile ground and successful agriculture. The success of Egyptian crops depended on the Nile River overflowing at a certain time of year. When that did not happen, the crops failed. And when the crops failed, so did the livestock. During the worst of such famines, the Egyptians even resorted to cannibalism, choosing to eat their own children rather than starve.

Because of the Nile River's essential role in Egyptian agriculture, the Egyptians came to associate it with a fertility god called Hapi. They credited Hapi as Egypt's source of life. In Pharaoh's dream in Genesis 41, he was standing by the Nile and saw cows and wheat come out of it. Cows and wheat were key resources for Egypt, and Egyptians saw the Nile River as the source that gave life to both of these agricultural staples.

It was rare for famine to hit Egypt and Canaan at the same time, as it did in the Joseph story, because Canaan depended on rainfall for its irrigation while Egypt depended on the Nile River overflowing at the right time. That is why Abraham was able to sojourn in Egypt during a previous Canaanite famine (12:10). The famine foretold in Genesis 41, however, would extend to the entire Mesopotamian world (vs. 57). Such a famine certainly could have destroyed Jacob's small family. But God had planned well ahead of time for His people's protection.

Years before the famine came, God sent Joseph ahead to Egypt through the wicked schemes of his brothers. Then He placed Joseph right where he needed to be to interpret the dream of Pharaoh's cupbearer so that the cupbearer would remember him at just the right time. Then He gave Joseph the wisdom seven years ahead of time to plan how to save the land from famine.

When we face trials and persecutions today, we likely will not know how God has planned for His people's protection during that time, but we can be certain that He was preparing us for that trial long before we even knew it existed, just as He did for His "seed" in the Old Testament.

—Matthew Robinson

Guiding the Superintendent

In Genesis 41, Joseph revealed the interpretation of Pharaoh's dreams. Notice how repetition is used to emphasize God's attributes in the text.

DEVOTIONAL OUTLINE

1. Future foretold: God enables Joseph to interpret Pharaoh's dreams (Gen. 41:25-32). Joseph told Pharaoh what God was planning to do because God wanted to reveal His will. In verse 25, Joseph said, "God hath shewed Pharaoh what he is about to do," and later he stated, "What God is about to do he sheweth unto Pharaoh" (vs. 28). Similarly, in verse 32 Joseph said, "God will shortly bring it to pass." This narrative closely intertwines God's omniscience with His providence over human affairs. Not only did God foretell the famine, but He was the one bringing it about!

Why did God send the famine foretold in Pharaoh's dream? The wider context of Genesis shows us that God chose the famine as His method of getting Jacob's family to Egypt (cf. Gen. 42:3; 45:9). God told Jacob in "the visions of the night" that God's promise to make Abraham a great nation (12:2) would be fulfilled in Egypt (46:3; cf. 15:12-16). This may have been because the people of Canaan wanted to intermingle with and influence Jacob's family (cf. 34:14-18), which likely would have led to moral and spiritual deterioration (cf. 38:2, 12). The Egyptians, on the other hand, wanted to remain separate from the Hebrews (43:32; 46:33-34). Furthermore, Egypt would provide the stage for God to show Israel and the world His redemptive power (Ex. 9:16).

2. Famine relief plan: God gives Joseph life-saving wisdom (Gen. 41:33-36). When modern readers hear about dreams and their interpretation, there is a temptation to seek God's will in a similar manner. Christians should recall, however, that God's written Word in Scripture did not yet exist in Joseph's lifetime (Moses wrote the narrative later). Other than directly speaking to people (cf. Gen. 12:1), one of the ways God communicated His will in Genesis was through dreams (cf. Gen. 20:3, 6; 31:10-11). While dreams occurred in the New Testament (cf. Matt. 1:20), they were much less frequent than in Genesis, perhaps due to the availability of God's Word in Scripture. When Christians want to know what God will do and what they should do, they should look first to the Bible or advice consistent with it (2 Tim. 3:16-17).

Genesis 41 demonstrates the love of God for the world. Without Pharaoh's dream and God's revelation to Joseph, many Egyptians and people "in all lands" (Gen. 41:57) would "perish" (vs. 36). Joseph would later reflect about the lifesaving nature of God's providence, saying to his brothers: "But as for you, ye thought evil against me; but God meant it unto good, to bring to pass, as it is this day, to save much people alive" (50:20). Not only did God love the people He rescued from the famine, but in love He also preserved the line of Judah through the famine so the Savior of the world could come through his ancestry (cf. 49:10).

CHILDREN'S CORNER

Children need leaders with wisdom. Joseph recommended that a "discreet and wise" person carry out a food conservation plan (Gen. 41:33). The text does not indicate that this plan was revealed to Joseph in the dream. Joseph responded to God's revelation with wisdom. This text can help us reflect on how we are to act wisely in a way that benefits the well-being of those relying on our leadership, especially the children in our care.

—Matthew Swale

SCRIPTURE LESSON TEXT

ACTS 4:32 And the multitude of them that believed were of one heart and of one soul: neither said any *of them* that ought of the things which he possessed was his own; but they had all things common.

33 And with great power gave the apostles witness of the resurrection of the Lord Jesus: and great grace was upon them all.

34 Neither was there any among them that lacked: for as many as were possessors of lands or houses sold them, and brought the prices of the things that were sold,

35 And laid *them* down at the apostles' feet: and distribution was made unto every man according as he had need.

36 And Joses, who by the apostles was surnamed Barnabas, (which is, being interpreted, The son of consolation,) a Levite, *and* of the country of Cyprus,

37 Having land, sold *it*, and brought the money, and laid *it* at the apostles' feet.

5:1 But a certain man named Ananias, with Sapphira his wife, sold a possession,

2 And kept back *part* of the price, his wife also being privy *to it*, and brought a certain part, and laid *it* at the apostles' feet.

3 But Peter said, Ananias, why hath Satan filled thine heart to lie to the Holy Ghost, and to keep back *part* of the price of the land?

4 Whiles it remained, was it not thine own? and after it was sold, was it not in thine own power? why hast thou conceived this thing in thine heart? thou hast not lied unto men, but unto God.

5 And Ananias hearing these words fell down, and gave up the ghost: and great fear came on all them that heard these things.

6 And the young men arose, wound *him* up, and carried him out, and buried *him*.

7 And it was about the space of three hours after, when his wife, not knowing what was done, came in.

8 And Peter answered unto her, Tell me whether ye sold the land for so much? And she said, Yea, for so much.

9 Then Peter said unto her, How is it that ye have agreed together to tempt the Spirit of the Lord? behold, the feet of them which have buried thy husband *are* at the door, and shall carry thee out.

10 Then fell she down straightway at his feet, and yielded up the ghost: and the young men came in, and found her dead, and, carrying *her* forth, buried *her* by her husband.

11 And great fear came upon all the church, and upon as many as heard these things.

NOTES

God Sees Our Hearts

Lesson Text: Acts 4:32—5:11

Related Scriptures: Leviticus 10:1-11; Deuteronomy 15:1-11; Joshua 7:1-26; Psalm 34:11-22; 2 Corinthians 8:1-15

TIME: A.D. 30 or 31 PLACE: Jerusalem

GOLDEN TEXT—"Why hast thou conceived this thing in thine heart? thou hast not lied unto men, but unto God" (Acts 5:4*b*).

Introduction

What happened in the early church was truly astounding. Largely through Christian influence, care for the poor has become common in the modern world, but this practice would have been startling to a first-century Gentile like Theophilus, who was the recipient of the book of Acts. Not only did people in the church practice charity toward the poor, but they cared for others without thought of receiving something in return.

The early church transformed the surrounding culture. The rich became friends with the poor, meeting their financial needs without thought for personal gain. The responsibility of caring for the needs of all people was ingrained in the Christian mindset.

But the fledgling church also faced challenges that, if not stopped immediately, would threaten the church's ability to function as God's instrument to reach the world with the gospel.

LESSON OUTLINE

1. **OBEDIENT CARING FOR THE CHURCH—Acts 4:32-37**
2. **LYING TO GOD—Acts 5:1-11**

Exposition: Verse by Verse

OBEDIENT CARING FOR THE CHURCH

ACTS 4:32 And the multitude of them that believed were of one heart and of one soul: neither said any of them that ought of the things which he possessed was his own; but they had all things common.

33 And with great power gave the apostles witness of the resurrection of the Lord Jesus: and great grace was upon them all.

34 Neither was there any among them that lacked: for as many as were possessors of lands or houses sold them, and brought the prices of the things that were sold,

35 And laid them down at the apostles' feet: and distribution was made unto every man according as he had need.

36 And Joses, who by the apostles was surnamed Barnabas, (which is, being interpreted, The son of consolation,) a Levite, and of the country of Cyprus,

37 Having land, sold it, and brought the money, and laid it at the apostles' feet.

The unified community through Christ (Acts 4:32-33). Luke described the believers not in terms of their individual relationship to God but according to their inclusion in a group comprised of people who had trusted in Jesus Christ. Unlike the tendencies in modern-day Western culture, the believers did not view themselves individualistically but as inseparably connected to the group through the Holy Spirit who indwelled them.

{The believers had the same mindset toward one another. Luke described this mindset as being of one "heart" and "soul" (or mind).}[Q1] They were concerned for one another's well-being. This mindset is remarkable since they were not family, not longtime friends (though some may have been), and came from every strata of society.

The believers' caring mindset influenced their view of their possessions. Concern for the needs of other community members trumped their desire to hold on to their possessions for their own use. They shared their possessions as others in the church had need.

{The reason for their exemplary care of one another was Jesus Christ.} [Q2] The apostles were eyewitnesses of the resurrected Christ, and they diligently proclaimed that momentous event in Jerusalem (Acts 4:33). The credit, of course, goes to God, for He gave the apostles power and boldness of speech. Their message had God's unlimited might behind it. Obedience to the gospel resulted in God bestowing His great grace upon this unified assembly.

Caring for the community (Acts 4:34-35). {The early believers' Christ-oriented mindset also resulted in practical societal benefits (vs. 34). The poor, whom Jesus affirmed would always be present in a sinful world (Matt. 26:11), had needs met through the generous giving of other believers. The law of Moses included instruction for the care of the poor (cf. Deut. 15:11), but the Jewish leaders of the first century failed to carry it out (cf. Luke 20:47). In contrast, the new covenant community fulfilled God's expectations of caring for the poor by following the guidance of the indwelling Holy Spirit.}[Q3]

Luke explained how the believers ensured the poor would be taken care of. "As many as were possessors of lands or houses sold them, and brought the prices of the things that were sold" (Acts 4:34). Believers who were landowners sold properties and used the proceeds to help their fellow Christians who were in need. This was a voluntary activity, not a demand by the believing community or the apostles. {Luke did not imply that having possessions was evil or a sign of a lack of reliance on Christ's provision. Wealthy individuals did not gain greater standing with God, the apostles, or the believing community as a result of their generosity.}[Q4]

{Nor was this a Christian version of communism. There was no requirement for everyone in the community to share their possessions with everyone else. One-time gifts would help alleviate temporary problems, but they did not change societal status. Rich believers remained rich (though with fewer possessions), and the poor remained poor (though their temporary needs were met). The money was not distributed equally to everyone; it was given only to selected individuals who had financial needs.}[Q5] Selling possessions was not a philosophical response to social inequality but a practical expression of caring for the needs of fellow believers.

In Luke's Gospel, Jesus told a rich young ruler to sell all his possessions and give to the poor (18:22), but that was a different situation from what Luke recorded in Acts 4. Jesus knew the rich man's possessions were an idol that he needed to turn from if he was going to follow Christ, but in Acts, Luke described committed followers of Christ who voluntarily used their possessions to care for their fellow Christians who were in financial need.

Believers did not give to the poor directly but gave the money from the sale of their property to the apostles, so they could distribute the money as needed (vs. 35). There is no record of the apostles requesting that the money be given to them rather than directly to the poor, but that was the method preferred by the church at Jerusalem. There is no prohibition against helping the poor directly, but that was not how it was done at this time in the early church.

The apostles handled the distribution of the gathered funds personally. The church trusted them to use the money for its intended purpose: the care of the poor. Soon the apostles would find the task of distributing finances too time-consuming, robbing them of time they needed to spend in prayer and preaching the gospel, so others were appointed to the task (6:1-4).

Example of obedient caring (Acts 4:36-37). Luke provided an example of one individual who sold property and brought the proceeds to the apostles (vs. 36). He introduced Joses, whom the apostles called Barnabas. The name Barnabas, meaning "son of consolation," likely was given to him as a description of his character.

Later in Acts, Luke reintroduced Barnabas as playing a pivotal role in bringing Paul to the Jerusalem church (9:27). Later Barnabas would travel to the church at Antioch (11:22) and then go to Tarsus to find Paul (vs. 25). Barnabas and Paul would later be sent out from Antioch to spread the gospel to other regions (13:1-4). Barnabas's missionary travel records were no longer documented by Luke after Barnabas and Paul had a disagreement and decided to go on separate missionary journeys (15:36-39).

Barnabas was a Levite from the island of Cyprus (4:36). While Levites were not allotted land by the Lord as was done for the other tribes of Israel (cf. Num. 18:20, 24), there was no prohibition against owning land. There are Old Testament examples of Levites owning land (cf. Jer. 1:1; 32:5-15), and the practice in first-century Israel seems to have changed from what it was in Old Testament times. After Barnabas sold his property, he brought the money to the apostles, the same practice that Luke described as the general pattern of the church.

LYING TO GOD

5:1 But a certain man named Ananias, with Sapphira his wife, sold a possession,

2 And kept back part of the price, his wife also being privy to it, and brought a certain part, and laid it at the apostles' feet.

3 But Peter said, Ananias, why hath Satan filled thine heart to lie to the Holy Ghost, and to keep back part of the price of the land?

4 Whiles it remained, was it not thine own? and after it was sold, was it not in thine own power? why hast thou conceived this thing in thine heart? thou hast not lied unto men, but unto God.

5 And Ananias hearing these words fell down, and gave up the ghost: and great fear came on all them that heard these things.

6 And the young men arose, wound him up, and carried him out, and buried him.

7 And it was about the space of three hours after, when his wife, not knowing what was done, came in.

8 And Peter answered unto her, Tell me whether ye sold the land for so much? And she said, Yea, for so much.

9 Then Peter said unto her, How is it that ye have agreed together to tempt the Spirit of the Lord? behold, the feet of them which have buried thy husband are at the door, and shall carry thee out.

10 Then fell she down straightway at his feet, and yielded up the ghost: and the young men came in, and found her dead, and, carrying her forth, buried her by her husband.

11 And great fear came upon all the church, and upon as many as heard these things.

Planned hypocrisy (Acts 5:1-2). {Luke then contrasted Barnabas and his generosity with two fellow members of the Jerusalem church, Ananias and his wife, Sapphira.}[Q6] They were also property owners, and as Barnabas and others had done, Ananias and Sapphira sold some of their property.

Barnabas gave the apostles the full amount that he received for his property, while Ananias and Sapphira decided to give only part of the money they received (vs. 2).

We do not know why the couple decided to give only a portion of the sale to the apostles. {God owns everything, and Jesus was pleased with the paltry sum given by the poor widow (Luke 21:1-4), so the amount is not what matters to God. As Luke explained in Acts 5:4, the issue was not the amount of money given but the deceptive intent behind the action.}[Q7]

Ananias brought the money to the apostles and laid it at their feet, the same action as when Barnabas brought his gift (cf. 4:37). That act, which suggests submission to authority, came from the heart when offered by Barnabas, but Ananias and Sapphira did it to increase their esteem in the eyes of the church. What may seem to be a small matter to human beings was a large transgression in the eyes of the all-knowing and wise Judge.

Lying to the church and God (Acts 5:3-4). Peter, perhaps the leader or at least the spokesperson of the apostolic group, responded to Ananias's gift with divine insight. He knew that Ananias's gift was not the full sale price for the property. While Luke did not record it, it is implied in Peter's accusation that Ananias claimed to be giving the entire proceeds from the sale.

Peter's words cut to the heart of the issue. He recognized Satan's influence leading to Ananias's action. A Christian's thoughts and actions should be guided by the Holy Spirit (cf. Gal. 5:16), but Ananias chose to follow Satan's temptation instead. The reference to Satan's influence reminds us of Satan's role in Judas Iscariot's betrayal of Jesus (Luke 22:3).

{But the fact that Ananias listened to Satan's influence was not the worst part of Peter's condemnation. Not only did Ananias listen to Satan and keep back part of the selling price, but he also lied to the Holy Spirit.}[Q8]

Peter explained the nature of what Ananias did (Acts 5:4). The property was Ananias's to do with as he wished. He could have kept it, or he could have sold it and done whatever he wanted with it, and God and the church would have been happy with Ananias's decision. But Ananias had other motives. He wanted the praise of people for his show of generosity. Jesus condemned such hypocrisy (Matt. 6:1-2).

{Blinded by his sinful desire, Ananias failed to consider God's nature and His relationship to His church. He did not take into account that God sees and knows everything. While he thought it was a harmless matter to lie to the church for his own benefit, God's relationship with His church is of such a nature that to lie to the church is to lie to God. The church is comprised of His children, indwelled by God's Holy Spirit (Eph. 2:19-22). By lying to God, Ananias failed to give Him the honor due to Him.}[Q9]

Judgment for sin (Acts 5:5-10). Peter's questioning was instantly fatal to Ananias (vs. 5). He "gave up the ghost," meaning that he lost the life in him. As soon as he heard the rebuke roll off of Peter's tongue, he fell down and died. This was an unexpected and rare miracle. In the Old Testament, Aaron's sons Nadab and Abihu were among the few Israelites who could approach God in worship (cf. Ex. 24:1, 9). But they offered before the Lord fire that was, in some way, unauthorized by the Lord. God judged them immediately because their action violated God's holiness (Lev. 10:1-3).

{As a result of Ananias's death, great fear came upon everyone who heard about it.}[Q10] God was serious about His relationship with the followers of Jesus Christ. The church was not just a social gathering of people; it was as sacred a gathering as when the priests offered sacrifices in the temple. The young men of the church buried Ananias immediately, without mourning for him or even notifying his wife (Acts 5:6). In this regard, he was treated as a rebel, just as Nadab and Abihu were (cf. Lev. 10:3).

When Sapphira appeared about three hours later, Peter asked whether she sold the land for the price that Ananias had told him (Acts 5:7-8). When she said yes, Peter pronounced judgment upon her as well. Peter revealed that Ananias and Sapphira's action was the result of their conspiring together to "tempt," or test, the Holy Spirit (vs. 9). The people who buried Ananias buried Sapphira as well (vs. 10).

Warning to all (Acts 5:11). The death of Ananias and Sapphira had a profound effect. Great fear came upon the church. They understood that they must not treat the fellowship of believers in a cavalier way. The gathering of believers is holy ground, for the Lord is present in His church. The church at Corinth had to learn that painful lesson as well (cf. 1 Cor. 11:29). The news was not hidden from the unbelieving community either. They too had great fear of what God was doing in the world through the followers of Jesus Christ.

—Glenn Weaver

QUESTIONS

1. How did Luke describe the mindset of the early church?
2. Why did the early church demonstrate extraordinary care for one another?
3. What societal benefits occurred because of the church's mindset?
4. According to Luke, is it evil to have wealth? Why or why not?
5. Why is the early church's practice not considered to be communism?
6. Against what did Luke contrast Ananias and Sapphira's wickedness?
7. What was the issue that caused Ananias and Sapphira's gift to be rejected?
8. What two reasons did Peter include in his condemnation of Ananias? Which was the more severe reason?
9. What did Ananias fail to consider when he committed his deceit?
10. What happened as a result of Ananias's judgment? Do you think it was effective?

—Glenn Weaver

Preparing to Teach the Lesson

This lesson continues to explore the doctrine of omniscience, which means God knows everything. We will explore some accounts in the Bible that show us that His knowledge extends to knowing our hearts.

TODAY'S AIM

Facts: to understand that God sees everyone's heart.

Principle: to realize God knows the thoughts and intentions of our heart.

Application: to live honestly before the Lord, who knows all.

INTRODUCING THE LESSON

What are some phrases or sayings that are used about the heart? Who can name a song or two about the heart? When we speak about the spiritual, romantic, and poetic heart, we obviously aren't speaking of the organ that pumps blood.

The heart is the seat of our emotions, the home of our will, the center of our being. Today we will learn that God sees our heart.

DEVELOPING THE LESSON

1. The Lord sees generous hearts (Acts 4:32-37). Although our text today primarily focuses on the wicked acts of Ananias and Sapphira, the first part of the text reminds us that God sees generosity in our hearts.

In Acts 4 and 5 we read of the first church in the days immediately following Pentecost. This was the exciting birth of the church. At the end of Acts 4, we read that the early church had one heart and soul (vs. 32). People were generous and shared their belongings, so no one was needy. A man named Barnabas, for example, sold some land and gave the proceeds to the church.

The principles of generosity extend back to the Old Testament. In Deuteronomy 15, we see God's law regarding the forgiveness of debts. Every seven years, the people of Israel were to cancel debts owed to one another. God was going to take care of their every need, so they did not have to worry about holding debt over each other. God commanded obedience, promised blessings, and told His people not to be hard-hearted. He wanted His people to be generous and not give with a grudging heart. The Lord will always take care of His children. He knows when our hearts are generous.

In the New Testament, we see this lived out, for example, in 2 Corinthians 8:1-15. In his letter to the Corinthian church, Paul praised the church in Macedonia for their great financial sacrifice. Even though they were poor and persecuted, they actively and strategically gave beyond their ability to support the missionary efforts led by Paul and Titus.

The apostle said he wanted the Corinthians to be like the Macedonians, not because he needed the money but because the Corinthians needed to experience the grace of giving.

2. The Lord sees the sinful heart (Acts 5:1-11). Strangely, people believe they can lie to the Lord. In Acts 5, we are introduced to a married couple named Ananias and Sapphira. We do not know much about them because bad things begin to happen quickly. They were part of the first church and lived among this group of generous believers. They had just seen Barnabas do something very generous and be publicly acknowledged for his great gift. They also had some land and sold it. But they lied. They did not have to sell their land or give all the money to the church. But they sold the land, kept some of the money, gave the rest to the church, and lied by saying they had given all the proceeds to the church.

When Ananias publicly gave the offering, the apostle Peter asked him two questions related to his heart: "Why hath Satan filled thine heart to lie to the Holy Ghost?" and "Why hast thou conceived this thing in thine heart?" (vs. 3). After these simple questions, Ananias fell and died! Then his wife came, and Peter confronted her. He asked her whether they had sold the land for a certain amount and why she tested the Holy Spirit. She also fell and died!

God sees and judges the wickedness in people's hearts. This story is similar to the Old Testament account of Nadab and Abihu, two of the sons of Aaron the high priest. God was very clear in His law about how He wanted the Israelites to live and worship Him. In Leviticus 10:1-11 we read the disturbing account of Nadab and Abihu, who tried to worship God with strange fire. Instead of the smoke and incense they were supposed to offer with their censers, they were reckless and decided to try something new. We do not know the reason, but God knew what was in their hearts. When they tried it, God killed them instantly.

A few decades later, Achan committed a similar sin (Josh. 7). The Israelite conquest of the Promised Land was going well, but then they lost the battle of Ai, and some of them were killed. They had won a tremendous victory, but now they were defeated. Scripture says "the hearts of the people melted" (vs. 5). When Joshua went to the Lord in prayer, God (who knows the hearts of all people) told Joshua that someone had stolen things they were commanded not to take. A man named Achan admitted to stealing valuable clothing, silver, and gold. His heart was greedy. He did not trust God to provide for his family, so he stole. He and his family were executed for breaking the law of God and endangering the entire nation. Sinful hearts lead to sinful decisions.

Psalm 34:11-22 teaches us how to honor the God who knows our hearts. His eyes are upon us. His ears are attentive. His face is against those who do evil. He hears our cries and is near the broken-hearted.

ILLUSTRATING THE LESSON

God knows our hearts. We cannot hide our thoughts and intentions from him as Ananias and Sapphira tried to do.

CONCLUDING THE LESSON

God saw the hearts of each person that we discussed today: Ananias and Sapphira, Nadab and Abihu, and Achan. The Lord saw their wickedness and did not let their evil hearts destroy His work. His law of generosity was shared by Moses in Leviticus and by Paul in 2 Corinthians. In all these situations, we understand that the God beautifully described in Psalm 34 has never changed.

ANTICIPATING THE NEXT LESSON

Next week, we will continue this theme by reading Jesus' encounter with a man named Nathanael.

—Adam Clagg

PRACTICAL POINTS

1. Christian community can be a welcome relief for those who have only experienced the loneliness of an individualistic culture (Acts 4:32-33).
2. Members of Christ's church should ensure that poor church members have their basic needs met (vss. 34-35).
3. The righteous actions of one believer can set a pattern for others to follow (vss. 36-37).
4. Believers are not immune to sin's deceitfulness, even concerning their relationship with the church (5:1-2).
5. Lying to the church is the same as lying to God (vss. 3-10).
6. God can use the consequences of sin to promote righteousness (vs. 11).

—Glenn Weaver

RESEARCH AND DISCUSSION

1. What can we do to emulate the concern for one another that was present in the early church?
2. In what ways were the situations in the early church similar or dissimilar to today?
3. What are some ways a church can help its members who need financial help?
4. How did extraordinary acts of compassion help the early church mature?
5. How can the sinful actions of church members be damaging to the church?
6. Why did God take such swift action to judge Ananias and Sapphira but does not in the church today?

—Glenn Weaver

ILLUSTRATED HIGH POINTS

Were of one heart and of one soul (Acts 4:32)

A young man moved 1,500 miles from his parents to attend seminary. He graduated and immediately suffered a traumatic brain injury.

His medical situation caused great financial burdens for the family, but the church he attended while at seminary rallied behind him and his family, providing for his family's needs.

His parents, who had stopped going to church years ago, were astonished by the care and compassion that the church expressed to them and their son.

They traveled to visit their son, and while there, they visited the church that had been so kind to him. They met the people who befriended their son and felt great kindred with them. Through the Christlike example of that church, they determined that they would return to church when they arrived back home.

His wife also being privy to it (5:2)

There was a young man who was easily dissatisfied. For a high school student, he had a good job with a caring boss. But that did not stop him from wanting an exorbitant pay increase that the boss could not provide, so the young man walked out of work before his shift ended.

When he walked out, he convinced another young man to depart with him. The second young man liked the job and the boss and was not disappointed with the pay he received. But he was swayed by the appeals of his friend, so he left as well.

Peer pressure can be used for good or for evil. In this case, it was for evil. But the boss convinced the second young man to return to work, and this influenced the first young man to see the error of his decision.

—Glenn Weaver

Golden Text Illuminated

"Why hast thou conceived this thing in thine heart? thou hast not lied unto men, but unto God" (Acts 5:4*b*).

Often when a person tells a lie, their face subtly gives it away. That is, the face exhibits certain tics and signals when one is not telling the truth. A face's tics are irrelevant to God, however, for He sees the secrets of the heart. A liar might fool another man, but God is never fooled, because "all things are naked and opened unto the eyes of him with whom we have to do" (Heb. 4:13).

This is precisely what we see in the disturbing scene of Acts 4:32—5:11. With the early church exploding with conversions and the grace of God overflowing in the generosity of the saints toward one another, Ananias and Sapphira saw an opportunity. It was their chance to receive fame, recognition, applause, and human accolades. Like many others in the church, they sold a piece of property and donated the proceeds to the general fund to be distributed to those in need. However, they did not donate all the proceeds, and they lied about it.

As Peter made clear later, Ananias and Sapphira were not obligated to give anything to the church—let alone the full amount. The money was theirs to do with as they pleased. What they could not do was lie about the amount they were donating. On the surface, their generosity looked just as generous as any other donation. There were no facial tics or signals to give them away. Yet what they had conceived was in the plain sight of God, and He eventually killed them for their treachery (cf. 5:10). Here are two principles and applications from Acts 5:4, which we would do well to pay attention to:

1. The heart is not secret to God. Peter said to Ananias: "Why hast thou conceived this thing in thine heart?" Ananias forgot that the innermost secrets of the heart are as visible to God as open rebellion. There is no safe place to sin. There is no darkness into which the vision of God cannot penetrate. God alone "knowest the hearts of all the children of men" (1 Kgs. 8:39), and the most secret sins are always seen by Him "in the light of [His] countenance" (Ps. 90:8).

This reality should produce in saints a longing for sincere and blameless lives. Knowing that God sees all and knows all helps prevent His people from having shallow, external faith performed only for the eyes of other people.

2. Sin that fools man is sin against God. The point is obvious, but it carries great weight. We are often comfortable with white lies, half-truths, and other forms of sanitized deception if they win the favor of people (or help us temporarily avoid unpleasant consequences). But sins that might fool people infuriate God. Peter said to Ananias, "Thou hast not lied unto men, but unto God" (Acts 5:4). Whether or not people believed Ananias's self-exalting fable was irrelevant. The only thing that mattered was that Ananias lied to the God of truth, and he paid for it with his life. This serves us well with a powerful remedy against all forms of deception. Ananias did not deny the Trinity or the deity of Christ. He only fudged a few numbers. Yet what received applause from men received a death blow from God. This is yet another reminder to us that "the Lord looketh on the heart" (1 Sam. 16:7).

—Jerod A. Gilcher

Heart of the Lesson

When someone wishes to commit a sin and remain unseen, they often seclude themselves and deceive themselves into thinking that no one can see them. Yet there is One who is always present. The Bible is clear that God knows and sees all, even "the secrets of the heart" (Ps. 44:21). That is the lesson driven home in a shocking way in Acts 4:32-5:11.

The truth of God's piercing, penetrating knowledge of the secrets of the heart produces three effects in the life of the faithful: 1) dependence on God's transforming grace; 2) deterrence from sin; and 3) delight in God's presence.

1. The all-seeing eyes of God produce a dependence on His transforming grace (Acts 4:32-37). As the first church grew in numbers in Jerusalem, everybody marveled with a sense of awe at the work of the Lord (vss. 32-33). Many people sold their goods and gave generously to the poor (vss. 34-37).

True believers know that God is both near in proximity and eager in generosity. That is, He is always with us in the fullness of His being, ready to be called upon for all the power we need to do what He commands. God is present not just as a spectator of our deeds but as the ready Sanctifier of our lives.

Ananias and Sapphira had the opportunity to confess their need for grace but were far too enticed by gold. We remember, however, that the presence of God provokes our dependence upon the power of God. Indeed, God commands us to be holy, but He is also always present to make us holy.

2. The all-seeing eyes of God produce a deterrent from sin (Acts 5:1-11). Ananias and Sapphira saw an opportunity to cash in on the recognition and applause of men (5:1-2), so they lied to both men and God. For this, they lost their lives (vss. 3-10). Both husband and wife were struck dead by God, and their frightening death sobered the church (vs. 11).

Ananias and Sapphira failed to realize that God "weigheth the spirits" (Prov. 16:2). That is, He knows the motives of the heart. Our "secret sins" are "in the light of [His] countenance" (Ps. 90:8), and even before a word is on our tongue, the Lord knows it (139:4).

The all-seeing eyes of God also move true believers to delight in His presence. God is everywhere, of course, but believers know that in His presence "is fulness of joy" and that at His "right hand there are pleasures for evermore" (Ps. 16:11).

True believers are moved to holy living in the secret moments of life, not merely because God can see them, but because God is there in the fullness of His being. When one is persuaded that God is a treasure and satisfies us more than the fleeting pleasures of sin, the delight of secret sin loses its deceptive appeal. Of that Ananias and Sapphira were not persuaded. For them, God was a tiny treasure compared to what could be obtained in monetary wealth and the applause of men. Had they truly understood the all-seeing and all-satisfying God, they would not have lied to God.

Ananias and Sapphira's private scheming revealed that they had been duped by the "deceitfulness of riches" (Mark 4:19). Believers, however, know that the God who satisfies the deepest longings of the soul is always close and that joy in His presence is found through the means of His Word.

—Jerod A. Gilcher

World Missions

The team had left their sending base in the Pacific Northwest and headed down to El Paso, Texas, for several weeks of mission training that would focus on language learning. They would meet with local people on both sides of the U.S.-Mexican border, seeking to practice language skills while weaving a gospel witness into their conversations. On the weekend, they would cross the border into Ciudad Juarez, which was safer then (in the late 1980s) than it became later, and seek opportunities to share the gospel of Jesus with both local Mexican folks and the many American soldiers who would come to party.

Toward the end of their time in El Paso, they arranged to cross the border and travel several hours into the mountains, where those learning Spanish would have many opportunities to practice and the few fluent Spanish speakers in the group could also build *their* skills in language learning by interacting with a local tribal language.

They reached the border and stopped for the border officials to see their documents. The officials, though, refused to allow them to cross into Mexico! They prayed and went on to another border crossing to try again, but once again they were prevented from crossing the border. They prayed again and asked God to reveal whether anything *in them* was creating this literal road block that prevented their entrance.

As they returned to their accommodations, they began to discuss matters. Tempers began to fray, and an argument broke out between two members of the team. It suddenly became clear to them what the issue was: there had been hidden sin and disunity "in the camp," and they needed to rectify that before the Lord would allow them to move forward.

Slowly, the arguing students began to confess their sin against one another. That led to other students also expressing their shortcomings and inner disarray. God allowed these things to come to the surface so that, as dross is skimmed off the top of heated metal, so the students' spiritual and social impurities would be lifted off. They went to prayer once more and *this* time had a real sense of the power of God. The next day, they approached yet another border crossing, but this time they were able to cross without difficulty.

What was going on in this situation? Here was a team that had been preparing for outreach in Mexico but, more than that, was part of a training program designed to prepare long-term Christian workers among some of the most unreached people in the world. God was fully aware of what was going on in the heart of each member of the team, and He knew that the sin in the camp (cf. Josh. 7) would infect the team as a whole and taint everything else that they did. Graciously, He intervened.

As we engage in missions, we must understand that we cannot lie to or hide anything from God (cf. Acts 5:4). In order to engage in fruitful, relational ministry, our own relationship divisions must at some point be exposed and rooted out.

In her beautiful memoir *Tramp for the Lord*, Corrie Ten Boom described a teaching visit to Uganda with her assistant Connie. They were visited by the deeply spiritual William Nagenda, a key figure in the East African Revival, who asked them if they were "walk[ing] in the light" with one another (1 John 1:7). Reflecting on his exhortation, they, like the team in Mexico, realized that they needed to make things right.

—Matthew Friedman

The Jewish Aspect

God began with one man, Abraham, when He began His plan to gather a group of people to call His own. From Abraham's descendants came the nation of Israel.

But God's people needed instructions about how to relate to Him and how to function as God's community. God made a covenant with His people through Moses to guide them in these things, including how to treat the poor among them (Deut. 15:7-11). The covenant provided almost everything they needed.

What the people lacked was a way to change the sinful human heart. God's plan from the very beginning was for Jesus Christ to provide that crucial change.

When Jesus came to earth, He clarified how people were to relate to God. His death and resurrection provided the one-time sacrifice that satisfied a holy God's requirements for payment of sins. Then, after Jesus ascended to heaven following His resurrection from the dead, He gave His disciples everything they needed to form a new community. He bestowed on them the indwelling Holy Spirit to guide them and left the apostles to provide leadership (cf. Eph. 4:1-16).

This new community grew out of the nation of Israel, but it was a very different type of organization. Israel was a nation, but God designed the church to be a group of individuals that could function within any nation. While the nation of Israel was comprised of Abraham's ethnic descendants, the church would incorporate individuals from every ethnic group.

As the new community formed, God went to great lengths to protect it. That protection included swift judgment on people like Ananias and Sapphira, who mocked the holiness of God and threatened to corrupt the holiness of the church.

The immediacy of God's judgment may sound harsh to us, but it makes sense in light of several Old Testament parallels.

For example, shortly after Moses built the tabernacle, two of Aaron's sons, Nadab and Abihu, offered unauthorized fire before the Lord. God's judgment came immediately (Lev. 10:1-2). Nadab and Abihu served as a reminder to the fledgling nation not to treat God in a cavalier way.

Another lesson for God's people occurred when they entered the Promised Land. God forbade Israel from taking anything from Jericho for themselves when they conquered the city. The city and all it contained was dedicated to the Lord for destruction (Josh. 6:17-19). But Achan's eye was drawn to some of the city's riches, and he took them and hid them in his tent (7:1, 20-21). Because of Achan's sin, Israel lost thirty-six men during their attack on the city of Ai (vss. 3-5). To satisfy God's righteous judgment, Israel stoned Achan and his household to death and burned the forbidden items (vss. 22-26).

Those examples of God's swift judgment each came when His people rebelled during the early days of a new phase of His redemptive plan. Such judgments protected His faithful followers and served as warnings to them.

Ananias and Sapphira's sin occurred at another key moment in redemptive history. They succumbed to Satan's deception soon after Jesus' ascension and the birth of the church (cf. Acts 1—2). Their deaths served as a warning to the church and community that God and His church were not to be treated lightly.

—Glenn Weaver

Guiding the Superintendent

When have you seen a believer's generosity bless your church? How does it feel when you realize that someone was pretending to be generous to get people to think more highly of them? Today's text compares grace-motivated giving with selfishly motivated giving.

DEVOTIONAL OUTLINE

1. Great grace: Generosity at the apostles' feet (Acts 4:32-37). Students should be encouraged to look for the repeated adjective "great" (4:33; 5:5, 11). This word demonstrates how the Lord grows the church in Jerusalem. "Great grace" (4:33), not great self-reliant effort, enabled the believers to be generous. Does your church—especially members in financial need—benefit from your generosity?

While believers are not commanded to sell their possessions to follow the practice in Acts 4:32-37, we expect God's Spirit to move believers in a similar fashion. Generosity should be motivated by God's grace, not by selfishness.

2. Great fear: God's discipline at the apostles' feet (Acts 5:1-11). "Great fear" resulted from the death of Ananias and Sapphira (vss. 5, 11), and that was a good thing, because it led to growth in the church (vs. 14). Acts 4:32—5:11 suggests that *great fear* of God urges believers to rely upon *great grace* from God. Barnabas lived more faithfully than Ananias and Sapphira because he relied upon God's *great grace* (cf. 4:36-37).

Participants may wonder what the deaths of Ananias and Sapphira mean for sin in their own lives. It should be stated at the outset that this is not a common means of the Lord's loving discipline of believers in the New Testament (cf. Heb. 12:7; Rev. 3:19). The only other New Testament example of people in the church dying because of sin occurred because of the Corinthians' abuses of the Lord's Supper (1 Cor. 11:30). Given the death-dealing nature of sin (Jas. 1:13-15), Christians should not be surprised that Ananias and Sapphira died but should be surprised that more people do not die when they sin.

Even when we keep in mind the wages of sin, however, many will naturally wonder why God killed Ananias and Sapphira rather than others who sinned in the early church. Luke, the writer of Acts, appears to have embedded an answer to the question by designing the story to intentionally mirror the Old Testament story of Achan (Josh. 7). In both stories, someone held something back (Josh. 7:1; Acts 5:2), God disciplined through death (Josh. 7:25; Acts 5:5, 10), and the people's fear quickly turned into expansion of their territory or numbers (Josh. 8:1; Acts 5:11, 14).

Why would Luke link the two stories? Both stories occurred at the beginning of a new phase for God's people. Israel was entering the Promised Land in Joshua 7, and the church had begun to form in Acts 1—4. God's action in Acts 5 is not common in the New Testament, so it appears that the Lord deals with sin in these stories to make a statement to His people about the danger of sin to their growth during an early, vulnerable stage.

CHILDREN'S CORNER

Children do not need to be protected from the serious consequence of Ananias and Sapphira's sin of lying to God and the church. It is OK to teach them about God's anger and wrath (cf. Prov. 6:16-19). God is the Truth and desires His children to always tell the truth and walk in the truth.

—Matthew Swale

SCRIPTURE LESSON TEXT

JOHN 1:43 The day following Jesus would go forth into Galilee, and findeth Philip, and saith unto him, Follow me.

44 Now Philip was of Bethsaida, the city of Andrew and Peter.

45 Philip findeth Nathanael, and saith unto him, We have found him, of whom Moses in the law, and the prophets, did write, Jesus of Nazareth, the son of Joseph.

46 And Nathanael said unto him, Can there any good thing come out of Nazareth? Philip saith unto him, Come and see.

47 Jesus saw Nathanael coming to him, and saith of him, Behold an Israelite indeed, in whom is no guile!

48 Nathanael saith unto him, Whence knowest thou me? Jesus answered and said unto him, Before that Philip called thee, when thou wast under the fig tree, I saw thee.

49 Nathanael answered and saith unto him, Rabbi, thou art the Son of God; thou art the King of Israel.

50 Jesus answered and said unto him, Because I said unto thee, I saw thee under the fig tree, believest thou? thou shalt see greater things than these.

51 And he saith unto him, Verily, verily, I say unto you, Hereafter ye shall see heaven open, and the angels of God ascending and descending upon the Son of man.

NOTES

God Sees Nathanael

Lesson Text: John 1:43-51

Related Scriptures: Genesis 28:10-17; Matthew 3:13-17; Luke 24:44-48; John 2:23-25; 7:40-52

TIME: A.D. 26 and 30 PLACE: east of Jordan

GOLDEN TEXT—"Nathanael saith unto him, Whence knowest thou me? Jesus answered and said unto him, Before that Philip called thee, when thou wast under the fig tree, I saw thee" (John 1:48).

Introduction

Have you ever heard someone call Jesus "just a good teacher"? Many of us struggle to reach out to the lost or respond to objections to the faith. This story might surprise us, as we find Jesus going to an unexpected place and talking to unexpected people. Jesus did not go where he could have found the best-educated and most promising candidates to be His disciples. He went to uneducated Galilee.

We also see a disciple who does not answer questions but still leads a friend to Christ (literally). Additionally, there are Old Testament allusions hiding just below the surface of the text that provide great depth and meaning to this story. This is not simply the story of a random event early in the ministry of Jesus. It provides powerful insight into who Jesus claims to be and how we should respond.

LESSON OUTLINE

1. **JESUS CALLS PHILIP— John 1:43-33**
2. **PHILIP INVITES NATHANAEL— John 1:45-46**
3. **JESUS AND NATHANAEL— John 1:47-51**

Exposition: Verse by Verse

JESUS CALLS PHILIP

JOHN 1:43 The day following Jesus would go forth into Galilee, and findeth Philip, and saith unto him, Follow me.

44 Now Philip was of Bethsaida, the city of Andrew and Peter.

{Jesus did not seek the most educated candidates to be His disciples. He was in Galilee, hardly the center of Jewish culture or learning. He was likely near Bethsaida along the Sea of Galilee (cf. vss. 43-44).}[Q1] Andrew and Peter were fishermen (Matt. 4:18), and it is possible Philip was as well.

Jesus' call to Philip was simple; He wanted him to follow Him. It was a total, unconditional call. Jesus did not explain to Philip all the details of what would happen if he followed Him; He simply told him to follow. Jesus would later teach that this call to follow Him is costly and involves taking up a cross—a violent, humiliating, painful form of execution (Matt. 16:24-28). Yet despite the cost, Jesus promised everlasting rewards that made this costly, unconditional call well worth it.

Jesus calls people the same way today. We are to count the cost of being His follower and renounce all that we have (cf. Luke 14:25-33), but we do not know up front exactly what that will entail. Jesus calls us to follow Him wherever He goes and do whatever He asks of us (John 12:20-26). The details are unknown, and the cost may be high. However, Jesus is good and worthy of our trust, and He demands our complete obedience. When Philip faced this call, he chose to listen and obey. We should follow his example.

PHILIP INVITES NATHANAEL

45 Philip findeth Nathanael, and saith unto him, We have found him, of whom Moses in the law, and the prophets, did write, Jesus of Nazareth, the son of Joseph.

46 And Nathanael said unto him, Can there any good thing come out of Nazareth? Philip saith unto him, Come and see.

Philip's invitation (John 1:45). {After meeting Jesus, Philip was excited. The first thing he did was find Nathanael and share the news that they had found the one of whom Moses and the prophets wrote.}[Q2] Even today, many people immediately react with excitement and a desire to share the good news with friends or family when they first encounter Jesus.

{When talking about the Old Testament, Jews often spoke of the Law, the Writings, and the Prophets. This threefold distinction encompassed the entire Old Testament, and sometimes they used further subdivisions, such as the Former Prophets and the Latter Prophets. However, sometimes they used a twofold distinction: the Law and the Prophets.}[Q3]

When Jesus spoke about the Old Testament, He often named the Law and the Prophets. In this common scheme, the Law referred to the first five books of the Bible, the Torah, or the Pentateuch. Included in the Prophets were all the remaining books of the Old Testament, including the histories, wisdom texts, and the prophets. However, in Luke 24:44, Jesus used the threefold model when He mentioned the Psalms as well. From the fact that Jesus used both models to talk about the Old Testament, we see that one was not right and the other wrong. They were simply shorthand terms.

In the threefold model, the Law referred to Genesis through Deuteronomy, and the Prophets included historical books, including Joshua, Judges, Samuel, and Kings, as well as the books we often refer to as prophets today. Finally, the Writings, or Psalms, referred to all the remaining books. This is the order in which the Jewish Bible is organized. Although the books in our Old Testament today are the same, the order is different.

Philip's claim that Moses and the prophets wrote about Jesus effectively asserted that Jesus was the one whom all Scripture had been anticipating. It meant that Jesus was the culmination of thousands of years of expectation. It was no small statement.

Nathanael's response (John 1:46). Perhaps unsurprisingly, Nathanael was skeptical. Just as many Christians casually assume that Christ will not return in their lifetime, Nathanael assumed that the Messiah would not come from Nazareth. {Whether that was because he knew that the Messiah was supposed to come from Bethlehem (Mic. 5:2) or because he was prejudiced against Nazareth is not entirely certain. His question, however, seems more likely to indicate that he looked down on Nazareth, not that he was contemplating messianic prophecies from the Old Testament.}[Q4]

{Philip did not try to explain that Jesus fulfilled the Old Testament prophecies because He had actually been born in Bethlehem (cf. Matt. 2:1; Luke 2:1-7), and perhaps he did not even know that Jesus was from Bethlehem. He did not try to argue with Nathanael about the likelihood of the Messiah coming from Nazareth. Instead, he simply invited him to come and see Jesus for himself.}[Q5] We do not need to have answers to every objection that skeptics might raise to invite others to come and see Jesus for themselves.

To Nathanael's credit, he followed Philip. He may have had doubts and prejudices, but he was able to put them aside enough to follow Philip and meet Jesus.

JESUS AND NATHANAEL

47 Jesus saw Nathanael coming to him, and saith of him, Behold an Israelite indeed, in whom is no guile!

48 Nathanael saith unto him, Whence knowest thou me? Jesus answered and said unto him, Before that Philip called thee, when thou wast under the fig tree, I saw thee.

49 Nathanael answered and saith unto him, Rabbi, thou art the Son of God; thou art the King of Israel.

50 Jesus answered and said unto him, Because I said unto thee, I saw thee under the fig tree, believest thou? thou shalt see greater things than these.

51 And he saith unto him, Verily, verily, I say unto you, Hereafter ye shall see heaven open, and the angels of God ascending and descending upon the Son of man.

Jesus knows Nathanael (John 1:47). {When Nathanael approached, Jesus declared that there was no deceit in him. By commenting on Nathanael's character, Jesus suggested that He knew this man who had never seen Him before.}[Q6] He was claiming supernatural knowledge.

Nathanael was far from perfect, and Jesus was not claiming otherwise. But Nathanael was honest and not prone to flattering deception—as evidenced by his blunt response to Philip earlier. Perhaps Jesus was even hinting that He knew how Nathanael had replied when Philip had first told him about Jesus. He had not sugar-coated anything. His honesty was to be commended. Still, his honesty did not justify his prejudice.

Nathanael responded by asking how Jesus knew him. Nathanael's question could indicate that he was skeptical about Jesus' claim, or it could indicate that Nathanael understood that Jesus knew him. Considering Nathanael's declaration that Jesus is the Son of God and King of Israel in verse 49, it seems quite likely that the second explanation is correct. Nathanael may have been prejudiced against Nazarenes, but he was honest. Jesus knew who Nathanael was, and that made Nathanael curious.

Jesus' knowledge of people's hearts reveals who He is. After all, who knows what someone is thinking and feeling except for that person (cf. 1 Cor. 2:10-11)? Only God can look inside us and know our thoughts (1 Sam. 16:7; Ps. 139:1-4). Jesus' ability to look inside Nathanael (and us) reveals His divine nature. As Jesus described to Nathanael what he was like in John 1, Nathanael realized that Jesus knew him and was from God.

Under the fig tree (John 1:48-50). Jesus told Nathanael that He saw him before Philip called him under the fig tree. Some people argue that being "under the fig tree" referred to meditating on God's Word. In much later Jewish tradition, the phrase "sitting underneath a fig tree" became a way of metaphorically describing discussions about the books of the law. If Jesus intended that meaning, then He was declaring that He knew what Nathanael was thinking while he was praying to God. That may have opened the door for Nathanael to make some startling conclusions. While he had been contemplating God's Word and talking to God, Jesus was aware of what he was doing. Perhaps that was why he immediately jumped to the realization that Jesus was the Son of God, even though he likely did not know all the implications of that statement.

Others point to Old Testament passages promising future hope that include fig trees (cf. Mic. 4:4). If Jesus had these passages in mind, Zechariah 3:10 is particularly illuminating. There the prophet recorded his messianic vision in which God's Anointed removed the land's guilt, and everyone rested under their fig trees (vss. 9-10). Proponents of this interpretation understand Jesus to have been orienting His followers toward these messianic prophecies. He announced that the prophetic hope was coming to fruition.

Finally, many think that there is no need to read metaphors or figures of speech here. Jesus' statement about seeing Nathanael can be taken literally. Nathanael could have been under a physical fig tree when Philip met him. Jesus had not been present at that meeting, so this straightforward reading carries with it the same implication of supernatural knowledge on Jesus' part as the other interpretations. Such a detail would have been convincing evidence for the skeptical Nathanael.

{Regardless of one's interpretation of John 1:48, the detail about the fig tree revealed that Jesus is no ordinary man. He possesses supernatural knowledge. Nathanael immediately dropped his preconceptions about what a man from Nazareth could or could not be.}[Q7] He did not stubbornly cling to his old views but recognized that he had been wrong.

Nathanael called Jesus "Rabbi," meaning "teacher." Rabbis studied and taught God's law. Jesus is indeed a teacher. Sometimes we forget how radical Jesus' teachings were in the first century; He called people to treat those below them with respect and to love their enemies. In a self-centered world, Jesus' teaching of self-denial and sacrifice is still radical today, and sorely needed. Sadly, many today try to limit Him to only being a good teacher, which we must reject. Jesus is not less than a teacher; He is more. He is the Son of God (John 1:49).

Jesus seemed almost amused at how quickly Nathanael changed his opinion of Jesus. All it took was a simple comment for him to completely change his mind about Jesus. Jesus promised that he would see much greater things than that. Jesus stated that Nathanael would see heaven opened and angels ascending and descending on the Son of Man.

Jacob's ladder (John 1:51*a*). {The promise about heaven opening and angels ascending and descending seems to be a clear reference to Jacob's ladder (Gen. 28:12-16). In that story, Jacob was on the run from his brother Esau and slept. He had a vision of a ladder (or stairway) coming down from heaven and angels ascending and descending on it. There God renewed His covenant with Abraham's line. After Jacob awoke, he named the place Bethel, which means "house of God."}[Q8] The angels did not do much in the Genesis narrative besides provide a celestial background and awe Jacob. Likewise, the emphasis here is not on the angels who are ascending and descending but on Jesus, the Son of Man.

In Jacob's vision, the ladder connected heaven and earth, and the angels traveled along it. Jesus said that Nathanael would see the angels ascending and descending on Him. {In other words, Jesus is the ladder of Jacob's vision. Jesus connects heaven and earth. Through His perfect life and death, Jesus opened a way for fallen humanity to reach God (cf. John 14:6; Heb. 10:19-20). On the cross, Jesus reconciled the relationship between God and man. Man had been separated from God by sin, but Jesus died for sin and metaphorically bridged the gap.}[Q9] Did Nathanael understand all of this? Probably not. He might have understood that Jesus was declaring Himself the connection between God and humanity, but he would not have understood how that would come about. One day, however, he would recognize who Jesus truly is as the Son of Man.

The Son of Man (John 1:51*b*). What does it mean that Jesus is the Son of Man? This is Jesus' most common name for Himself in the Gospels (cf. Matt. 20:28). He used it frequently, but only once did someone else refer to Him in that way (Acts 7:56). The title was used repeatedly in the Old Testament, however. Ezekiel was called "son of man" over ninety times (cf. Ezek. 2:1; 5:1)! In Ezekiel, the title often contrasted Ezekiel's humanity with God's glory. But there is another prominent use of "son of man" in the Old Testament with a very different meaning. In the book of Daniel, one like a son of man came in glory before God's throne and received an everlasting kingdom that will never be destroyed (7:9-14). He is distinct from the Ancient of Days, who sat on the great throne. The son of man in Daniel is glorious and rules forever over all nations.

{Jesus fulfills both meanings of "Son of man." He is fully human and shared in our weaknesses (Heb. 2:14-18). This correlates with Ezekiel's usage of the title. But He is also the glorious One, who comes on the clouds and rules the nations (Matt. 26:64). This correlates with Daniel's use of the title.}[Q10]

Jesus never denied it when Nathanael or others called Him the Son of God or the King of Israel, but He did not draw undue attention to Himself before the proper time. If He had frequently and openly called Himself the Son of God, He might have been crucified before His time (John 7:3, 30). By using the humble title "Son of man," he claimed a title that would not draw charges of blasphemy but still hinted at His identity.

—Tom Greene

QUESTIONS

1. Where was Jesus when He called Philip?
2. What was Philip's immediate reaction?
3. What were the two ways Jews sometimes divided the Old Testament?
4. Why was Nathanael initially skeptical?
5. How did Philip respond to Nathanael's skepticism?
6. How did Jesus first display supernatural knowledge of Nathanael?
7. What convinced Nathanael of Jesus' identity?
8. What Old Testament story did Jesus refer to?
9. What did it mean that Nathanael would see angels ascending and descending on Jesus?
10. What does it mean that Jesus is the Son of Man?

—Tom Greene

Preparing to Teach the Lesson

The theme for this week's lesson is divine self-revelation. The main text and the supporting texts show God revealing Himself.

TODAY'S AIM

Facts: to discover that God does not hide His identity.

Principle: to realize that God reveals Himself in various ways.

Application: to think about how God has revealed Himself to us.

INTRODUCING THE LESSON

Sharing the good news is an integral part of following Christ. We follow Him and invite others to join us. Ask members of the class how they first learned about Jesus Christ. Whether it was from a family member, a friend, a total stranger, or a preacher, most of us came to Christ because someone told us about Him.

DEVELOPING THE LESSON

1. Philip invites Nathanael to meet Jesus (John 1:43-46). Jesus chose twelve men as His main disciples. In our first verse, we see the simple invitation of Christ to Philip: "Follow me." He was from a town called Bethsaida. This is the same hometown as Andrew and Simon Peter. The Bible records multiple miracles that Jesus performed near there, including His walking on water (Mark 6) and the healing of the blind man (chap. 8). It was also near this town that Jesus fed the five thousand (Luke 9:10-17).

Philip quickly went to tell his friend Nathanael. (Nathanael is probably another name of the disciple called Bartholomew in Matthew, Mark, and Luke.) We can see instant application to our lives. One of the most important things we can do during the days we have left on this earth is to tell our friends about the Lord. We can almost hear the excitement in Philip's voice as he told his friend that they had finally found the One who was prophesied by Moses and the prophets! Philip added He was "Jesus of Nazareth, the son of Joseph."

We see an instantaneous and honest argument between the friends. Nathanael asked if anything good can come out of Nazareth. It was small, in the middle of nowhere, not near the water or any major city. If you have maps in the back of your Bible, you can find the three places mentioned in our text: Galilee, Bethsaida, and Nazareth. But Philip did not give up on his friend. He told him to come and see. Later, in John 7:40-52, we see another time when people debated whether Jesus is the Messiah. Some believed, but others did not. Jesus' hometown was part of this doubt. The Old Testament said the Messiah would come from Bethlehem. Of course, we know from the Christmas story that Jesus was born in Bethlehem but was raised in Nazareth. But many people who met Jesus may not have known that.

2. Jesus knows Nathanael's actions (John 1:47-48). As Nathanael approached, Jesus gave him a compliment that likely revealed that He knew Nathanael was proud of his Israelite heritage and the honest life he led. This is also interesting because of the connection to Jacob (known for not being honest) in verse 51. When Nathanael met the Lord for the first time, Jesus said the very things Nathanael wanted to hear, and he asked Jesus how He knew him. Jesus then revealed that He knew where Nathanael was and what he was doing before his friend Philip found him. In John 2:23-25, we read that Jesus "knew all men" and "he knew what was in man." This is an interesting aspect of the omniscience of God. When Jesus was on the earth, He displayed supernatural knowledge. This is something we can apply to our lives today. The Lord knows what you care about. He knows where we are and what we are doing.

3. Jesus is acknowledged as deity and royalty (John 1:49-51). As soon as Jesus revealed this knowledge, Nathanael declared that Jesus is truly the Son of God and the King of Israel. Notice the difference in Nathanael after he met Jesus. He made the true declaration that would be shared many times and would ultimately be used as a charge against Jesus before the crucifixion.

Also, notice the contrast to the earlier description of Jesus. Instead of the son of Joseph, He is called the Son of God. He is more than a country boy from rural Nazareth—He is the King.

The Lord's reply in verse 50 may have been a bit sarcastic, as if to say, "You believe these amazing things just because I saw you under a fig tree?! You will see greater things than that!"

Jesus told Nathanael in verse 51 that he would see heaven open with the angels of God ascending and descending upon the Son of Man (yet another title Christ used). This referenced the Old Testament story of Jacob found in Genesis 28:10-22. Jesus was making an obscure comparison between honest Nathanael and Jacob who cheated his brother.

Jesus was revealed as the Son of God multiple times in the Gospels. One of the most memorable came at His baptism. God spoke from heaven to say that Jesus is His Son who is greatly loved and pleasing to Him.

ILLUSTRATING THE LESSON

Philip could not help sharing the good news of Jesus with his friend.

CONCLUDING THE LESSON

As we begin our week, let us try to live each moment knowing that God sees every detail of our lives. He knows what we are doing. He knows where we are. This can be comforting but also convicting.

Holy living is part of being a child of God. If we are not careful, we may find ourselves in situations where the temptation to sin is strong.

Let us acknowledge Jesus for who He is: the Son of God and King of the universe. He has proven this time and time again. But even if there are situations in which this is not obvious, it is still true.

Let us follow the example of Philip and tell a friend about Jesus this week. Maybe you have talked to them before, and they didn't want to talk to you about the Lord. Again, follow Philip's example of not giving up. Change how you word things. Be excited about the living Savior.

ANTICIPATING THE NEXT LESSON

Next week, we will conclude this unit's theme, "God is all-knowing," with the encounter Jesus had with the Samaritan woman in John 4. In today's lesson, a disciple brought someone to Christ. In next week's lesson, Jesus goes out of His way to meet the Samaritan woman and offer her everlasting life.

—Adam Clagg

PRACTICAL POINTS

1. Jesus calls us to follow Him unconditionally (John 1:43).
2. All the Old Testament points to Jesus. We should read it looking for ways it points to Him (vss. 44-45).
3. We should invite others to come to Jesus (vs. 46).
4. Jesus knows everything about us. We can come to Him even when we have doubts and skepticism (vss. 47-48).
5. When we truly encounter Jesus, we will confess that He is far more than merely a man (vs. 49).
6. We should expect God to work in mighty (though often unexpected) ways in our lives (vss. 50-51).

—Tom Greene

RESEARCH AND DISCUSSION

1. Should we always respond to skepticism about Jesus the way Philip did?
2. What might Nathanael have been thinking of when he doubted that the Messiah could come from Nazareth (cf. Mic. 5:2)? How should we respond when someone says something about God that we are not sure is true?
3. How should we respond to doubts? How does Jesus respond to doubt in the Gospels?
4. Who do you relate to more in the text, Philip or Nathanael? How has your understanding of who Jesus is grown over time?
5. What do you think it meant that Nathanael would one day see angels ascending and descending on Jesus?

—Tom Greene

ILLUSTRATED HIGH POINTS

Follow me (John 1:43)

"Jeff" was the son of a fabulously wealthy family in the Middle East. As a teenager he had his own sports car and horse. When his brother traveled abroad and converted to Christianity, his father was furious. Jeff was sent to persuade his brother to come back, but instead, he also converted to Christianity.

In response, his father put a bounty on Jeff, who sought international asylum. Although he gave up millions, he insisted that following Jesus was worth it. We are called to follow Jesus unconditionally, regardless of what it costs us.

Come and see (vs. 46)

A notable professor was a lesbian activist for nearly a decade. While researching for a paper on the religious right, she wrote an article criticizing an evangelical organization. A pastor wrote her a letter and invited her to dinner. She accepted and began investigating Christianity. Two years later, she converted and left her lesbian partner. Once she began investigating Jesus, she could not resist Him. When we meet people who have objections, we should try to answer them. But we should also simply try to get them to listen to Jesus.

Because I said unto thee, I saw thee (vs. 50)

Three women in the back row of a church glanced at each other. The visiting preacher did not know them, but he had just described each of them in detail, going down the row in order, while giving illustrations. Afterward, one of them came up to talk to him.

Sometimes we may get the feeling that a pastor has wiretapped our house! But it is God who knows everything about us and loves us.

—Tom Greene

Golden Text Illuminated

"Nathanael saith unto him, Whence knowest thou me? Jesus answered and said unto him, Before that Philip called thee, when thou wast under the fig tree, I saw thee" (John 1:48).

While Deism affirms that there is a God who created all things, it wrongly asserts he is not involved in daily life. The "god" of Deism is distant, detached, and disinterested in the details of our lives. He is indifferent and virtually irrelevant to the people he has made. How different is the God of the Bible who revealed Himself in Jesus Christ!

Rather than keeping Himself remote and removed from us, the Son instead "was made flesh, and dwelt among us, (and we beheld His glory, the glory as of the only begotten of the Father)" (John 1:14). One bright beam of this glory that was displayed in Christ was the attribute of His omniscience.

John 1 presents four consecutive days on which Jesus gathered His first disciples. In verses 43-51, Nathanael became persuaded to join himself to Christ. What persuasive power did Christ use to silence Nathanael's skepticism? It was nothing less than the majestic display of His perfection of omniscience.

The day before Nathanael met Christ, Philip declared Jesus as the Messiah (cf. vs. 45). Nathanael, however, scoffed and slighted Christ's hometown, ruling out Nazareth as a place too lowly for the Messiah to come. The next day, however, Nathanael encountered the stranger from Nazareth and had his life changed forever. Upon seeing Nathanael, Christ declared, "Behold an Israelite indeed, in whom is no guile!" (vs. 47). Nathanael, surprised and confused, retorted, "Whence knowest thou me?" And Jesus answered—behold the glory of Christ—"Before that Philip called thee, when thou wast under the fig tree, I saw thee" (vs. 48).

Notice first the *time* Christ saw Nathanael: "*Before* that Philip called thee." Christ was already involved in Nathanael's life even before Philip approached him.

Second, notice the *place* Christ saw Nathanael: "When thou wast under the fig tree, I saw thee." At a specific moment in time and location, Christ saw Nathanael—not merely that he existed, but who he was down to the very thoughts of his heart and the DNA of his soul.

From this brief episode, we may derive two comforts for our own lives.

Comfort #1: Christ does not just know about humanity in general but about every individual—and not just *that* they exist but their condition and location at every moment. Christ is not the indifferent spectator deity of Deism, keeping His distance from the events of our lives. Instead, He is *in* every moment, watching, sustaining, and always ready to provide for every need. Never hesitate to call upon this near and present Christ!

Comfort #2: As with Nathanael, Christ has a plan for His disciples today. And what do disciples do but make more disciples (cf. Matt. 28:19)? In Matthew 28:20, what did Christ declare to those first disciple-makers? "Lo, I am with you alway, even unto the end of the world." Christ is present, not merely for our comfort, but to make us competent for His global mission. Go out into the world and make disciples and call upon this near and present Christ!

—*Jerod A. Gilcher*

Heart of the Lesson

It is fascinating to explore the various ways Jesus invited people to be His disciples. Nathanael was won over to Christ in one of the more interesting ways. As we read that story, we see that the supernatural knowledge of Christ was what convinced and converted Nathanael from being a doubter to being a disciple. The scene also furnishes some crucial implications for our lives today.

1. Christ's omniscience implies intimate knowledge of the details of our lives (John 1:43-48). First, Jesus found and called Philip. Then Philip found Nathanael and told him about Jesus. Nathanael, though, scoffed at Jesus' origins from Nazareth. He could not believe that anything good—let alone the Messiah—could hail from there.

When Nathanael approached Jesus, however, he received a surprise, as Jesus seemed to know him already. Nathanael asked how Jesus knew him, and Christ gave this staggering reply: "Before that Philip called thee, when thou wast under the fig tree, I saw thee" (vs. 48).

Christ was not merely aware of Nathanael's existence; He saw him *before* Philip even called him. Nathanael was *already* known by Christ before he had ever heard of Jesus. Also, Christ saw Nathanael when he was sitting under a fig tree. Christ even knew the type of tree under which he sat before Philip found him, which reminds us that God sees us (and is present with us) in our lives as well, no matter where we are. Jesus' nature as God means that there are no details outside of His knowledge.

2. Christ's omniscience implies His deity (John 1:49*a*). Nathanael responded to Christ's astonishing revelation by becoming His eager disciple. He declared, "Rabbi, thou art the Son of God" (vs. 49). To call Him the "Son of God" may have been a recognition of His identity as God, though Nathanael likely had only a partial understanding of this. He would come to understand it better with time. To be the Son of God is to be God the Son—the Second Person of the Trinity. With all of its challenges to human logic, theology of multiple individualities within the Godhead was not entirely unknown by the Jews in that day, but it was certainly a divisive point for most.

Nathanael could perceive that this Nazarene "nobody" was actually the greatest Somebody in history. He was God in flesh, even if Nathanael did not realize it yet. The omniscience of Christ implies His deity, and His deity reminds us that He possesses all power.

3. Christ's omniscience implies His authority as King (John 1:49*b*-51). Nathanael could immediately surmise that Jesus was qualified to be the Messiah of Israel foretold throughout the Old Testament. He declared, "Thou art the King of Israel!" (vs. 49). Jesus was the long-awaited Messiah. Nathanael's exclamation in no way limited Jesus' kingship to merely one nation; rather, God had chosen Israel as the source of blessing for all nations (Gen. 12:3), and only the true King of Israel could bring that to fruition.

Upon Christ's Second Coming, He will take back the entire rebel planet and bring it into full subjection under His holy authority. Yet, He provides great comfort and consolation to our souls today as well. All authority in heaven and earth belongs to Him (cf. Matt. 28:18). As our omniscient King, He flawlessly rules the universe and our lives.

—Jerod A. Gilcher

World Missions

The young man was as rough as they come. Hailing from the Karen, a tribal people who had awaited the gospel for centuries, Ko Tha Byu had left his parents' home at the age of fifteen to take up a life of crime, robbing and killing across the countryside. Soon, however, he had to sell himself into servitude to pay off his massive debts. He was picked up by a Burmese Christian, Shwe Be, who sought to teach him to read.

Shwe Be introduced Tha Byu to the man who was discipling him, an American missionary named Adoniram Judson. Judson had been working on translating the Scriptures into the Burmese language of the majority community there. Slowly, the two men began to share the gospel with Tha Byu. He seemed to grasp the potential implications that the gospel had for his own people. The Karen had largely avoided the Buddhism of the majority population, clinging instead to their monotheistic indigenous faith and prophecies of restoration of relationship when a messenger would come with God's *book.*

As Tha Byu began to grasp the Bible and the faith described therein, he became excited, realizing that this could be the very book and the very message for which his people had been waiting! Tha Byu spent most of the remainder of his life traveling to the villages of Burma, proclaiming the message of salvation in Jesus.

God can and does use and call people like Tha Byu, who come from the least likely backgrounds imaginable. But God also calls people from historically Christian families to join with Him in His mission.

We see God calling both kinds of people in Scripture. Jacob was an example of someone called by God despite his suspect background and character. He was a bit sketchy ethically; even his name meant, effectively, "cheater." And he lived up to his name, especially in his relationship with his brother, whom he manipulated to take his birthright. He then deceived their father, too, and got the blessing that his father had meant to give to his older brother.

After that second deception, Jacob's mother realized that his life was in danger, because his own twin brother might very well kill him if he did not leave. So off he went—the child of promise, possessor of his remarkable family's birthright and blessing, and would-be inheritor of the Promised Land. Exhausted, he stopped for the night at a place called Luz.

That night Jacob had a remarkable dream. He saw God at the top of a stairway, with angels ascending and descending, and there, in an expression of pure grace, God declared that He would be with him, provide for his needs, and bring him back to the very land from which he was fleeing. In awe, Jacob vowed to follow God if He fulfilled the promise He had just given him (Gen. 28:10-22).

Centuries later, Jesus called Nathanael in Galilee. When he approached, Jesus saw him and said, "Behold an Israelite indeed, in whom is no guile!" (John 1:47) Perhaps Jesus knew that here was someone whose character was solid, something to build on. And just as the trickster Jacob was given a vision of angels ascending and descending, so Jesus said Nathanael would see angels ascending and descending on the Son of Man (vs. 51).

Regardless of our past failings or faithfulness, God knows us, and God can and will give us the call we need to find our place in His purposes.

—Matthew Friedman

The Jewish Aspect

Philip told Nathanael that Moses and the prophets wrote about Jesus, which was a way of saying that *all* the Scriptures were about Jesus. Many of the titles that are ascribed to Jesus in today's lesson text have their roots in the Old Testament. Here are just a few of them.

Lamb of God. When John the Baptist called Jesus "the Lamb of God, which taketh away the sin of the world" in John 1:29, he recalled the Passover lamb that was sacrificed the night before Israel left Egypt (Ex. 12:1-13). The Israelites spread lambs' blood on the doorpost of their houses in order to avoid the tenth plague that fell on Egypt. All the firstborn sons of the Egyptians would suffer God's judgment that night, but anyone with the lamb's blood spread on their doorpost would be delivered. Passover celebrated that deliverance.

When Jesus instituted the Lord's Supper, He did so at the Passover meal, imbuing it with further meaning (Mark 14:12-25). This title also recalled Isaiah's prophecy of the Suffering Servant, who would be like a lamb led to the slaughter and bear the sins of others (Isa. 53:7-12). Through His death on the cross, Jesus perfectly fulfilled these prophecies. He is celebrated in heaven as the Lamb who was slain to redeem people from every tribe, language, people, and nation (Rev. 5:5-14).

Son of God. John and Nathanael called Jesus the Son of God (John 1:34, 49). In the Old Testament, Israel was called God's son (Ex. 4:22-23; Hos. 11:1). Likewise, David was called God's son, as was Solomon (Ps. 89:27; 1 Chr. 17:13). However, Jesus was God's Son in a way that the nation of Israel and its kings only hinted at (Acts 13:33). His usage of the name Son of God was considered blasphemous (John 19:7). When Jesus used the phrase, He made Himself equal to God (5:16-18). Christians are also called sons and daughters of God, but Jesus is God's Son in a unique way (1:12-13; 3:16).

Messiah. God promised David that his offspring's throne would be established forever (2 Sam. 7:12-14). God also promised that this offspring would build a temple. Clearly, the first fulfillment of that promise was David's son Solomon, who built a physical temple in Jerusalem. However, Solomon did not reign forever. The Lord's anointed king was His Son and would one day rule over the nations (Ps. 2:1-12). Solomon did not rule over all the nations, and he was not the final fulfillment of the promise. Faithful Old Testament Jews rightly looked forward to a future Messiah who would fulfill all the Old Testament promises in a way no king ever had. Jesus declared that He is this Messiah (John 4:25-26).

King of Israel. Before Jesus was born, an angel came to Mary and promised her that her son would be the Son of the Most High and would sit on the throne of David. He would reign forever, and His kingdom would never end (Luke 1:28-35). Jesus is both the Son of God and the King of Israel. He and His kingdom did not look the way people expected (John 18:36). Instead of coming in triumphant glory, Jesus came in humility, quietly going about His work (Matt. 13:31-33). However, when He comes again one day, He will do so triumphantly and in glory, judging all the earth (25:31-46).

Jesus is not unrelated to the Old Testament. Instead, He is the culmination of all the Old Testament hopes and expectations.

—Tom Greene

Guiding the Superintendent

As you study today's text, it would be beneficial to invite people to think about who helped them realize that Jesus is the Savior and Son of God. Philip helped bring Nathanael to Jesus in today's text.

DEVOTIONAL OUTLINE

1. "Follow me": Philip meets Jesus (John 1:43-44). Jesus told Philip to follow Him. Philip then found Nathanael and told him about Jesus. Philip's wise words, "come and see" (John 1:46), demonstrate how the kingdom grows: new disciples tell others, who repeat the process. John reported more about Philip than the other Gospels, perhaps because, according to church tradition, they ministered in nearby cities. Philip is prominent in three additional stories in John (6:5-7; 12:20-22; 14:8-9).

2. "Come and see": Nathanael meets Jesus (John 1:45-49). Jesus Christ is fully human and fully divine. Jesus had an earthly father (vs. 45). Jesus had a hometown—and not a reputable one (vs. 46).

Unlike any other human, however, "Moses in the law, and the prophets, did write" about the birth, life, ministry, death, resurrection, and exaltation of Jesus (vs. 45). Additionally, unlike any other human, Jesus knew Nathanael's location before meeting him (vs. 48). That omniscient insight convinced Nathanael that Jesus is divine: "thou art the Son of God; thou art the King of Israel" (John 1:49). He believed because Jesus truly saw him.

3. "Thou shalt see": Heaven meets earth (John 1:50-51). After Nathanael's confession, Jesus told him that he would see greater things (vs. 50). While Jesus' concluding words about angels "ascending and descending" on Jesus may have surprised the listeners (vs. 51), it is a logical conclusion from what the story reveals about Jesus. If Jesus is fully human and fully divine (what theologians call the hypostatic union), then He possesses an unparalleled relationship with both God's realm (heaven) and the human realm (earth).

Jesus alluded here to an event in Jacob's life when Jacob dreamed of a ladder reaching to heaven. God explained to Jacob the point of the dream by reiterating the promises to Abraham and Isaac, which were now being extended to Jacob: God would give him land (28:13; cf. 12:7) and many descendants (28:14; cf. 12:2), and God promised that "in thy seed shall all the families of the earth be blessed" (28:14; cf. 12:3). God would reach from heaven to earth to reverse sin's curse with the blessing of salvation (cf. Gen. 3:17; Gal. 3:10-14).

Jesus' allusion to Genesis 28 constitutes at least two claims. First, Jesus was claiming to be the fulfillment of the promise of Genesis 28. In Jesus Christ, the promised blessings of heaven can flow to earth. Second, Jesus was claiming to be the access point between heaven and earth. Jesus Christ is the true house of God and the ladder that extends between heaven and earth.

Through the Genesis 28 imagery, Jesus previewed how He would bless the world: providing access to heaven only available through faith in Him. Jesus' allusion to Genesis 28 anticipated His later claim that "no man cometh unto the Father, but by me" (John 14:6).

CHILDREN'S CORNER

Children may wonder how they can talk to their friends about faith in Jesus Christ. They can simply do what Philip did. Jesus knew what Nathanael needed to hear. God is omniscient; we are not. Believers can simply try to show Jesus to others and let Him do the rest. Our mission, like Philip's mission, is to follow Jesus and tell others to "come and see."

—Matthew Swale

SCRIPTURE LESSON TEXT

JOHN 4:5 Then cometh he to a city of Samaria, which is called Sychar, near to the parcel of ground that Jacob gave to his son Joseph.

6 Now Jacob's well was there. Jesus therefore, being wearied with *his* journey, sat thus on the well: *and* it was about the sixth hour.

7 There cometh a woman of Samaria to draw water: Jesus saith unto her, Give me to drink.

8 (For his disciples were gone away unto the city to buy meat.)

9 Then saith the woman of Samaria unto him, How is it that thou, being a Jew, askest drink of me, which am a woman of Samaria? for the Jews have no dealings with the Samaritans.

10 Jesus answered and said unto her, If thou knewest the gift of God, and who it is that saith to thee, Give me to drink; thou wouldest have asked of him, and he would have given thee living water.

11 The woman saith unto him, Sir, thou hast nothing to draw with, and the well is deep: from whence then hast thou that living water?

12 Art thou greater than our father Jacob, which gave us the well, and drank thereof himself, and his children, and his cattle?

13 Jesus answered and said unto her, Whosoever drinketh of this water shall thirst again:

14 But whosoever drinketh of the water that I shall give him shall never thirst; but the water that I shall give him shall be in him a well of water springing up into everlasting life.

15 The woman saith unto him, Sir, give me this water, that I thirst not, neither come hither to draw.

16 Jesus saith unto her, Go, call thy husband, and come hither.

17 The woman answered and said, I have no husband. Jesus said unto her, Thou hast well said, I have no husband:

18 For thou hast had five husbands; and he whom thou now hast is not thy husband: in that saidst thou truly.

19 The woman saith unto him, Sir, I perceive that thou art a prophet.

28 The woman then left her waterpot, and went her way into the city, and saith to the men,

29 Come, see a man, which told me all things that ever I did: is not this the Christ?

NOTES

God Sees the Samaritan Woman

Lesson Text: John 4:5-19, 28-29

Related Scriptures: Exodus 17:1-7; Nehemiah 9:15-21; Isaiah 12:1-6; Jeremiah 2:9-13; John 7:37-39

TIME: between A.D. 26 and 30 PLACE: Sychar

GOLDEN TEXT—"Come, see a man, which told me all things that ever I did: is not this the Christ?" (John 4:29).

Introduction

Jesus left Judea because of the threat of persecution from the Pharisees (John 4:1-3). His actions of cleansing the temple (2:13-17) and gathering disciples made Him a target of the Jewish leaders. Jesus would remain in Galilee for a time because the Jewish leaders sought to kill Him (7:1). Jesus' travel to Galilee took Him through Samaria, where He would meet the woman at the well.

Samaria would be a key part of the apostles' mission after Jesus ascended to heaven (Acts 1:8). Jesus' ministry in John 4 prepared the Samaritan region to enter God's kingdom alongside Jews.

LESSON OUTLINE

1. **JESUS' ARRIVAL IN SAMARIA—John 4:5-6**
2. **JESUS' REQUEST FOR WATER—John 4:7-9**
3. **JESUS' OFFER OF LIVING WATER—John 4:10-12**
4. **JESUS' OFFER OF ETERNAL LIFE— John 4:13-15**
5. **JESUS THE PROPHET—John 4:16-19**
6. **JESUS THE MESSIAH—John 4:28-29**

Exposition: Verse by Verse

JESUS' ARRIVAL IN SAMARIA

JOHN 4:5 Then cometh he to a city of Samaria, which is called Sychar, near to the parcel of ground that Jacob gave to his son Joseph.

6 Now Jacob's well was there. Jesus therefore, being wearied with *his* journey, sat thus on the well: *and* it was about the sixth hour.

{Jesus entered a Samaritan area that was rich in religious heritage. The events of this account took place in the valley between Mount Ebal and Mount Gerizim. Jacob, one of Israel's patriarchs, had a well there (though we do not have a record of it from the Old Testament), and his son Joseph was buried at the nearby town of Shechem (cf. Josh. 24:32).

The location has significant meaning for Jesus' discussion with the Samaritan woman. Mount Ebal and Mount Gerizim were important landmarks when Israel entered the land under Joshua. According to Moses' instructions, half of the nation was to stand on Mount Ebal, and the other half was to stand on Mount Gerizim. In a large antiphonal choir, the curses of Deuteronomy 27 were spoken from Mount Ebal, and blessings of Deuteronomy 28 were spoken from Mount Gerizim (cf. Deut. 11:29; Josh. 8:33).}[Q1]

Abraham and Jacob both built altars to worship God in the region (cf. Gen. 12:6-7; 33:18-20)—a fact that the Samaritan woman mentioned later in her conversation with Jesus (John 4:20). The Jewish historian Josephus claimed that a priest named Manasseh became high priest over a temple built on Mount Gerizim during the Persian period (*Antiquities of the Jews* 11.306-10). That temple was later destroyed by John Hyrcanus in 128 B.C.

{There was much more to this meeting than Jesus talking with a woman who needed salvation. Jesus was preparing the way for His church to reach the Samaritans with the gospel after His ascension. The complicated history of the relationship between Samaritans and mainline Jews required Jesus to overcome the obstacles that could jeopardize the church's mission in that part of the world.}[Q2]

The town of Sychar was near the land that Jacob gave to Joseph (vs. 5). This was likely the field mentioned in Genesis 48:22 and Joshua 24:32. Jesus stopped at the well to get a drink because He was weary from His travels (vs. 6). It was the sixth hour, which is noon, when the sun is highest in the sky and the day is hot.

JESUS' REQUEST FOR WATER

7 There cometh a woman of Samaria to draw water: Jesus saith unto her, Give me to drink.

8 (For his disciples were gone away unto the city to buy meat.)

9 Then saith the woman of Samaria unto him, How is it that thou, being a Jew, askest drink of me, which am a woman of Samaria? for the Jews have no dealings with the Samaritans.

Jesus initiates the conversation (John 4:7-8). {Ordinarily, women would come to draw water when the day was cooler, perhaps in the morning or evening, but this woman chose to draw water at noon instead. It appears that she was alone. No one else was involved in the conversation, and the woman later went to town to tell others of her talk with Jesus. Perhaps she sought to avoid contact with others because of her immoral living arrangement, which Jesus would soon bring up.}[Q3]

{Jesus did something unexpected for a Jewish man, especially for someone who was considered a rabbi. He spoke to the woman. According to rabbinic traditions, rabbis would not speak to women in public for fear of what others would think.}[Q4] But Jesus did not have such fears. He was concerned for the spiritual well-being of the woman, and no social prohibitions or potential slander would dissuade Him from accomplishing His task.

His request, at first glance, was a simple one. He asked the woman for a drink of water. But this was no ordinary woman. She was a Samaritan. {The long-held hatred the Jews had for the Samaritans led the Jews to believe that Samaritans, especially Samaritan women, were ceremonially unclean.}[Q5] Yet here was Jesus, asking her to draw water with her jar and to give Him a drink from it!

The disciples were not present to see Jesus as He discounted this unfounded bigotry. They had gone into the city to obtain food (vs. 8). Right now, He needed to have a conversation with this woman. The time for instructing the disciples would come later.

The woman responds in surprise (John 4:9). The woman was shocked that Jesus would speak to her and questioned why He would do so (vs. 9). She knew the barriers between Jews and Samaritans and between men and women. John added a clarifying note to inform his readers that Jews were concerned with becoming unclean through contact with Samaritans. But Jesus did not answer her question. He let His continuing conversation provide His answer as to how little social prohibitions meant to His ministry.

JESUS' OFFER OF LIVING WATER

10 Jesus answered and said unto her, If thou knewest the gift of God, and who it is that saith to thee, Give me to drink; thou wouldest have asked of him, and he would have given thee living water.

11 The woman saith unto him, Sir, thou hast nothing to draw with, and the well is deep: from whence then hast thou that living water?

12 Art thou greater than our father Jacob, which gave us the well, and drank thereof himself, and his children, and his cattle?

After discussing physical matters, Jesus shifted the discussion to spiritual matters. He began by suggesting there were some things that the woman did not know. {She did not know God's gift or the identity of the person talking to her.} Q6 If she had known those, she would have asked Jesus for a drink of "living water"—that is, running water—not the stagnant water found in a cistern, and He would have given her a drink!

Of course, this was a confusing statement to her (vs. 11). Jesus had no jar to draw water, and the well was too deep to get water without some means of retrieving it. What water was Jesus talking about? She assumed Jesus was talking about common drinking water. Like many people today, she was focused upon her daily material needs and wants, so she was slow to realize the meaningful spiritual discussion that Jesus was attempting to have with her. But Jesus knew how to gain her attention and turn her thoughts to the weightier spiritual matters that, whether she knew it or not, were crucial for her eternal destination.

The woman's heritage was rich and meaningful to her (vs. 12). Abraham's grandson Jacob, one of the respected patriarchs of Jewish and Samaritan history, was credited with providing the well from which the woman drew water. Certainly, Jesus did not consider Himself to be greater than Jacob, did He? To think so was preposterous in her mind.

JESUS' OFFER OF ETERNAL LIFE

13 Jesus answered and said unto her, Whosoever drinketh of this water shall thirst again:

14 But whosoever drinketh of the water that I shall give him shall never thirst; but the water that I shall give him shall be in him a well of water springing up into everlasting life.

15 The woman saith unto him, Sir, give me this water, that I thirst not, neither come hither to draw.

Jesus did not allow the conversation to be diverted by a challenge about whether He is greater than Jacob. He is greater, of course, but the woman knew a lot about Jacob and nothing about Jesus. Instead, Jesus continued to talk about the water that He offers.

The water in Jacob's well, as refreshing as it may have been, could not give lasting relief from thirst. The woman would need to return to the well day after day to gain the water's short-lived benefits.

{But the water that Jesus offers is eternally satisfying (vs. 14). It quenches all thirst. The water that Jesus provides is of a completely different nature. It is a free-flowing fountain of water resulting in eternal life!}Q7

The woman continued to misunderstand the magnitude of Jesus' offer (vs. 15). She was still thinking in terms of physical water, though she liked the idea of special water that only has to be drunk once. She would not have to carry a heavy water jar ever again! She did not realize that Jesus was talking about spiritual realities. She did not yet understand God's gift that Jesus had mentioned earlier (vs. 10).

JESUS THE PROPHET

16 Jesus saith unto her, Go, call thy husband, and come hither.

17 The woman answered and said, I have no husband. Jesus said unto her, Thou hast well said, I have no husband:

18 For thou hast had five husbands; and he whom thou now hast is not thy husband: in that saidst thou truly.

19 The woman saith unto him, Sir, I perceive that thou art a prophet.

Jesus' knowledge (John 4:16-18). The Samaritan woman still did not know who Jesus was, leading her to misunderstand His offer of eternal life. So Jesus shifted the conversation to help her consider His identity.

{Again He used practical life issues to further a spiritual discussion (vs. 16). Jesus told the woman to go, call her husband, and then come back to the well.}Q8

The woman responded that she had no husband (vs. 17). Jesus told her that she answered truthfully. She had been married five times, and she was not married to the man with whom she was living (vs. 18).

The woman's acknowledgment (John 4:19). Jesus' response was calculated to draw a specific response from the woman. She had never met Him before. {She could think of no way He could know about her past relationships or her current living arrangement unless it was through God's insight into her life. She concluded that Jesus must be a prophet (vs. 19).}Q9

At last she was beginning to think about spiritual things. Her knowledge of Jesus' identity was improving as well. At this point she brought up the main religious distinction between the Jews and the Samaritans—the place where God is to be worshipped.

The Samaritans asserted that the proper location to worship God was on the nearby Mount Gerizim. A temple had been built there, and Jewish priests who had disagreed with the priesthood in Jerusalem had served in the new temple. The Jews had subsequently destroyed the temple on Mount Gerizim, but that did not extinguish the Samaritans' zeal for their views. The Samaritan woman reminded Jesus of the barrier between them.

But Jesus circumvented the Jewish-Samaritan barrier and made the issue personal to the Samaritan woman (vss. 23-24). Rather than focusing on the proper *place* to worship God, Jesus described the proper *attitude* with which to approach worship. Worship is not through a community-endorsed method but by a heartfelt devotion to God driven by scriptural truth and, as Jesus would later elaborate in John's Gospel, by the Holy Spirit indwelling each believer. Jesus, as the Messiah, causes these things to come to pass.

Jesus' statements had directed the woman toward His identity. She knew the Messiah was coming sometime, and He would reveal everything (vs. 25). She had not yet identified Jesus as the Messiah, but she knew He was a very special teacher.

Jesus' response was blunt (vs. 26). Jesus rarely asserted His identity as Messiah during His earthly ministry, perhaps because of the likelihood that people would have mistaken Him as a political figure who would rescue the Jews from Roman control. But He had no hesitation with the Samaritan woman. She was ready to hear who He really is. He told her that He is the Messiah, the One for whom she had been waiting.

Up to that point, the disciples were not at the well, so they missed the conversation between Jesus and the woman (vs. 27). When they arrived after their trip to town for supplies, they were surprised that Jesus was speaking to a woman. The disciples had the same prejudices as other Jewish men toward women.

They did not share Jesus' insight into the woman's spiritual needs or the opportunity to minister to the Samaritan community. They did not ask Jesus anything about the woman and her needs. They were still bound by the cultural and historical pressures that would hinder their gospel ministry until they saw humanity from God's perspective.

JESUS THE MESSIAH

28 The woman then left her waterpot, and went her way into the city, and saith to the men,

29 Come, see a man, which told me all things that ever I did: is not this the Christ?

When Jesus' disciples arrived at the well, the Samaritan woman departed and returned to the city. She was in a hurry to leave the scene. Her original reason for going to the well was no longer important to her. She left her water jar at the well because it was large and would slow her down.

When she arrived in the city, she discussed the man she encountered at the well. The woman urged the people to follow her back to Jesus (vs. 29). She had met a man unlike anyone she had ever met. He had displayed intimate knowledge of her, knowing the good and the bad, the past and the present. A stranger could not have such knowledge unless he had a unique relationship with God.

{She asked a very direct question: Can this be the Messiah? The way it is phrased in the Greek text normally expects a negative answer, but that was not her intention. The townspeople needed to come to their own conclusion about Jesus.}[Q10]

Jesus effectively used His knowledge of the background and life situation of the woman to make her consider His identity and the salvation He offered. In response, the woman pointed others to Jesus by telling them about the profound impact that He had on her life.

—Glenn Weaver

QUESTIONS

1. What was the religious significance of Samaria?
2. How was Jesus' meeting with the Samaritan woman significant for the early church?
3. Why was Jesus able to talk uninterrupted with the Samaritan woman?
4. Why was it unusual that Jesus spoke with the Samaritan woman?
5. What was the Jewish attitude toward the Samaritans?
6. What were the two important pieces of information that the Samaritan woman did not know?
7. What was special about the water that Jesus offered to the Samaritan woman?
8. How did Jesus further the spiritual discussion with the woman?
9. What was the woman's conclusion when Jesus described details of her personal life?
10. What did the woman do in order to have the townspeople consider Jesus' claim to be the Messiah?

—Glenn Weaver

Preparing to Teach the Lesson

Christians can be guilty of forgetting how much the Lord loves the world and desires for all to be saved. The account of Jesus and the Samaritan woman reminds us that the Lord will go the extra mile to reach one lost soul.

TODAY'S AIM

Facts: to see Jesus offer living water.

Principle: to understand the gift He has given to believers.

Application: to praise God for living in us.

INTRODUCING THE LESSON

Many of us struggle when we share the gospel with unbelievers. We may have done our very best to explain God's gift of salvation, but the person is not interested.

In today's lesson, we get to watch Jesus offer eternal life to a woman who had never met Him before. Of course, He completely knew her because He knows everything.

DEVELOPING THE LESSON

1. Jesus breaks barriers to reach the Samaritan woman (John 4:5-9). At the beginning of the chapter, we see Jesus leaving Judea and traveling to Galilee. But He did not take the normal route. Jesus had a divine appointment with the Samaritan woman. Knowing how and when to find her, He arrived at Jacob's well at noon. Most people would get their daily water in the morning because it is a cooler time of day. Also, getting water in the morning provided cool water for the whole day. Mornings would also be crowded with other women at the well, making it a social time. This is the first hint about her.

In verse 7, we see Jesus initiating a conversation. The woman's purpose was clear: she came to draw water. Jesus asked her to give Him a drink. Verse 8 gives more information about the event, saying the disciples had gone into town to buy food. This statement implies that Jesus and the woman were alone. That led her to point out the obvious absurdity to the Lord: He was a Jew, and she was a Samaritan woman. How could He ask her for a drink? For hundreds of years, the Jews and Samaritans did not associate with one another. So we see her changing the subject to a controversial topic of racism and prejudice. This can be a way that people avoid a discussion about their personal sins.

2. Jesus offers living water to the Samaritan woman (John 4:10-19). In verse 10, Jesus made a profound announcement of the gospel. He shows us how to rise above arguments and distractions and focus on His power to change lives. He told the woman that if she knew the gift of God and who He is, she would ask from Him and He would give her living water. This is an interesting term not used very often in Scripture. Jeremiah 2:13 records the Lord calling Himself "the fountain of living waters" and shows His disgust over people choosing their own broken cisterns. The woman refuted Jesus' statement by saying He could not give her water because He had nothing to draw with and the well was deep.

She used another tactic to avoid discussing her spiritual condition. She attempted to attack Him personally and appealed to historical evidence by asking Him if He was greater than Jacob. Samaritans and Jews both revered the patriarch Jacob.

You may have friends who will attempt to have religious, historical, or personal arguments instead of discussing their own need for a Savior. The mention of Jacob and his family literally drinking from that same well may reveal her connection to traditions, sentimentality, and possibly superstition.

Jesus pressed further with His evangelistic message that whoever drank from that well would thirst again, but whoever drinks from the water He gives will never thirst again. The promise of salvation includes a well of water springing up into eternal life. Just like the prophet Isaiah said, "Therefore with joy shall ye draw water out of the wells of salvation" (Isa. 12:3).

In verse 15 we see the Samaritan woman's move toward the gospel offer. She wanted living water so she would never be thirsty for water or have to keep coming to the well to draw water every day.

Jesus continued the gospel discussion by highlighting her sinful lifestyle. God has full knowledge of our sins. He told the woman that He knew that she had had multiple husbands and was now living with another man. The woman was amazed that Jesus knew her life and acknowledged Jesus as a prophet.

3. The woman tells her town that Jesus is the Messiah (John 4:28-29). It is always amazing to witness God's saving power in a person's life, At the beginning of the chapter, the woman was an outcast living with shame, but now she had met the Master.

She was so excited that she left her water jar, hurried back to town, and told everyone to come meet a man who knew everything about her. Because of what He said to her, she asked her neighbors if He could be the Christ, or Messiah.

ILLUSTRATING THE LESSON

Jesus offers living water.

CONCLUDING THE LESSON

Many people fear and dread the fact that God knows their sins. But here we see the power of the gospel. When our sins are brought to light, God can wash them away as we confess and repent.

Later, in John 7:37-39, Jesus boldly preached that anyone thirsty can come to Him and drink. By believing in Him, rivers of living water will flow from within them. John clarified the message by saying that Jesus was referring to the Holy Spirit.

In Exodus 17, we read the story from the wilderness journey of Moses and the Israelites when they were very thirsty. They whined and complained to Moses, wishing they were still in Egypt. Then (at the same place that God appeared to Moses in the burning bush in Exodus 3) God told Moses to strike the rock and refreshing water would come out for the people to drink. Many years later, in Nehemiah 9, we read the prayers of the Levites recalling this amazing event.

ANTICIPATING THE NEXT LESSON

Next week we will begin the third unit of this quarter by studying God's omnipotence: He is all-powerful! We will begin the unit next Sunday in 1 Corinthians 2:6-16 by studying the Holy Spirit's power to give us wisdom.

—Adam Clagg

PRACTICAL POINTS

1. Everyday activities can provide a segue into a spiritual discussion (John 4:5-9).
2. Even spiritual discussions that are not understood immediately can result in great benefit (vss. 10-12).
3. Jesus offers what the world cannot, if we are willing to receive it (vss. 13-15).
4. Jesus can provide what we need, for He knows everything about us (vss. 16-19).
5. A person can prioritize spiritual matters over physical needs if properly motivated (vs. 28).
6. Life transformation can lead to bold witness for God (vs. 29).

—Glenn Weaver

RESEARCH AND DISCUSSION

1. Why is it significant that John spent so much time writing about the Samaritan woman?
2. Why are people often slow to understand the meaning of spiritual discussions? What steps can we take when someone does not understand the concepts we are trying to convey?
3. What traditions often lead people to reject biblical teaching?
4. What pitfalls may we encounter if we bring up the sinful lifestyle choices of others?
5. When might it be appropriate to discuss the sinful personal choices of others?
6. Is it more difficult to witness to an individual or to a group? How might you have to adjust your approach in each situation?

—Glenn Weaver

ILLUSTRATED HIGH POINTS

Jews have no dealings with the Samaritans (John 4:9)

When I was in grade school, I was a big fan of the Pittsburgh Steelers football team—but only because they had recently won the Super Bowl. I did not like the New England Patriots football team—but only because some of my classmates disliked them.

Bigotry is contagious. We often fear those we don't know. Differences of color, societal class, or background can be viewed as bad if we aren't careful. We are all equal at the foot of the Cross.

He would have given thee living water (vs. 10)

Near my childhood home was a spring that flowed from a small hill behind the house. On hot summer days, the flowing water was cool and refreshing. How different was the water in the nearby pond! It had green algae and was lukewarm. The smell reminded you that there were fish in it.

Too often people are content to live their lives drinking the stagnant water of this world's values. They reject the fresh, life-giving water that God offers freely through Jesus Christ.

I have no husband (vs. 17)

When I was young and living in a small-town community, it was shocking to hear of people who were getting a divorce or of an unmarried man and woman living together.

There was a sense of shame, such that people avoided talking about their living arrangements, even with friends.

Fortunately for us, God knows all about our situation. He knows our living situation, our failing, and our heartbreak, and He offers His loving compassion and forgiveness in Christ.

—Glenn Weaver

Golden Text Illuminated

"Come, see a man, which told me all things that ever I did: is not this the Christ?" (John 4:29).

We are not very different from the Samaritan woman Christ encountered at the well in John 4. She was, like us, someone who longed for satisfaction. And yet, like so many of us, she spent much of her life chasing after things that would never truly satisfy her soul. She had, like many of us, made sinful decisions that left her empty. And yet, she had a life-changing encounter with the only One who can both save and satisfy the soul, Jesus Christ Himself.

Christ was sitting at a well in Samaria (a region typically avoided by Jews) when suddenly a Samaritan woman showed up at the well to draw water. Christ asked her for a drink, which surprised her (vss. 7-9), but His request for water was an evangelistic tool to reach her soul. In verse 10, Christ offered the woman "living water." The woman, although intrigued, missed the point. She was thinking only in physical terms. At first, *He* was thirsty, and *she* had the water. But now, all of a sudden, Jesus spoke to her as if *she* were the thirsty one, and *He* was the One who had the water! Although He initially asked *her* for a drink, it was she who needed a drink from *Him*! When the woman expressed interest in His "living water," Jesus urged her to call her husband. The woman said she was not married, to which Christ replied: "Thou hast had five husbands; and he whom thou now hast is not thy husband" (vs. 18). This moment helped convince the woman that this stranger at the well was the Christ.

This prompted the woman to quickly run into the city and proclaim to all who would listen, "Come, see a man, which told me all things that ever I did" (vs. 29). It was thus the omniscience of Christ that compelled the woman not only to believe but to invite others to listen to this stranger as well. Two thousand years later, this stranger also knows us with absolute perfection. The omniscience of Christ supplies us with four reasons why He deserves our worship, trust, and allegiance.

Reason #1: Jesus Christ has all authority. Since Christ has exhaustive knowledge of all things (including the hidden deeds and secret thoughts of our heart), He is qualified to speak with authority on all matters.

Reason #2: Jesus Christ is the source of absolute truth. Having perfect knowledge of all things means that all Christ reveals and says is absolute truth and absolutely trustworthy.

Reason #3: Jesus Christ is the preeminent Object of trust. If Christ were deficient in knowledge, it would be a risk to trust Him with our souls. But knowing all things makes Him the only perfect Object of faith and trust.

Reason #4: Jesus Christ knows perfectly what we need at every moment for every situation. For every anxiety, fear, struggle with sin, relationship difficulty, and longing, Christ not only *knows* what is best but has *stated* what is best through His Word (although He does not specifically tell us what to do in every situation). The sufficiency of Christ is revealed to us through the Scriptures, and that makes Him no longer a stranger but our all-sufficient Savior.

—Jerod A. Gilcher

Heart of the Lesson

Everyone wants a friend, companion, or spouse who understands and "gets" them, knows how they think, and can help them with their problems. We value people who give good counsel, help us see our blind spots, and help us overcome challenges.

The unnamed but famous Samaritan woman in John 4, however, found so much more than that kind of friend. She met a man who did not merely understand her, "get" her, and help her with her problems, but also saved her soul. She met Jesus Christ the Messiah, the Savior of the world.

1. Jesus, who knows all things, is able to save our souls (John 4:5-19). The scene opens with thirsty, exhausted Jesus asking the Samaritan woman for water at a well (vs. 7). Three verses later, however, Jesus revealed to her that she was the one who needed a drink from Him (vs. 10). After offering the woman water that satisfies the soul forever, Jesus revealed that He knew everything about her life, her choices, and her long history of sinful decisions that led to her current sad situation (vss. 16-18). So much more than a friend who could merely give advice, Jesus revealed Himself to be the all-knowing Savior and source of eternal life (vss. 19-26).

Jesus offered the woman "the gift of God" (vs. 10), which He later called a "well of water springing up into everlasting life" (vs. 14). This is a Savior who knows that the deepest plight of the human soul is the sin that separates us from God. As the all-knowing prophet, Messiah, and Savior of the world, He offers water that gives eternal life to anyone who drinks. How can that not increase our boldness with the gospel? We bring to sinners the only salvation message of the only One who can save souls.

2. Jesus, who knows all things, is able to satisfy our souls (John 4:28-29). After speaking with Jesus, the woman left for the city, seeking to bring others to meet this stranger at the well. As she did so, she left her water bucket behind, signaling that she believed Jesus to be the true Satisfier of her thirst. The evidence she used to convince the townspeople was: "Come, see a man, which told me all things that ever I did: is not this the Christ?" (vs. 29).

She recognized that the claims of Jesus to satisfy the soul were verified by His supernatural knowledge of her life. The One who knew all things could also solve all problems. The Messiah who knows our hearts has the ability not just to sympathize with us but to satisfy the deepest longings of our souls.

That is why He described salvation in terms of "living water" (vs. 10). The One who can see the secret caverns of the soul is the One who perfectly knows what alone can fill those caverns: "Whosoever drinketh of this water shall thirst again; but whosoever drinketh of the water that I shall give him shall never thirst; but the water that I shall give him shall be in him a well of water springing up into everlasting life" (vss. 13-15). Jesus frees us from the empty, counterfeit pleasures of sin that pretend to do what only He can do.

In Jesus, we have so much more than a friend who "gets" us and understands us. Jesus is the Friend of sinners who knows and provides what sinners need the most. His salvation both saves and satisfies the soul forever.

—Jerod A. Gilcher

World Missions

The young Muslim international student and his Christian friend conversed easily into the evening. They had become friends and had many common interests. When they had first met, the Muslim student was grateful to realize that, unlike many American students at his college, this new friend did not seem to need drinking, drugs, and immorality to get through his week. He clearly believed in God, even though he knew that they did not quite believe the same things *about* God.

Once, the Muslim student expressed a common cultural fear about the dangers of the presence of *jinn*, a kind of demonic entity. When he saw that his friend recognized the reality of the spiritual world, he asked him how Christians dealt with people who were oppressed by such entities. His friend, recognizing the genuine spiritual hunger behind the question, guided the conversation to a discussion of the name of Jesus and how He alone has all authority in the spiritual realm.

In some ways, that interaction with the Muslim student paralleled Jesus' encounter with the Samaritan woman at the well. Toward the end of the eighth century B.C., men and women from other countries that had been conquered and exiled by the Assyrians settled in Samaria and mixed with the remnant of poor Israelites. By the first century A.D. Samaritans followed what was essentially an alternate form of the Jewish religion, centered on Mount Gerizim instead of in Jerusalem.

In John 4, a Samaritan woman had a transformational encounter with Jesus beside a well. She had been trying to run from her own shame, which is likely why she came to the well at an unusual hour, seeking to avoid other women who might call out the source of her shame. She was doubtless surprised to encounter Jesus there and even more so to hear Jesus, a Jew, ask her for water.

As they went back and forth in their conversation, Jesus exposed the root of her shame—the brokenness of multiple marriages and immorality. She initially responded by seeking to retreat into a traditional, religious response. Jesus, however, knew that she was really thirsty for the truth and the life that only He could give her. He promised to give her *living* water (vs. 10), which would satisfy the deepest thirst of her heart—and the hearts of her kinfolk too. She ran off to tell the people of her town all about Jesus: "Come, see a man, which told me all things that ever I did: is not this the Christ?" (vs. 29).

How often we are desperate and in need of the One who can satisfy our deepest thirst, and yet we flee from Him into our own wisdom. We become like those about whom the prophet Jeremiah wrote, "They have forsaken me the fountain of living waters, and hewed them out cisterns, broken cisterns, that can hold no water" (Jer. 2:13).

Jesus invites us to come to Him, not only to be satisfied ourselves but also to be a source of life to others. He promised, "He that believeth on me, as the scripture hath said, out of his belly shall flow rivers of living water" (John 7:38). Through our testimony, He will satisfy the thirst of many others. As He said to His disciples, "Lift up your eyes, and look on the fields; for they are white already to harvest" (4:35)

For those seeking to reach Muslim friends like the young man in the opening illustration, God offers us wisdom in showing how Jesus alone can meet their spiritual hunger.

—Matthew Friedman

The Jewish Aspect

Ancient roads in Israel were not well developed until the time of the Romans. The routes were dictated by geographic features such as ridges, mountains, and rivers.

There were few main roads in and near ancient Judea, though several smaller roads existed to connect local destinations. Perhaps the most developed highway was the international Great Trunk Road, which went from Egypt to Babylon. It ran along the coast of Israel to the city of Megiddo in the Jezreel Valley and continued through Galilee toward Syria. The King's Highway, which is often referenced in the Old Testament, extended from the Red Sea across the plains of Moab until it joined the Great Trunk Road at Damascus. Another road was the Central Ridge Route, which was smaller but important for Jesus' time. This road went from Egypt through Beersheba to Jerusalem and north to Shechem, then to Galilee by way of Samaria.

It was this third route, the Central Ridge Route, that Jesus likely took in John 4 on His way to Galilee. It was the shortest route to Galilee from Jerusalem, but often the Jews chose to cross the Jordan River and travel on a smaller road to Galilee, even though it was a longer journey. They took the longer path to avoid Samaria because the Jews did not like the Samaritans.

The rivalry between the Jews and Samaritans had gone on for centuries. Samaritans claimed that mainstream Judaism had abandoned the true faith by changing the approved worship site from Mount Gerizim to other locations, eventually Jerusalem.

The Jewish traditions, on the other hand, claimed that the Samaritan people originated when the Assyrians repopulated the Northern Kingdom with other conquered people from Mesopotamia (cf. 2 Kgs. 17:24-41).

The animosity between the two groups continued into the New Testament era. The Jewish leaders, when confronting Jesus, slandered Him by claiming that He was a Samaritan and had a demon (John 8:48). The Samaritans were not fond of the Jews either. When Jesus traveled from Galilee and tried to enter a certain Samaritan town, they would not welcome Him because He was traveling to Jerusalem. James and John responded with hatred befitting Jewish prejudice, asking Jesus if they should call down fire to consume the townspeople! Of course, Jesus said no (Luke 9:51-56).

Jesus did not participate in the Jewish hatred of the Samaritans. He recognized that they were estranged from Israel, however. They were counted as foreigners (cf. 17:11-19). When sending out the twelve disciples, Jesus instructed them to go to the house of Israel, not to the Gentiles or the Samaritans (Matt. 10:5-6).

At other times in the Gospels, Samaritans are cast in a good light. Jesus used a Samaritan as the compassionate hero in His illustration of a good neighbor (Luke 10:25-37). In the account of the ten lepers, only a Samaritan showed gratitude to Jesus for healing him (17:11-19).

Healing the ancient rift between the Jews and Samaritans was important for the spread of the gospel. Jesus named Samaria as a key destination for the disciples to evangelize after He ascended to the Father (Acts 1:8). Acts 8 records Philip going to the city of Samaria and having a fruitful ministry in that region. The gospel overcame the separation between Jews and Samaritans that persisted for centuries by reconciling both groups to God in Christ.

—Glenn Weaver

Guiding the Superintendent

When were you the thirstiest, and what did it feel like to finally drink water? Why do you think the Bible uses this experience as a spiritual metaphor?

Jesus thirsted. After a long journey, He asked a Samaritan woman for a drink from Jacob's well. Jesus used this encounter to transform a woman's life and her community as He spread His truth about Himself and God's Kingdom. In this narrative about the woman at the well, John used cultural and biblical history, prophetic imagery, and dialogue to convey his portrayal of Jesus.

DEVOTIONAL OUTLINE

1. Setting (John 4:5-6). Culturally, Jesus broke a catalogue of social norms in John 4. Most pious Jews would walk around Samaria, not through it, because they hated Samaritans. Jesus, however, wanted to take the shortcut right through the village. He was weary from His journey and rested at Jacob's well.

Jesus initiated the dialogue by asking the woman at the well for a drink. The woman, surprised that a rabbi would talk to her, expressed several significant cultural issues: "How is it that thou, being a Jew, askest drink of me, which am a woman of Samaria?" (John 4:9). John used the dialogue between Jesus and the woman to reveal the cultural norms of society as well as information about the characters speaking. Jewish animosity toward Samaritans had existed for a long time. After God's judgment against Samaria in the eighth century B.C., people from various regions and religions settled in Samaria (cf. 2 Kgs. 17:24-34). Those peoples worshipped many different gods. Some even sacrificed their children in the fire (vs. 31).

2. Conversation (John 4:7-19). In biblical history, Isaac (Gen. 24), Jacob (Gen. 29), and Moses (Ex. 2) all found their wives at a well. Betrothal and marriage had repeatedly failed this woman (John 4:17-18), however, so here John subverted the traditional scene at a well by portraying her finding a different kind of love and a never-ending satisfaction that romance cannot offer.

Jesus explained the nature of His salvation through the metaphor of "living water" (vs. 10). The Old Testament prophets used the imagery of living (that is, moving) water to refer to God as Israel's life-source (Jer. 2:13) and to the salvation God would provide (Isa. 12:3). Isaiah declared that such water would be given free of charge to anyone who wanted it (55:1). By promising to give eternal, living water, Jesus identified Himself as the divine source of salvation. Later, John identified the living water as the Holy Spirit, whom Jesus would send (John 7:37-39).

3. Testimony (John 4:28-29). Jesus' dialogue with the woman also revealed His supernatural knowledge. The Samaritan woman recognized that when she said, "Come, see a man, which told me all things that ever I did: is not this the Christ?" (John 4:29). Her testimony led to the townspeople likewise believing in Jesus as the promised Messiah (vs. 42).

CHILDREN'S CORNER

Because of sin, all people are like the woman at the well—in need of Jesus' offer of salvation. Help children recognize that by reminding them that Jesus knows everything about them, just like He knew everything about the woman at the well. Ask the children if there is anything they would not want Jesus to know about their lives. Then tell them all they need to do is ask to receive Jesus' free gift of forgiveness and eternal life with Him.

—Matthew Swale

SCRIPTURE LESSON TEXT

1 COR. 2:6 Howbeit we speak wisdom among them that are perfect: yet not the wisdom of this world, nor of the princes of this world, that come to nought:

7 But we speak the wisdom of God in a mystery, *even* the hidden *wisdom*, which God ordained before the world unto our glory:

8 Which none of the princes of this world knew: for had they known *it*, they would not have crucified the Lord of glory.

9 But as it is written, Eye hath not seen, nor ear heard, neither have entered into the heart of man, the things which God hath prepared for them that love him.

10 But God hath revealed *them* unto us by his Spirit: for the Spirit searcheth all things, yea, the deep things of God.

11 For what man knoweth the things of a man, save the spirit of man which is in him? even so the things of God knoweth no man, but the Spirit of God.

12 Now we have received, not the spirit of the world, but the spirit which is of God; that we might know the things that are freely given to us of God.

13 Which things also we speak, not in the words which man's wisdom teacheth, but which the Holy Ghost teacheth; comparing spiritual things with spiritual.

14 But the natural man receiveth not the things of the Spirit of God: for they are foolishness unto him: neither can he know *them*, because they are spiritually discerned.

15 But he that is spiritual judgeth all things, yet he himself is judged of no man.

16 For who hath known the mind of the Lord, that he may instruct him? But we have the mind of Christ.

NOTES

Power to Impart Wisdom

Lesson Text: 1 Corinthians 2:6-16

Related Scriptures: Proverbs 8:12-31; Isaiah 63:15—64:4; John 3:1-8; 1 Corinthians 1:18—2:5; Ephesians 1:15-21

TIME: between A.D. 54 and 56 PLACE: from Ephesus

GOLDEN TEXT—"We speak the wisdom of God in a mystery, even the hidden wisdom, which God ordained before the world unto our glory" (1 Corinthians 2:7).

Introduction

The word for "wisdom" occurs about fifteen times in the first three chapters of 1 Corinthians and only twelve other times in all of Paul's writings. Wisdom was something of an obsession with the Corinthians, prompting Paul to address and correct their thinking using their own favorite terms.

Wisdom in the Greco-Roman world was closely associated with the worldly philosophers who delved into deep speculations about the divine nature and other convoluted controversies. In contrast, in Christian thinking, wisdom has more to do with the practical: "The fear of the Lord is the beginning of knowledge: but fools despise wisdom and instruction" (Prov. 1:7).

Contrary to pagan philosophy, God's divine wisdom conveys that Jesus the Messiah was sent by the Father to save sinners by enduring the shame of the cross. Believers are challenged to bear gladly the reproach of the cross, for it leads to the incomparable greatness of the glory that comes with it at the final resurrection (1 Cor. 15:40-42). And the Holy Spirit is the only one who has the power to impart that wisdom to us.

LESSON OUTLINE

1. **WISDOM AMONG THE MATURE—1 Cor. 2:6-11**
2. **WISDOM AND THE MIND OF GOD—1 Cor. 2:12-16**

Exposition: Verse by Verse

WISDOM AMONG THE MATURE

1 COR. 2:6 Howbeit we speak wisdom among them that are perfect: yet not the wisdom of this world, nor of the princes of this world, that come to nought:

7 But we speak the wisdom of God in a mystery, even the hidden wisdom, which God ordained before the world unto our glory:

8 Which none of the princes of this world knew: for had they known it, they would not have crucified the Lord of glory.

9 But as it is written, Eye hath not seen, nor ear heard, neither have

entered into the heart of man, the things which God hath prepared for them that love him.

10 But God hath revealed them unto us by his Spirit: for the Spirit searcheth all things, yea, the deep things of God.

11 For what man knoweth the things of a man, save the spirit of man which is in him? even so the things of God knoweth no man, but the Spirit of God.

Paul had written all kinds of positive things in his opening greeting, but he quickly transitioned to some concerns that turned out to be major. Corinthian fascination with worldly knowledge and wisdom had taken them away from the message of the cross, which was the very heart of Paul's gospel. Satan had managed to focus so much of their attention on the glitz and glitter that is achieved through high rhetoric and eloquence that the Corinthians' respect for Paul had diminished.

Paul did not correct the Corinthians' diminished appreciation for him. He was glad to lack any such rhetorical skills. In fact, he had just said that in his ministry to the Corinthians, he had resolved to know nothing except the crucified Messiah (2:2)—probably a very emphatic way to convey that he had no interest in impressing his audiences with outward performance features.

The wisdom of the world versus the wisdom of God (1 Cor. 2:6-9). Before letting go of the wisdom issue, Paul circled back to correct the Corinthians' misgivings. **{**He did, in fact, preach a message full of wisdom but of a kind completely unfathomable to the Corinthians in their present immaturity (vs. 6).**}**[Q1]

Paul conceded that the gospel's wisdom could not be recognized as such by the standards of this age or by those elites who controlled the culture of his day. The very existence of those cultural gatekeepers was soon to pass. In contrast, Paul came speaking the wisdom of God ordained from eternity past (vs. 7). It was shrouded in mystery so that God's enlightened people might share in God's glory while those who oppose Him are brought to naught.

Paul added the explanatory note that the "princes" of this present age (who have no authority in the coming age already inaugurated by Christ's death and resurrection) did not know this wisdom, for had they known, they would not have crucified the Lord of glory (vs. 8). **{**The comment makes clear that Paul was speaking about the rulers and influencers who brought about Jesus' crucifixion.**}**[Q2] Irony abounds. How foolish were the self-proclaimed wise people to have shamefully crucified humble Jesus, who was, in actuality, the Lord of glory!

Paul affirmed his assessment with an allusion to Isaiah 64:4, which depicts God as acting incomparably to save His people (1 Cor. 2:9).

The wisdom of God revealed (1 Cor. 2:10-11). Paul argued that God had revealed incomparable glory to believers only through the Holy Spirit (vs. 10), countering the shame that the so-called wise might heap on them.

Status-holders who claim to have a monopoly on wisdom might think they have plumbed great depths of wisdom, but their best efforts at philosophizing are nothing compared to the wisdom revealed to believers by the Holy Spirit, who searches all things, even the "deep things" pertaining to God (vs. 10). **{**Accordingly, only the Holy Spirit can truly know the thoughts of God, just as only individual persons understand their own thoughts (vs. 11).**}**[Q3]

Paul's point that God's wisdom is unfathomable was important for the Corinthians. They had poorly interpreted their giftedness (1:5-7; 4:8) and wisdom (1:5; 4:10) as indicators of status in their competitive environment, as Paul's extended correction about tongues in 1 Corinthians 14 suggests. While the Corinthians assumed that their experience of the Spirit made what they did with their own physical bodies irrelevant to Christian maturity (whether engaging with prostitutes in 6:12-20 or withholding sexual relations from their spouses in 7:1-7), Paul argued that their experience of the Spirit was meant to help them understand the mind of God. It was not meant to give them ecstatic experiences or to grant them license to sin with their bodies. {It was meant to impart an understanding of God's will, leading them into Christian maturity.}[Q4]

More than once in 1 Corinthians Paul urged the Corinthians to imitate his example (4:16; 11:1). Paul's experiences before he first came to Corinth would have served as an example for the Corinthians about what Spirit-imparted wisdom looks like in action.

On Paul's second missionary journey, God interrupted his plans (Acts 16:6-15). The team had planned to go one way, then the next, and yet again in a third, but the Holy Spirit stopped them. Meanwhile, the team likely devoted itself to serious prayer and team worship as they sought the Lord's direction. When we find ourselves at a standstill, awaiting something to break and get the waters flowing again, we should remember that waiting is not a waste and that God often works when we stand quiet before Him.

The Lord then led the missionary team to Philippi. Though their ministry was successful there, Paul and Silas were severely beaten and locked in stocks in prison (vss. 16-24). Their disposition, however, was that it was better to be locked up in a tortuous dungeon with the Lord in their midst than to enjoy freedom on the outside without the Holy Spirit.

When released, Paul's priority was to safeguard the new believers, so he made sure that the city elders, who had illegally tortured them, escorted them out of the city with honor and respect. Paul's request was not motivated by self-vindication. Instead, he made a point that the city officials pass by Lydia's house, where other believers were gathered, to pay proper respect to the new church.

Despite the harsh treatment in Philippi, the missionary team dared to go to Thessalonica (Acts 17:1; cf. 1 Thess. 2:2). Opponents in Thessalonica were accusing Paul of using flattery to deceive the Thessalonians and of employing religion to turn a profit. Paul asserted that his ministry there was driven by pure motives, and the people knew that was true. Paul also stressed that he did not impose on them to supply even his basic needs; he had worked night and day to avoid being a burden to the Thessalonians. Instead of using the Thessalonians to serve his needs, he shared his very own life with them. Such is the model of the cruciform life.

{That was Paul's recent experience when he came to Corinth, where he undoubtedly modeled the same cruciform life and servant's heart. Therefore, the news that the Corinthians were now pursuing and celebrating status distressed Paul, prompting him to emphasize Jesus, the crucified Messiah who gave His life for others.}[Q5] Although the cross of Christ carried a stigma of shame, the glory of that same cross will endure while the glitz and glitter of this present evil age passes away.

WISDOM AND THE MIND OF GOD

12 Now we have received, not the spirit of the world, but the spirit which is of God; that we might know the things that are freely given to us of God.

13 Which things also we speak, not in the words which man's wisdom teacheth, but which the Holy Ghost teacheth; comparing spiritual

things with spiritual.

14 But the natural man receiveth not the things of the Spirit of God: for they are foolishness unto him: neither can he know them, because they are spiritually discerned.

15 But he that is spiritual judgeth all things, yet he himself is judged of no man.

16 For who hath known the mind of the Lord, that he may instruct him? But we have the mind of Christ.

The natural person does not know the things of God (1 Cor. 2:12-14). Paul now tried to bring the Corinthians toward maturity. When they came to faith, they were not given "the spirit of the world"—that is, they were not given a new worldly outlook and competency, earning them the respect of great pagan thinkers (vs. 12). Nor were they enabled to delve into false teaching or speculations about God's divine nature, as their pagan counterparts did. {Rather, God's Spirit enabled them to understand the gospel. That is what Paul meant when he wrote that they received the Spirit in order to "know the things that are freely given to us of God" (vs. 12).}[Q6] Since the Spirit they received did not come from the world, they should stop thinking and behaving like the world.

Paul's wording in verse 12 alludes to the opening thanksgiving, where he commended the Corinthians for having been enriched and lacking no spiritual gift (1:5-7). When Paul first preached to them and they received the gospel, the Holy Spirit granted them superior wisdom and depth of insight that would make the world's wisdom seem puny and inconsequential. It is that simple godly wisdom that Paul proclaimed to them. It explains spiritual truths with Spirit-taught words (vs. 13).

{Paul's message was that God sent Jesus Messiah to be crucified and save sinners (1:23-24).}[Q7] That message is eternal. In contrast, worldly wisdom, with all its speculation, passes away, along with the elites who cherish it.

To clarify his point in theological terms, Paul now asserted that humans, in their unsaved natural state and prior to the Holy Spirit's work in their lives, lack the capacity to welcome or accept the truths taught by God's Spirit (2:14). Such unbelieving people, since they lack the Holy Spirit, naturally think that the truths taught by Him are pure foolishness; they cannot grasp spiritual truths, for those truths can only be discerned through the Holy Spirit.

{That inability of unbelievers to grasp spiritual truth reflects the doctrine of human depravity.}[Q8] God did not create humans as depraved. When God created anything, it was "very good" (Gen. 1:31). Depravity became a human trait at the Fall (3:1-7), and now it is transmitted from one generation to another. (Some may wish that the Bible were clearer on how that happens!)

Our personal experiences reinforce the doctrine of depravity. Most Christians can remember a time when they found the gospel either foolish or repulsive. They may have vigorously opposed conversion, but over time, the Holy Spirit began working more and more in their hearts until they were so overwhelmed by the convicting and powerful drawing of the Holy Spirit that they cast themselves on God's mercy, pleading for forgiveness for their sins and committing their hearts to serve Christ.

How God works to bring people to salvation has some degree of mystery, but our lesson passage teaches that, in any case, unbelievers cannot understand spiritual things without the miraculous intervention of the Holy Spirit.

The spiritual person knows the things of God (1 Cor. 2:15-16). After negatively asserting that the natural, unspiritual person cannot know the things of the Spirit, Paul now added its positive corollary: the person who lives under the control of the Holy Spirit discerns everything. {Paul was speaking ideally; while Spirit-controlled believers discern everything, the Corinthian believers were not living up to the ideal.}[Q9]

{Paul then added, perhaps to chide the Corinthians for their judgmental attitude toward him, that spiritually led people, who thoughtfully discern all things, are not to be judged by those who are spiritually immature.}[Q10] Paul would later add a caveat that claims about spiritual truth must be tested by other discerning believers (cf. 12:10; 14:29), thus preventing Christians from assuming that their opinions are always beyond question.

Paul's point was that he had received God's Spirit, who enabled him to judge in truth. In contrast, the Corinthians judged him according to the standards of an unredeemed Greco-Roman culture. In their judgment, Paul was not learned, wise, eloquent, or even conversant in speculative philosophies! Later, Paul told the Corinthians that he cared little about how they judged him; what counted to him was how the Lord judges His servants (4:3-4).

To support his argument, in 2:16 Paul cited Isaiah 40:13, which praises God for His unfathomable greatness and wisdom that no one can (naturally) discern. But believers, Paul quickly added, have the mind of Christ, making them capable of such discernment.

The Spirit searches the deep things of God (1 Cor. 2:10). By this comment, Paul did not mean that the Spirit reveals to us esoteric aspects about God's nature, as if we could divine the proverbial number of angels that could dance on a pinhead. Paul had in mind, rather, the idea that the Spirit can help us discern more practical matters, such as a person's motives (see Paul's rebuke of Elymas in Acts 13:9-10) or whether we should orient ourselves in one direction in ministry or another (see how the Spirit directed the church in Antioch to set aside Paul and Barnabas for missions in Acts 13:1-3). The Spirit helps us discern true holiness in action and to sift things that have the mere appearance of spirituality from matters that are truly spiritual.

—James M. Leonard

QUESTIONS

1. Why did the Corinthians not recognize the wisdom of Paul's message about the cross?
2. Who were the "princes of this world" (1 Cor. 2:8)?
3. What comparison did Paul make between the Holy Spirit and a person's knowledge of his or her own thoughts?
4. What is the purpose of our experience of the Holy Spirit?
5. How did Paul's recent experiences before coming to Corinth likely influence his reaction to the Corinthians' love for the wisdom of the world?
6. What does it mean to "know the things that are freely given to us of God" (vs. 12)?
7. What was the content of Paul's "spiritual" message (vs. 13)?
8. What doctrine is taught in verse 14?
9. Does every true believer exhibit perfect spiritual wisdom? How do we know that from the context of 1 Corinthians?
10. Why might Paul have been eager to point out the inability of the spiritually immature to judge those who are spiritual (vs. 15)?

—Matthew Robinson

Preparing to Teach the Lesson

The wisdom of God is different than the wisdom of man. Many people think they are intelligent but are not wise. Today's lesson discusses the ability that only God has to reveal wisdom to us by and through the Holy Spirit.

TODAY'S AIM

Facts: to know that God gives believers wisdom through the Holy Spirit.

Principle: to realize only Almighty God can reveal supernatural wisdom.

Application: to seek the wisdom of God by depending on the Holy Spirit and the revealed Word of God.

INTRODUCING THE LESSON

Some people in our lives are smart but not wise. It can be frustrating to live or work with someone who has no common sense. Not only is there a difference between intelligence and common sense, but there is also a significant difference between the wisdom of God and the wisdom of man.

We often discuss the gifts and fruit of the Spirit, but we neglect to discuss the wisdom of the Spirit. God's power is revealed when the Holy Spirit gives supernatural wisdom to ordinary people.

DEVELOPING THE LESSON

In 1 Corinthians 1, the apostle Paul teaches about the wisdom of God. Unbelievers see the message of the cross as foolishness, but we know it is the power of God!

As a missionary to the Greeks, Paul knew one of their main quests in life was knowledge. That could be a stumbling block to Christianity, for he was asking them to believe in a supernatural God who does things that do not always make sense. But if they could have faith in Him, they would gain wisdom given by the Creator.

1. True wisdom comes from God (1 Cor. 2:6-8). People can be divided into groups in multiple ways: age, ethnicity, gender, religion, politics, and more. In the Bible, we see that believers can also be divided into groups of maturity and immaturity. In verse 6, the apostle Paul says that those who are mature in their faith understand the wisdom of God. This is a different kind of wisdom than the wisdom of the world. Those with worldly power and their ways of thinking will die.

The wisdom preached by Paul and the other apostles is directly from God but has been a mystery hidden from unbelievers. An effective way to understand this use of the word mystery is as a sacred secret that is only made known by divine revelation. If the so-called powerful people in the world possessed God's wisdom, they would not have crucified Jesus Christ, the Son of God, the Lord of glory!

2. The Holy Spirit freely gives believers wisdom (1 Cor. 2:9-13). In verse 9, the apostle Paul quoted Isaiah 64:4. This is a popular Bible verse that means that we mere humans cannot comprehend the vast wisdom of God. But God revealed these things to us through the Holy Spirit. Some people mistakenly use this verse to refer to the things awaiting believers in heaven. When we read this verse in the context of the surrounding paragraphs, we see that these "things" are the mysteries of God that He has revealed to His children.

The Holy Spirit searches all things, even the deep things of God. There are things about a person that no one will ever know except that person and God. Deep in a person's spirit lie personal secrets. Here we see a glimpse into the mystery of the Trinity, when verse 11 explains that a person's spirit understands everything about that person, and God's Spirit knows and understands everything about God. Now, because of the work of Christ, He sent the Holy Spirit to live in us. So that same Holy Spirit who knows everything now lives in us and teaches us. Jesus, in His conversation with Nicodemus, said that believers are born again by the work of the Holy Spirit in their lives (John 3:8).

Because of this powerful indwelling of the Holy Spirit, spiritual people can teach other spiritual truths using the Spirit's wisdom and words. The actual words of the Bible are important for us to know, understand, and teach. We should not oversimplify some of the deep things of God. Spiritual people can understand spiritual concepts.

3. Unbelievers cannot understand the things of God (1 Cor. 2:14-16). People without the Holy Spirit cannot receive the truth of God's Word without the intervention of the Spirit. They believe spiritual truth to be foolishness. But the power of the Holy Spirit enables those He indwells to understand the mysteries of God. God empowers a Spirit-filled person to make sound judgments. Discernment is a spiritual gift (1 Cor. 12:10; 1 John 4:1). Since there is a spiritual world, God gives wisdom to judge whether something is from Him or not. Paul was not saying that Christians are above criticism, nor was he saying that some Christians should be the judge of everyone's lives. Rather, Paul was contrasting the divine wisdom Christians have and the lack of wisdom of those who do not believe. This is a preview of his teaching in 1 Corinthians 6 to not sue each other and end up in front of an unsaved judge.

First Corinthians 2:16 begins with another quote from Isaiah. "Who hath known the mind of the Lord, that he may instruct him?" Of course, the answer to that question is no one. No person, angel, or creature in heaven or on earth can discern the Lord's thoughts or teach Him. He is too powerful for that! But He has given us a wonderful gift: we have the mind of Christ.

ILLUSTRATING THE LESSON

True wisdom is given to believers by the Holy Spirit.

CONCLUDING THE LESSON

Because of the power of the Holy Spirit, we can have the wisdom and knowledge of God. We can pray the words of Ephesians 1:15-20 for one another to receive the wisdom and knowledge of God. We pray that we can know Him better, that the eyes of our hearts will be enlightened, for one another to know the hope of His calling, and that we would understand the glorious riches of our inheritance and the greatness of His mighty power in our lives.

ANTICIPATING THE NEXT LESSON

Next week we will study God's power in the parting of the Red Sea in Exodus 14, which reminds us that God uses His power to provide for His children.

—Adam Clagg

PRACTICAL POINTS

1. Unlike God's wisdom, the worldly wisdom so many adore is soon passing away (1 Cor. 2: 6-7).
2. Worldly wisdom leads to utterly foolish actions (vs. 8).
3. Loving God makes His wisdom known to us through His Holy Spirit (vss. 9-10).
4. We learn God's ways through God's indwelling Spirit (vss. 11-12).
5. The wisdom we preach is salvation through a crucified Messiah (vs. 13).
6. Unbelievers cannot understand godly wisdom without the Holy Spirit's intervention (vs. 14).
7. Believers have the mind of Christ and should remember that daily (1 Cor. 2:15-16; cf. Phil. 2:5).

—James M. Leonard

RESEARCH AND DISCUSSION

1. What things made Corinth unique and challenging to Paul's ministry (Acts 18; 1 Cor. 16:10-18)?
2. What differences are there between wisdom that is revered today by the world's elite and Christian wisdom (1 Cor. 4:8-13; cf. Prov. 1:7)?
3. How do you discern godly wisdom from worldly wisdom (cf. 1 Cor. 12:8; Ps. 119:105)?
4. What has the Holy Spirit taught you about the deep things of God (1 Cor. 2:10)?
5. When you share God's wisdom with unbelievers, how can you help them understand it (14:24-25)?
6. In what way do believers have the mind of Christ (1 Cor. 2:16; cf. Phil. 2:5)?

—James M. Leonard

ILLUSTRATED HIGH POINTS

We speak wisdom among them that are perfect (1 Cor. 2:6)

Dan and Darla were disturbed by their daughter Danielle's decision to move away with her infant to a far-off state into an unstable situation. Despite their efforts, Danielle would not change her mind. Finally, they asked, "Which of your godly friends is telling you this is a good idea?" Danielle, however, did not have spiritually mature friends and had made this decision apart from God's wisdom. Months later, Danielle returned very disappointed.

God grants wisdom to those who ask for wisdom (Jas. 1:5). One of the best ways to find wisdom is to be friends with mature believers in the church.

The things which God hath prepared for them that love him (1 Cor. 2:9)

Joe was a middle-aged appliance repairman. In recent years, he had grown spiritually, and his church even asked him to preach on occasion. He sensed that God was calling him into ministry. He attended a Bible college, although college was something new to him. He was amazed that God had brought him there. Assured by his home church, Joe came to understand that God had been preparing him for this.

But we have the mind of Christ (vs. 16)

Two sisters fiercely competed against each other in softball for years. In the championship game, the elder sister knew her younger sister so well that she called for a high fast pitch, knowing that her sister could not resist.

Paul calls us to have the mindset of Jesus and to serve one another (Phil. 2:5). If we are to have the mind of Christ, we must always turn our eyes to Him so that we may know Him.

—James M. Leonard

Golden Text Illuminated

"We speak the wisdom of God in a mystery, even the hidden wisdom, which God ordained before the world unto our glory" (1 Corinthians 2:7).

An old hymn declares: "Immortal, invisible, God only wise, in light inaccessible hid from our eyes." (Smith, Immortal, Invisible, God only Wise). This captures the sentiment of the apostle Paul in our text that the wisdom of God is mysterious, hidden, and beyond human comprehension.

This raises the question: What does it mean that God is "wise"? While humans can be wise, we know that the wisdom of God is vastly different. Because God is infinite in knowledge, unlimited in power, and sovereign over all things, His wisdom includes His skill to unfold His plan. To be wise means that one knows how to use the best means to achieve the best possible outcome, and God's wisdom is God navigating all of history to the ultimate outcome, namely, to reveal his character, full of truth and grace. God's wisdom means that He fulfills His plan despite the raging and plotting of human and demonic opposition.

The clearest display of God's wisdom, however, was found in the death of His own Son. This is the context of our Scripture, and Paul goes on to say in verse 8 that the rulers of this would did not understand God's wisdom, "for had they known it, they would not have crucified the Lord of glory."

This raises a question about what it means for us to be wise as believers and how we may obtain that wisdom. The rest of this feature will explore the following questions: 1) What is wisdom? 2) How do we obtain wisdom? And 3) What are the practical effects of wisdom in our lives?

What is wisdom? If God's wisdom includes fulfilling His plan in a way that brings Him glory, so too wisdom for us means commitment to God's glory. Wisdom applies God's Word to every area of life, which leads to the glory of God. Putting it another way, wisdom is living in God's way, according to God's Word, by God's power, for God's glory. This leads to the next question, however.

How do we obtain wisdom? How do we become wise people? The answer is simple: by thinking God's own thoughts after Him and adopting His perspective on everything as our own. In other words, while experience and education may furnish a type of wisdom, the only true source is the Word of God itself: "the testimony of the Lord is sure, making wise the simple" (Ps. 19:7). The more saturated with Scripture we are, the wiser we will become. This leads to the final question.

What are the practical effects of wisdom in our lives? What kind of transformation does wisdom bring about in our lives? First, wisdom results in holiness. Proverbs 14:16 says, "A wise man feareth, and departeth from evil." Second, wise people edify and equip others. Proverbs 15:7 says, "The lips of the wise disperse knowledge." Third, wise people have self-control over anger. Proverbs 29:8 says, "Wise men turn away wrath." Fourth, wise people bring spiritual healing to others with their words. Proverbs 12:18 says, "The tongue of the wise [brings healing]." There are many more effects of wisdom as well.

Wisdom matters, and the glory of God matters. We should desire His glory above all things. This requires a commitment to the Word of God as the fountain of wisdom.

—Jerod A. Gilcher

Heart of the Lesson

What does it mean that our great God Almighty is "wise"? By comparison, if humans are wise, we are wise only in a *creaturely* sense. We are limited by finite knowledge and power and subject to a future we cannot predict, so human wisdom can only go so far and do so much.

The wisdom of *God*, however, knows no limitations. God is infinite in His knowledge, power, and authority. (That includes knowing all things that might happen in the future.) God's wisdom, then, refers to His skill in bringing to fulfillment His perfect plan despite the waywardness and rebellion of His creation, and he does so in the way that is true to his character as full of grace and truth.

This, then, raises the question as to how believers might obtain the wisdom of God. How can we, as finite people, gain access to the transcendent, supernatural wisdom "not . . . of this world" (1 Cor. 2:6) and gain the spiritual skill of bringing God glory with our lives? The means to gaining that supernatural wisdom will be explained below in two points of simple application.

1. True, spiritual wisdom can only be obtained through the Word of God (1 Cor. 2:6-9). God's wisdom was most clearly displayed in the death of His own Son. Paul spoke of a wisdom "not . . . of this world, nor of the princes of this world" (vs. 6). He said that wisdom was hidden in a mystery, which "God ordained before the world unto our glory" (vs. 7).

The most striking statement about that wisdom, however, comes in verse 8. Paul declared that if the rulers of this world understood God's wisdom, "they would not have crucified the Lord of glory." What an astonishing statement! This truly is a wisdom not of this world! An incarnate Messiah slain for the sins of the human race transcends human thoughts and wisdom (vs. 9). As God says in Isaiah 55:8-9: "For my thoughts are not your thoughts, neither are your ways my ways, saith the Lord. For as the heavens are higher than the earth, so are my ways higher than your ways, and my thoughts than your thoughts."

Because the gospel about that unexpected Messiah is anticipated in the Old Testament and recorded in the New Testament, Scripture is the first source for us to obtain God's wisdom.

Paul prayed for the Colossians that they "might be filled with the knowledge of his will in all wisdom and spiritual understanding" (Col. 1:9). And that "will" of God is spoken and revealed to us in His Word. Only through the means of the Word of God—read, studied, meditated on, memorized, absorbed, and lived out—can the people of God gain the wisdom of God that transcends the wisdom of man.

2. True, spiritual wisdom is only for those who have been born again by the Spirit (1 Cor. 2:10-16). It is not enough, however, merely to know the content of the gospel message. Only the Holy Spirit can enable us to understand and apply that message. Paul said, "But the natural man receiveth not the things of the Spirit of God: . . . neither can he know them, because they are spiritually discerned" (vs. 14).

By a "natural man," Paul meant one not yet born again by the Spirit. Such a person cannot receive the "things of the Spirit." But being born again by the Spirit, believers have access to a wisdom "which the Holy Ghost teacheth" (vs. 13), and through the Spirit's instruction, we even "have the mind of Christ" Himself (vs. 16).

—Jerod A. Gilcher

World Missions

The Christian workers had spent a good deal of time together in prayer. They sought God's direction for the best strategy to establish themselves in the society and for where God would open the door for them to find an apartment. Beyond that, however, they were also concerned with what kind of role they should have in the community. They began to develop a strong sense that God was guiding them to enroll in a program of studying the local language in one of the local universities. They began visiting the universities, collecting material that described each program, and making inquiries about the details of each.

Slowly, they began to make inquiries about each of the schools and to speak with locals who knew about each one. At the same time, they prayed and sought to know God's direction. They certainly knew that they could not merely rely on their own wisdom in pursuing a ministry opportunity such as this. As they prayed, they all felt a strong sense that the Lord was guiding them to apply for a program focused on the local language in a large university in the south part of their city.

As they began to ask others, though, including a fellow believer who was teaching at the school, it seemed that everyone discouraged them from entering the program there. Several suggested that they apply to a famous university outside of the city. Others sought to push them toward an institute that featured classes in a number of languages. Finally, they were told that the class to which they sought admission was *no longer offered* at the university. They went to prayer again and still sensed, with a high degree of confidence, that this was the place to which they should go.

Finally, they returned to the university itself and were able to get an appointment with the dean of the school in which the language program had been listed. As they spoke with him, he shook his head and initially *confirmed* that the language program had not been offered in a number of years. He suggested that they consider one of the institutions that others had recommended to them. At the close of the conversation, however, his tone suddenly shifted, and he informed them that, in fact, *the school was considering offering the language program again in the year ahead*. They could come and apply once the public advertisement was published in the newspaper!

They ended up applying for and gaining admission to the program—and it turned out to be a perfect fit for them as they engaged in ministry in their community. As university students, not only were their language skills being greatly enhanced, but now their local friends could relate to them much more readily. Neither they nor the various people they had contacted could have known that the program would be revived in that very year. God, however, is *never* surprised. He knew all along and directed their steps to that very program that so wonderfully facilitated all that God was doing through them.

The Word of God has made it clear that God is the source of all wisdom. Speaking in the persona of wisdom, Proverbs 8:14 says, "Counsel is mine, and sound wisdom: I am understanding; I have strength." The wisdom God provides is for the greater purpose of being able to share the riches of the gospel with others, to impart the "hidden wisdom" of God in Christ (1 Cor. 2:7), and to show His love for people from every nation, tribe, and language.

—Matthew Friedman

The Jewish Aspect

Throughout the ancient Near East, there was a well-developed wisdom tradition. Sayings were created and applied to various situations, which either proved the saying or proved the situation to be exceptional. In Egypt, kings would pass down collections of wisdom sayings to their sons. Such traditions made their way to Israel, where King Solomon became famous for his wisdom and wisdom sayings, as recorded in the book of Proverbs. Accordingly, we are to take Solomon's comments that address the reader as his "son" to refer historically to the eventual heir to his throne. Solomon's intense pleas that his son pursue wisdom were meant for the future prosperity of the kingdom after Solomon's death.

Other biblical books from the Old Testament period came to be understood as wisdom literature. These include Job, Ecclesiastes, and some (or all!) of the Psalms. Other later Jewish writings associated with wisdom include Sirach and the Wisdom of Solomon. Sometimes the New Testament book of James is viewed as wisdom literature.

Biblical wisdom literature is practically oriented. It is not theoretical. It is grounded in everyday life, not in the false teachings and esoteric insights that an ancient philosopher might imagine. Proverbs 11:22 illustrates wisdom's practicality: "As a jewel of gold in a swine's snout, so is a fair woman which is without discretion."

After Alexander the Great's conquests, Jewish thinking became heavily influenced by Greek philosophies. In this period, wisdom moved from the practical to the theoretical. Where wisdom had been personified in Proverbs (e.g., Proverbs 8 depicts wisdom as a woman calling out persistently for people to learn from her), Jewish philosophers began to assign the abstract Greek concept *Logos* to wisdom. In John's Gospel, Jesus is identified as the Word (*Logos*) of God who spoke creation into existence.

Elsewhere in the Gospels, Jesus is depicted as all-wise. He created many practical wisdom sayings comparable to the sayings of Proverbs. Jesus' call to seek first the kingdom of heaven so that the other things will be attained as well (Matt. 6:33) is one such example. The Beatitudes (5:3-10) and other sayings in the Sermon on the Mount are wisdom-oriented. No wonder Jesus asserted Himself as someone "greater than Solomon" (Luke 11:31).

As Paul noted in 1 Corinthians 1:22, a major hindrance to Jewish belief in Jesus as Messiah was that their unspiritual wisdom could not allow for a crucified Messiah. Indeed, a crucified Messiah was totally contradictory to them. The very concept of the Messiah was built on one who would be a deliverer from the oppression of foreign powers.

To most Jews, then, Jesus was, by definition, disqualified as a messianic candidate. Rome, the world's most formidable power, had defeated Jesus in a way that highlighted Roman authority—by crucifixion, Rome's foremost means of reducing aspiring heroes to utter shame and defeat. A debased person could, in no way, be a candidate for the role of Messiah.

But it was the crucified Messiah that Paul preached: "we preach Christ crucified" (1 Cor. 1:23). Those who have God's wisdom through faith in Jesus clearly understand the crucified Messiah to be both the power of God and the wisdom of God (vs. 24).

—James M. Leonard

Guiding the Superintendent

This week's lesson begins a unit on the omnipotence (complete power) of God. First Corinthians 2:6-16 relates to that theme by asserting the Holy Spirit's power to impart wisdom from "the deep things of God" (vs. 10).

Pose some thought questions before studying the text: Who are the wisest people that you have ever known? Where do you think they gained their wisdom? What decisions led to their level of wisdom? What role do you think the Holy Spirit played in the development of their wisdom?

DEVOTIONAL OUTLINE

1. The world's wisdom rejects Christ (1 Cor. 2:6-8). In chapter 1, Paul identified the preaching of the cross as God's wisdom (vss. 18, 24). That wisdom does not come from the world, nor does it resemble what man teaches.

A slight shift occurs in verse 6 as Paul proclaims wisdom among mature believers. Therefore, the wisdom of God in verses 6-16 addresses the daily lives of believers.

2. The Spirit's wisdom imparts the mind of Christ (1 Cor. 2:9-16). Paul used the term "spiritual" to refer to those who are filled with the Spirit and led by Him.

In Paul's letters, the word "spiritual" always relates to the work of the Holy Spirit (Fee, "On Getting the Spirit Back into Spirituality," *Life in the Spirit*, IVP). First Corinthians 2:12-14 contrasts people who "have received . . . the spirit which is of God" with people who have not. The indwelling of the Holy Spirit distinguishes believers from unbelievers (cf. Eph. 1:13), and the presence of the Holy Spirit is what makes believers "spiritual." In Corinth, not all believers acted like people with the Spirit (cf. 1 Cor. 3:1), but they had the potential to do so through repentance, reliance, and obedience, because the Holy Spirit resided within them.

Paul referred to judgment in 2:15. Judgment necessitates wisdom, and God's wisdom is connected to the message of the cross, so here judgment is applying the wisdom of the cross to daily life.

Paul demonstrated that wise judgment in the rest of the letter as he systematically applied the message of the cross to all the issues of the church in Corinth.

For example, how does the wisdom of the cross apply to meat sacrificed to idols (8:1-10)? By helping those with knowledge to view the weak believers as those "for whom Christ died" (vs. 11). Or, how does the wisdom of the cross apply to abusing Communion (11:21-22)? By recognizing the Supper's role in proclaiming "the Lord's death till he come" (vs. 26) and in promoting the unity of Christ's body, the church (vss. 24, 29). The wisdom of the cross is central.

CHILDREN'S CORNER

Even the youngest believers can be spiritually mature just as adults can, but they can also face the same kinds of challenges. James 3:14-15 provides a wisdom diagnostic test: "But if ye have bitter envying and strife in your hearts . . . this wisdom descendeth not from above, but is earthly, sensual, devilish." When children become jealous of their friends or siblings, they exhibit spiritual immaturity, but with the Holy Spirit they are capable of acting humbly and lovingly toward others. Teach children that the best way to become spiritually mature is to think often about what Jesus did for them on the cross.

—*Matthew Swale*

SCRIPTURE LESSON TEXT

EX. 14:10 And when Pharaoh drew nigh, the children of Israel lifted up their eyes, and, behold, the Egyptians marched after them; and they were sore afraid: and the children of Israel cried out unto the LORD.

11 And they said unto Moses, Because *there were* no graves in Egypt, hast thou taken us away to die in the wilderness? wherefore hast thou dealt thus with us, to carry us forth out of Egypt?

12 *Is* not this the word that we did tell thee in Egypt, saying, Let us alone, that we may serve the Egyptians? For *it had been* better for us to serve the Egyptians, than that we should die in the wilderness.

13 And Moses said unto the people, Fear ye not, stand still, and see the salvation of the LORD, which he will shew to you to day: for the Egyptians whom ye have seen to day, ye shall see them again no more for ever.

14 The LORD shall fight for you, and ye shall hold your peace.

15 And the LORD said unto Moses, Wherefore criest thou unto me? speak unto the children of Israel, that they go forward:

16 But lift thou up thy rod, and stretch out thine hand over the sea, and divide it: and the children of Israel shall go on dry *ground* through the midst of the sea.

17 And I, behold, I will harden the hearts of the Egyptians, and they shall follow them: and I will get me honour upon Pharaoh, and upon all his host, upon his chariots, and upon his horsemen.

18 And the Egyptians shall know that I *am* the LORD, when I have gotten me honour upon Pharaoh, upon his chariots, and upon his horsemen.

19 And the angel of God, which went before the camp of Israel, removed and went behind them; and the pillar of the cloud went from before their face, and stood behind them:

20 and it came between the camp of the Egyptians and the camp of Israel; and it was a cloud and darkness *to them*, but it gave light by night *to these*: so that the one came not near the other all the night.

21 And Moses stretched out his hand over the sea; and the LORD caused the sea to go *back* by a strong east wind all that night, and made the sea dry *land*, and the waters were divided.

22 And the children of Israel went into the midst of the sea upon the dry *ground*: and the waters *were* a wall unto them on their right hand, and on their left.

NOTES

Parting the Red Sea

Lesson Text: Exodus 14:10-22

Related Scriptures: Exodus 5:15—6:1; 15:1-21;
Joshua 2:8-11; Psalm 106:1-12; 1 Corinthians 10:1-6

TIME: 1446 B.C. PLACE: Egypt

GOLDEN TEXT—"The Lord shall fight for you, and ye shall hold your peace" (Exodus 14:14).

Introduction

When the Israelites saw the Egyptian army bearing down on them, their gut reaction was to abandon the great salvation God was working for them and surrender to their old life of serving the Egyptians (cf. Ex. 14:12-13). Because the exodus foreshadowed our deliverance from slavery to sin, we can apply Israel's reaction directly to our lives today. For us, the temptation is to return to our old life of serving sin whenever our spiritual journey gets difficult.

When trials come, we need to remember what is at stake. The Israelites probably thought their reaction was reasonable. Wouldn't it have been better to live as slaves than to die before they received their freedom? But more than physical life and death was at stake. Their question should not have been *How can we stay alive?* but *Whom will we serve?* (cf. Josh. 24:15). The Red Sea crossing gives us confidence to continue serving the Lord when trials come. God will make a way for us to keep following His path even in impossible situations.

LESSON OUTLINE

1. **BATTLE MOVEMENTS—Ex. 14:10-19**
2. **DELIVERANCE THROUGH DIVISIONS—Ex. 14:20-22**

Exposition: Verse by Verse

BATTLE MOVEMENTS

EX. 14:10 And when Pharaoh drew nigh, the children of Israel lifted up their eyes, and, behold, the Egyptians marched after them; and they were sore afraid: and the children of Israel cried out unto the Lord.

11 And they said unto Moses, Because there were no graves in Egypt, hast thou taken us away to die in the wilderness? wherefore hast thou dealt thus with us, to carry us forth out of Egypt?

12 Is not this the word that we did tell thee in Egypt, saying, Let us alone, that we may serve the Egyptians? For it had been better for us to serve the Egyptians, than that we

should die in the wilderness.

13 And Moses said unto the people, Fear ye not, stand still, and see the salvation of the Lord, which he will shew to you to day: for the Egyptians whom ye have seen to day, ye shall see them again no more for ever.

14 The Lord shall fight for you, and ye shall hold your peace.

15 And the Lord said unto Moses, Wherefore criest thou unto me? speak unto the children of Israel, that they go forward:

16 But lift thou up thy rod, and stretch out thine hand over the sea, and divide it: and the children of Israel shall go on dry ground through the midst of the sea.

17 And I, behold, I will harden the hearts of the Egyptians, and they shall follow them: and I will get me honour upon Pharaoh, and upon all his host, upon his chariots, and upon his horsemen.

18 And the Egyptians shall know that I am the Lord, when I have gotten me honour upon Pharaoh, upon his chariots, and upon his horsemen.

19 And the angel of God, which went before the camp of Israel, removed and went behind them; and the pillar of the cloud went from before their face, and stood behind them.

Verses 10-19 capture three battle movements: the movement of Egypt toward Israel, the movement of Israel toward the sea, and the movement of the Angel of God to separate the two camps. These are indicated by the repeated use of the Hebrew verb "to set out"—rendered as "marched" in verse 10, "go forward" in verse 15, and "removed" and "went" in verse 19.

Egypt sets out toward the Israelites (Ex. 14:10-14). Pharaoh and the Egyptians had been so afraid after the tenth plague struck down their firstborn sons that they could not get rid of the Israelites fast enough (12:31-33). After the Israelites left, however, the Egyptians changed their minds and sent an army after Israel (14:5-9). {What led to such a sudden change? Verse 4 says it happened after the Lord hardened Pharaoh's heart.}[Q1] This heart-hardening is a central theme throughout the exodus story, so it is important to understand it.

First, note that the text alternates between saying that God hardened Pharaoh's heart and that Pharaoh hardened his own heart (cf. 7:3; 8:15). The actions of God and Pharaoh seem to have worked in tandem. God was indeed turning the heart of the king like a stream of water for His purposes (cf. Prov. 21:1), but He was not coercing Pharaoh to act sinfully. God did not force Pharaoh to do anything he did not already want to do.

Second, note the reason God hardened Pharaoh's heart. He did it so that He would gain glory over Pharaoh and the Egyptian army (Ex. 14:4). God *wanted* the Egyptians to pursue the Israelites so that He would be honored by Israel and Egypt alike when He miraculously defeated the Egyptian army.

When Israel saw Pharaoh's army marching, or setting out, after them (vs. 10), they too had a sudden change of heart. Understandably, they trembled with fear at the sight of Pharaoh's well-trained army bearing down on them and preparing to pin them against the Red Sea. {At first, they seemed to have the right response: they cried out to the Lord.

Quickly, however, their cries turned into a panicked desire to surrender and return to Egypt.}[Q2] Their question to Moses about graves in Egypt was sarcastic, as if to say, "Weren't there enough graves in Egypt already, Moses? Did we really need to go looking for a bigger one (the wilderness)?"

Israel's complaint quickly turned to irrational anger as they claimed it would be far better to continue serving

Egypt than to die where they stood. We might understand their panic given the circumstances, but this statement had serious implications. God was delivering Israel from slavery in Egypt so that they could serve Him rather than Egypt (8:1; 9:1, 13). Israel had been on board with the plan when the escape seemed to be going well, but the first time they encountered adversity, they wanted to run back to their old way of life.

Israel's panic even led them to misremember their original opinion of the exodus, claiming they had told Moses while they were still in Egypt that he should let them keep serving the Egyptians. While they did express disdain for the early results of Moses' interactions with Pharaoh (5:21), nowhere does Exodus record the comment they claim to have made, and nobody was complaining when Pharaoh actually let them go. Only when their circumstances darkened did they begin to doubt their decision to leave Egypt behind.

{Moses responded with words of assurance, giving the people three commands. First, he instructed them not to be afraid. Second, he told them to stand firm. They were not to go through with their plan to surrender and return to Egypt but instead were to hold their ground. Third, Moses told them simply to watch, because they would see God deliver them from their trouble, and the army pursuing them would vanish from their sight forever.}[Q3]

This would not occur by Israel fighting against them. While Israel watched, the Lord Himself would fight for them. They only needed to "hold [their] peace" (vs. 14), meaning they would not have to engage in the fight.

Israel commanded to set out toward the sea (Ex. 14:15-18). {Although Israel would not need to engage the Egyptians in battle, they were not to sit idly by. God asked Moses why he was crying out, then told him to instruct the Israelites to "go forward," or set out, presumably toward the sea (vs. 15).}[Q4]

God was not saying the Israelites' act of crying out to Him was bad *per se*. Earlier in Exodus, God spoke about Israel's cries as a positive motivation for Him to act (3:7). But their cries had given way to unbelief, and it was time for them to move forward in faith. Jesus would later rebuke His disciples in a similar way. When they cried to Him on their boat in the middle of a storm, He saved them from the storm but also admonished them for having little faith (Matt. 8:24-26).

God then instructed Moses to stretch out his staff over the sea. God would divide the sea, enabling the Israelites to walk through it on "dry ground" (Ex. 14:16). The term "dry ground" in this context is a clear callback to Genesis 1:9, when God caused the seas to recede and reveal the dry ground beneath it. The God who had originally commanded the seas not to go beyond their boundaries (Job 38:8-11) would now use His power over the sea to create a nation for Himself.

But what about the Egyptians? Wouldn't they just follow Israel through the sea? Yes, and that was part of God's plan! In fact, He would make sure they followed by continuing to harden their hearts (Ex. 14:17). {God did not yet reveal to Moses exactly what would happen next, but He assured Moses that by following Israel into the sea, Pharaoh and his army would become instruments for His "honour."}[Q5]

The Lord had identified Himself to Moses by His personal name, Yahweh, in Exodus 3:14. Throughout the exodus story, one of God's primary goals was for the people of Israel to recognize that He is Yahweh (6:7; 8:22; 10:2). In Exodus 14, He revealed that He wanted all of Egypt to know the same thing (vs. 18; cf. vs. 4). When the Egyptians saw His judgment coming on them, they would realize that

He was not just another god among many but the self-existent "I AM" who defends Israel.

The Angel of God sets out (Ex. 14:19). With the Egyptians bearing down on Israel, it was now the Angel of God's turn to set out ("remove") from His place in front of the Israelites and move behind them. At the same time, the pillar of cloud, which represented God's presence (13:21), also moved behind the Israelites.

Biblical scholars debate whether the terms "angel of God" and "angel of the Lord" in Scripture refer simply to an angel or to the presence of God Himself. In certain passages, the identification is clear. In Genesis 31:11-13, for example, the "angel of God" calls Himself the "God of Bethel." In other passages, there is a close connection but not an explicit identification. For example, when Moses encountered the burning bush in Exodus 3, the text seems to use the terms "angel of the Lord," "God," and "Lord" interchangeably. In other passages, there is no indication at all of who the "angel of the Lord" is.

Because a language can use the same term in different ways, we need to be careful not to assume immediately that the "angel of the Lord" is always identical with God Himself. We also need to realize that even in the passages that identify the angel of the Lord as divine, there is a reason the author chooses to call Him an angel rather than simply God. {Perhaps the best explanation in these cases is that because God cannot be seen, God's "angel" acted as a visible manifestation of His presence when He wanted to communicate with or guide someone on a personal level (cf. Gen. 16:7-11; 24:7).

In Exodus 14:19, we have reason to think that the "angel of God" is a manifestation of God's own presence.}[Q6] His movement is closely connected to the movement of the pillar of cloud (cf. 13:21), and it makes sense that Moses would identify the "angel of God" in this verse with the "angel of the Lord" from the burning bush. Just as Moses had promised the Israelites in 14:14, the Lord was moving into battle position on their behalf.

DELIVERANCE THROUGH DIVISIONS

20 And it came between the camp of the Egyptians and the camp of Israel; and it was a cloud and darkness to them, but it gave light by night to these: so that the one came not near the other all the night.

21 And Moses stretched out his hand over the sea; and the Lord caused the sea to go back by a strong east wind all that night, and made the sea dry land, and the waters were divided.

22 And the children of Israel went into the midst of the sea upon the dry ground: and the waters were a wall unto them on their right hand, and on their left.

The Angel of God divides the two camps (Ex. 14:20). God fought for Israel by dividing two things. First, the Angel of God used the cloud of God's presence to divide the camps of Israel and Egypt.

How would a cloud stop an entire Egyptian army? It seems that God did something similar to what He had done during the plague of darkness (10:21-29). {While the cloud cast darkness on the Egyptian camp, it "gave light by night" to the Israelites (14:20). Just as in the plague of darkness, God made a distinction between Egypt and Israel; only Egypt was covered in darkness, and the Egyptians could not come near Israel all night as a result (cf. 10:23).}[Q7]

During the plague of darkness, Moses confirmed Pharaoh's statement that they would never see each other again (10:28-29). That was ironic because the darkness over Egypt literally made it impossible for Pharaoh to see Moses (cf. vs. 23). At the Red Sea, Moses similarly promised the Israelites that they would never again see the pursuing Egyptians (14:13). And once again, God used darkness to fulfill that promise.

Despite popular movie depictions of the exodus, the text does not say that the Israelites looked back and saw the Egyptians pursuing them after they crossed the sea. Actually, the Egyptians were already retreating by the time the sea crashed back onto them (vss. 23-27). From the time the cloud divided the two camps, the Israelites never again saw the Egyptian army alive. The next time they saw them was the next morning when the Egyptians were lying dead along the sea (vs. 30).

{But this scene echoes more than just the ninth plague. It also echoes God's first act of Creation.}[Q8] God spoke into the darkness, and there was light. Then He divided the darkness from the light and called them "Night" and "Day" (Gen. 1:2-5). {Similarly, God brought light into the darkness at the Red Sea and separated the two so that the light lit the night in Israel's camp. This is more than an interesting similarity. This was God visibly signaling that Israel's exodus was the beginning of His plan for a restored creation.

The Lord divides the sea (Ex. 14:21-22). God continued to imitate His original acts of Creation by dividing the sea to reveal dry land beneath (cf. Gen. 1:9).}[Q9] Notably, He chose to do so through natural means—a strong wind from the east. This was certainly a miracle, but it did not happen instantaneously. The wind came from the east, which means the far side of the sea would have begun parting first. By the end of the night, it had progressed all the way to the Israelites' side of the sea. Earlier, Moses had instructed Israel to watch the Lord's salvation and be still while He fought for them (Ex. 14:13-14). As it turned out, they would have to watch and be still the entire night. When it was finally time to cross the sea, the waters were like two towering walls on either side of the Israelites.

In the following verses, we see how this miraculous deliverance fulfilled God's purpose of ensuring that both Israel and Egypt honored His name. {When the Egyptians tried to pursue, God threw them into chaos, and the Egyptians recognized that Yahweh fought for Israel (vs. 25). Then, after God plunged the sea back on top of the Egyptians, the Israelites praised the Lord for His immense power and believed in Him (vs. 31).}[Q10]

—Matthew Robinson

QUESTIONS

1. Why did the Egyptians change their minds about letting Israel go?
2. How did the Israelites respond when they saw the Egyptians pursuing them?
3. How did Moses respond to the Israelites' fear?
4. What was the Israelites' role in their deliverance?
5. Why did God plan to let the Egyptians follow the Israelites into the divided sea?
6. Who was the "angel of God" in Exodus 14:19?
7. How did the Lord's division of the two camps help Israel?
8. What two previous acts of God did the parting of the Red Sea echo?
9. How was the parting of the sea a callback to Creation?
10. How did God fulfill His purpose of getting honor for His name through the Red Sea crossing?

—Matthew Robinson

Preparing to Teach the Lesson

The parting of the Red Sea was an amazing event that the Israelites looked back on throughout the Old Testament as a witness to the power of God.

TODAY'S AIM

Facts: to observe the power of God as He protected the Israelites.

Principle: to understand that God will fight for His children.

Application: to realize that the same God who parted the Red Sea hears and answers our prayers.

INTRODUCING THE LESSON

The parting of the Red Sea was over 3,400 years ago, yet it is still celebrated today. Films like *The Ten Commandments* and *The Prince of Egypt* have dramatized the event with beautiful scenes of God's power and protection.

DEVELOPING THE LESSON

Our lesson begins in Exodus 14. God had already called and raised up Moses to lead His people. He (and Aaron) negotiated the release of the Israelites from Egyptian bondage multiple times, but Pharaoh's heart was hardened. God had already sent the ten plagues, including the death of the firstborn. Pharaoh had finally released the Israelites, and God was visibly leading them. In the day He appeared as a pillar of cloud, and at night He appeared as a pillar of fire. But then He seemingly led them to a dead end, and Pharaoh changed his mind again.

The Red Sea was in front of them. They could not go right or left, and Pharaoh's army was on their tail. This is where our Bible study begins.

1. Be still as the Lord fights for you (Ex. 14:10-14). In verse 10 we learn that the Israelites were afraid, and they prayed. We can relate to that. Pharaoh's mighty army was chasing them. They complained to their leader sarcastically. We can relate to that too. They asked Moses if there were no graves left in Egypt and if that was why he had brought them to the desert to die. They blamed Moses for taking them out of Egypt. They reminded him that they had told him to leave them alone so they could continue to be slaves to the Egyptians. Then they exclaimed that it would have been better for them to stay in Egypt than die in the desert. In Exodus 5:16—6:1, the Israelites similarly expressed distrust in Moses, and they blamed him and Aaron for Pharaoh's treatment of them.

With great patience and encouragement, Moses answered the people in 14:13-14. He told them 1) not to be afraid, 2) to stand firm, 3) to see the deliverance the Lord would bring, 4) they would never see these Egyptians again, 5) the Lord would fight for them, and 6) they only needed to be still. These were powerful promises that would soon come to pass!

2. The Lord gives specific instructions to Moses (Ex. 14:15-18). The Lord quickly responded to the situation and asked Moses why he was crying to God. He commanded Moses to tell the Israelites to keep moving. Then He shared His amazing plan with Moses in verse 16.

The Lord told Moses to pick up his staff and raise his hand over the sea. Interestingly, the Lord told Moses to divide the water, though Moses did not have the power to do that. God constantly asks us to do things we are unable to do while He accomplishes the task through us with His mighty power. The water would be divided, and the Israelites would cross on dry ground.

Verses 17 and 18 remind us of what the world is all about: the glory of God! Take notice when you read the Bible how many great miracles resulted in God receiving the glory He deserves. A few decades later, Rahab told Israelite spies that all the Canaanites knew that the Lord dried up the Red Sea for the Israelites. When they heard the stories, their hearts melted in fear because they knew that the God of the Israelites was the one true God (Josh. 2:8-11).

Part of God's plan was to harden the hearts of the Egyptians so they would follow the Israelites through the divided Red Sea. God's glory would be on display, and He would receive honor as Pharaoh and his powerful army fell into the trap.

3. God stands between us and our enemies (Ex. 14:19-22). The visible manifestation of God's presence moved from in front of the Israelites to the back, between Pharaoh's army and the Israelites. Many believe "the angel of God" (vs. 19) to be God Himself, or more specifically, God the Son. This is possible. But even if it was merely an angel, we know it was not a chubby baby with wings playing a harp. This was the mighty angel of God who had been leading God's people and was now defending them.

The cloud they had been following also moved in between the two groups. The cloud brought darkness to the Egyptian army but gave light to the Israelites.

In verse 21, Moses did as the Lord had commanded. He stretched out his hand over the sea, and the Lord created a dry road for them by blowing a strong east wind. Then the people of Israel walked through the middle of the Red Sea on dry ground with a wall of water on each side of them.

Ask someone to share a time when God protected them or a loved one. The Lord hears our prayers, and He is mighty to save!

ILLUSTRATING THE LESSON

When Moses obeyed God's command to hold his staff out, the waters of the Red Sea parted. While Moses held the staff, God used His power to divide the sea so that His people could pass through and escape Pharaoh's army. God is all-powerful. Nothing can stop Him from protecting His people, not even an Egyptian army—or the Red Sea!

CONCLUDING THE LESSON

In this Bible lesson, we can see clearly that God is very powerful. He is the most powerful Being in the entire universe. The Almighty God is your Heavenly Father. You can pray to Him anytime you want. The God who parted the Red Sea and protected the Israelites will fight your battles too. Nothing you face is too difficult for Him! Read Exodus 15 this week. It records the song Moses and Miriam led the Israelites in singing after this amazing miracle.

ANTICIPATING THE NEXT LESSON

Next week, we will continue to learn about the omnipotence of God by studying Mark 4, when Jesus calmed a storm. The Creator has more power than His creation. The laws of nature obey Him.

—Adam Clagg

PRACTICAL POINTS

1. Difficult trials can affect our reasoning (Ex. 14:10-12).
2. We will see God's power at work in our lives if we are willing to patiently surrender our circumstances to Him (vss. 13-14).
3. As God provided a way of escape from slavery to Egypt, so He provides a way of escape from slavery to sin (Ex. 14:15-16; cf. 1 Cor. 10:13).
4. One reason God may allow trials in our lives is because they will bring Him glory (Ex. 14:17-18).
5. The Lord is like a wall of defense between us and His enemies (vss. 19-20).
6. The power God used to create the universe is the same power He uses to redeem His people (vss. 21-22).

—Matthew Robinson

RESEARCH AND DISCUSSION

1. What can fear do to our walk with God (Ex. 14:10-12)?
2. Why was it so important for God to gain honor over Pharaoh and the Egyptian army (Ex. 14:17-18)?
3. Why don't we see God's power displayed today in the same ways it was displayed at the Red Sea? What other ways do we see His power displayed?
4. What kinds of trials make it difficult to keep following God today? Why is that? How can we prepare for those trials?
5. Why do you think God used natural means (a strong east wind) to part the sea rather than making it happen in an instant (vs. 21)?

—Matthew Robinson

ILLUSTRATED HIGH POINTS

The word that we did tell thee (Ex. 14:12)

Whenever a sports team's top draft pick doesn't play well his first year, many fans inevitably claim they saw it coming as soon as the pick was made. In reality, most of those fans were probably quite hopeful until things started going badly; their frustration with the team, however, leads them to misremember their original opinion.

That is similar to what happened on a much more serious level for the Israelites. As soon as the exodus started going badly, they claimed they had said all along that they should have stayed in Egypt. In reality, they had said no such thing.

The salvation of the Lord (vs. 13)

Church historians often refer to spiritual awakenings and revivals as echoes of Pentecost. They are not exact repetitions of the original event, but they bear similar features. Pentecost has become the point of reference, or paradigm, for all subsequent revivals because it was the defining moment that brought the church into existence.

In a similar way, the exodus became the paradigm for God's subsequent acts of salvation, because the exodus was the defining moment that brought Israel into existence as a nation.

Caused the sea to go back (vs. 21)

In 1958, a tsunami off the coast of Alaska produced a wave more than 1,700 feet tall. It flooded the land as far as five miles inland ("Wave that Shook the World: Once and Future Tsunamis," pbs.org). We have no way of knowing how high the walls of water were at the Red Sea crossing, but certainly this gives us a terrifying image of what came crashing down on the Egyptians.

—Matthew Robinson

Golden Text Illuminated

"The Lord shall fight for you, and ye shall hold your peace" (Exodus 14:14).

One thing that is clear about God's plan is that He loves to paint Himself into corners. God ordains events that are seemingly impossible so that He alone can get the glory when they are resolved.

For instance, God promised to make Abraham a great nation despite his old age and the barrenness of Sarah's womb.

In Judges 7, God reduced Gideon's army down from twenty-two thousand men to three hundred to defeat a much larger Midianite army.

Likewise, when the Lord Jesus hung weak and dying on a cross, His mission looked like a failure and a defeat.

In each of those scenarios, God looked cornered, weak, and even for a moment, foolish. Yet we know that God is anything but weak. He is absolutely sovereign (cf. Ps. 115:3; Isa. 46:9-10). Because of that, seeming setbacks to His plan will ultimately reveal His glory when He gains the victory.

That is precisely the scenario that unfolded in the exodus of Israel from Egypt. After fleeing the land of Egypt, the scrambling Israelites found themselves cornered at the Red Sea with the armies of Pharaoh closing in. At that moment, the Lord looked weak, shortsighted, or even cruel to put His people in such a situation. It was dangerous and seemingly impossible. But that is precisely the reason God planned it the way He did. That is why Moses declared to the people in Exodus 14:14, "The Lord shall fight for you, and ye shall hold your peace." The Lord orchestrated a scenario in which He alone would be displayed as the Hero. The scene ended with a crushing defeat of Pharaoh's armies as the Lord miraculously parted the sea, then caused it to crash back on the Egyptians (vss. 21-28).

God's mysterious ways in history and in the deliverance of His people offer us practical help that produces fearless faith in the midst of our trials.

First, we must remember that apparent setbacks are God's design. That includes both setbacks to our lives and to His sovereign plan as a whole. How freeing it is that the situations that seem to have no apparent resolution have God's fingerprints all over them! He deliberately allows them to ensure His glory when He comes through in the end.

Second, we must remember that God's design in trials is to increase our dependence upon Him. Despite claims to the contrary, God does give us more than we can handle in this life, that we may recognize our weakness and cast ourselves upon His power alone. That was the assertion of the apostle Paul, who declared that our afflictions are given by God "that we should not trust in ourselves, but in God which raiseth the dead" (2 Cor. 1:8-9).

Third, trials are designed to increase our joy in the glory of God. As we wait on God to do the impossible, we better position ourselves to see His glory. And this is one of the highest joys of the believer—to see God displayed for the treasure that He is and to declare to Him after He intervenes: "Who is like unto thee, O Lord, among the gods? who is like thee, glorious in holiness, fearful in praises, doing wonders?" (Ex. 15:11).

—Jerod A. Gilcher

Heart of the Lesson

The power over fear is... fear. That may seem like a riddle or a contradiction, but it is a deeply theological statement. We all have fears that haunt our hearts and lurk in our lives, and the secret to conquering the things in life that make us fearful is the fear of God Himself. Thus, the power over all earthly fears is the fear of God. That does not mean we should fear God as a monster, but we should tremble before His majestic holiness and power. Fearing God rightly involves trusting Him (Ps. 115:11). That is precisely what we see in the well-known account of the exodus.

1. Israel's fear and God's reassurance (Ex. 14:10-18). As the people of Israel were cornered at the Red Sea with Egypt's battalions closing in, they cried out in fear (vss. 10-12). Moses told the people not to fear and that the Lord would fight for them (vss. 13-14). What greater words of comfort could have been spoken? The Lord commanded Moses to stretch out his hand, promising to deliver the people and overthrow the Egyptian army (vss. 15-18).

2. God's fearsome deliverance (Ex. 14:19-22). Then God delivered His fearful people with an astonishing miracle, parting the Red Sea (vs. 19-22). After that, He crushed the Egyptian army. The scene ends with this conclusion: "And Israel saw that great work which the Lord did upon the Egyptians: and the people *feared* the Lord, and *believed* the Lord, and his servant Moses" (vs. 31; emphasis added).

That raises the question: What is it about the Lord that makes Him worthy to be feared and trusted? Further, how do we cultivate the fear of the Lord that conquers the fears in our lives? The celebratory poem in the next chapter of Exodus gives us many reasons to fear and trust the Lord.

First, we should fear and trust the Lord because He is supreme in power. Exodus 15:6 says that God is "glorious in power." That means God's glory is revealed in and through His sovereign power. That glorious power helps us fear Him as supreme and trust Him as sovereign.

Second, we should fear and trust the Lord because He is matchless in holiness. Exodus 15:11 asks, "Who is like unto thee, O Lord, among the gods? who is like thee, glorious in holiness?" The holiness of God does not merely speak of God's morality and ethical purity; it also describes His matchless, unrivaled divine nature. The only correct answer to the question, "Who is like God?" is absolute silence. The matchless worth of God produces fear of Him because He is infinitely above His creation. At the same time, however, it produces trust in Him because He is an incomparable treasure.

Finally, we should fear and trust the Lord because He has authority over the future. Exodus 15:18 declares, "The Lord shall reign for ever and ever." All earthly kingdoms—past, present, and future—are under the Lord's authority. His rule and reign will not be a temporary dominion but one that is eternal in nature. That produces fear of God as the undisputed sovereign ruler over all history, but it also cultivates trust in God who alone has the power to crush the powers of evil, establish the kingdom of His Son on the earth, and restore the paradise that once was lost.

God's supreme power, matchless holiness, and eternal authority produce an affectionate and trembling fear of God, and that fear conquers our fears in an evil world.

—Jerod A. Gilcher

World Missions

In the previous lesson, we described the miraculous manner in which God opened a door for a group of colleagues to study the local language at a local university, and we saw how God's Spirit guided them into His perfect will, even when that did not seem entirely obvious. In this lesson, we will see how God miraculously provided for the same group with admission, visas, and especially the resources needed to pursue their mission. We will observe how their experience demonstrated that it is truly the case that "the Lord shall fight for you, and ye shall hold your peace" (Ex. 14:14).

One young man in the group was still quite new on the field, and he was serving with a "faith mission," which means he had no minimum requirement for financial support. His monthly support was barely sufficient to get by each month. A month or two before our story began, he sent out a newsletter to those who were praying for him, and a month or so later, he received news that several times the usual amount of monthly support had come in for him.

When this young man and his colleague were granted admission into the program, they had to go through a wearisome process to get the required paperwork at the university. Finally, they received admission letters granting them less than two weeks to reappear with their student visas.

To get those visas, they had to travel to nearby countries. They booked tickets and traveled together to one nearby country, where one applied for his visa. They then traveled to a second nearby country, where the young man with the faith mission applied. Both of them received their visas on the final possible day, and the extra money that had come in for the young man proved to be precisely the amount needed to cover his visa and the expenses for the entire journey.

They returned to the university on the appointed day to present their new student visas to the wide-eyed university official, who had clearly not expected them to arrive back with their visas before the deadline. They marveled at how God had overcome apparent hostility to provide a place of study and ministry. The young man was grateful for those who had given so generously, apparently in response to his newsletter.

All of this was amazing and clearly directed by God. But there were even more miracles in this story than met the eye. After the young man's term was complete, he was to head home for a brief visit, from where he would apply for a visa for a second year of studies. Shortly before that, he received a letter from a friend in his home country who had been overseeing the typing, printing, and mailing of his newsletter. To the missionary's shock, the letter he received asked for his forgiveness. Amid a situation of unexpected personal hardship, the letter explained, the young man's friend had not sent out a single one of his newsletters in the past two years. That was a completely stunning admission—and terrifying in an age before social media or easy electronic communication.

It caused the young missionary to wonder, however: If his newsletter had not gone out at all, how had people known to give right after he thought the newsletter had gone out and before he even knew he would need the money for his unexpected journey? It became clear that God had moved in their hearts, even without any news at all. Surely, he could say, "The Lord is my strength and song, and he is become my salvation" (Ex. 15:2).

—Matthew Friedman

The Jewish Aspect

As the Israelites crossed the Red Sea, they were completely surrounded by pictures of God's original Creation. Behind them, light flashed forth from God's presence as He divided the light from the darkness (cf. Gen. 1:3-5). On either side of them, two mighty walls of water rose up, held back only by the command of the Lord (cf. Gen. 1:9; Job 38:8-11). Underneath them, dry ground appeared (cf. Gen. 1:9). And ahead of them lay a new life in the Promised Land (cf. 2:15).

Similar images of Creation are linked with God's major redemptive acts throughout the Old Testament. After the Flood, God made the waters recede and revealed dry ground just as He did at Creation (8:7, 14). When Israel crossed over the Jordan River into the Promised Land, He did the same thing (Josh. 3:17).

During Israel's exile, the prophets looked back to both the Creation and the exodus as their basis for hoping in a return to the land. Isaiah, for example, in his plea to the Lord for deliverance, declared that God was the one who "dried the sea, the waters of the great deep" and "made the depths of the sea a way for the ransomed to pass over" (Isa. 51:10). The first phrase recalls Creation, when God tamed "the deep" and revealed dry land (Gen. 1:2, 9). The second phrase recalls the Red Sea crossing, when God turned the sea into a road for His redeemed people.

Now, Isaiah declared, God would repeat His paradigmatic acts of Creation and re-creation by causing "the redeemed of the Lord [to] return" from their exile (Isa. 51:11).

Just as the Israelites had crossed through the Red Sea on a road cleared by God, so the scattered people of Israel would return from their exile (cf. Jer. 23:7-8). Some of those returnees were coming from Egypt and were truly retracing the steps of the exodus (Zech. 10:10).

Israel's return from exile was indeed glorious, but it also did not live up to the expectations suggested by the prophets. When the returned exiles rebuilt the temple, many of the leaders wept because that temple could not compare to Solomon's temple (Ezra 3:12). There was still another exodus event coming, a return from spiritual exile, not just physical exile.

That second exodus ultimately came through Jesus the Messiah. Matthew's Gospel in particular highlights the way Jesus' life and ministry paralleled the early history of Israel, including the exodus.

Like the family of Jacob, the family of Jesus fled to Egypt to save their lives and later returned (Matt. 2:13-14; cf. Gen. 46:2-3). The book of Matthew tells us that this fulfilled Hosea 11:1: "Out of Egypt have I called my son" (2:15). Interestingly, however, Hosea 11:1 is not a prophecy about a future event; it is a historical statement about Israel's exodus. Did Matthew misunderstand the Old Testament and take it out of context? No. Instead, Matthew was saying that the similarities between the exodus and the early events in Jesus' life were no coincidence. Israel's exodus reflected the pattern God had set for what Jesus' life would look like and what it would accomplish.

Luke 9:31 refers to Jesus' death as His "decease" (literally, His "exodus"). Just as the parting of the Red Sea had delivered Israel from their slavery to Egypt, so Jesus' death on the cross would deliver people from their slavery to sin.

—Matthew Robinson

Guiding the Superintendent

Everything about the exodus, from the ten plagues to the deliverance through the Red Sea, was designed to accomplish what God told Pharaoh in Exodus 9:16: "And in very deed for this cause have I raised thee up, for to shew in thee my power; and that my name may be declared throughout all the earth."

DEVOTIONAL OUTLINE

1. Reason: Israelites fear the Egyptian threat (Ex. 14:10-12). The Israelites were trapped and terrified. Their taste of freedom turned sour, and they thought they were better off as slaves. A major theme in Exodus is the ownership of God's people. Was Israel God's firstborn son (4:22) or Pharaoh's workforce (14:5)?

In 14:17-18, the Lord repeatedly said He would get "honour upon Pharaoh" (cf. vs. 4). This Hebrew verb (*kabed*) is related to the noun often translated as "glory" (*kabod*). The words connote heaviness or weight, implying that the one described is noteworthy. To receive honor, or glory, over Pharaoh meant that the significance of God's power both surpasses and defeats any rival claim to significance, weight, or ultimate noteworthiness.

2. Response: Moses addresses Israelite fear (Ex. 14:13-18). The Lord intentionally directed the Israelites in verses 1-2 into an avoidable, "terrible tactical situation, entrapped against the sea and easily pinned down by a military force" (Duane Garrett, *A Commentary on Exodus*, Kregel). The Lord did this so that Pharaoh would say, "They are entangled . . . the wilderness hath shut them in" (vs. 3). The Israelites did not understand at first how that could be a good thing. As it turned out, however, it maximized the Lord's opportunity to fight for the helpless Israelites against the arrogant Egyptians. Moses told the Israelites to fear not and stand still.

3. Redemption: God saves the Israelites by dividing the sea (Ex. 14:19-22). God's plan worked. He made His glory known throughout the earth by parting the Red Sea. God's way of gaining glory was twofold: by saving Israel and by judging Egypt.

Moses described the event as salvation in verse 13. Because God was saving Israel from Pharaoh's intention to re-enslave them (vs. 5), however, there would be no salvation without judging Pharaoh. Forty years later, and many miles away, Rahab told the Israelites, "We have heard how the Lord dried up the water of the Red sea for you . . . And as soon as we heard these things, our hearts did melt" (Josh. 2:10-11). Rahab's testimony displays the impact God's judgment had on Israel's enemies.

Exodus 14:10-22 is about the Lord's glorious redemption of His people from slavery. As such, teachers should resist relating the narrative to one's personal Red Sea predicament. God may indeed miraculously intervene in our specific situations, but sometimes He chooses not to. Instead, the Red Sea crossing primarily foreshadowed Christ's powerful salvation from sin and shame. We cannot redeem ourselves or secure God's redeeming love, because in Christ the Lord does the fighting and redeeming, "and ye shall hold your peace" (Ex. 14:14).

CHILDREN'S CORNER

Children often fear things (like large but friendly dogs) that adults know will not ultimately harm them. These lesser fears provide opportunities to teach kids that just as they can trust their earthly parents to take care of them in those situations, so they can trust God to take care of them in any situation that makes them afraid.

—Matthew Swale

SCRIPTURE LESSON TEXT

MARK 4:35 And the same day, when the even was come, he saith unto them, Let us pass over unto the other side.

36 And when they had sent away the multitude, they took him even as he was in the ship. And there were also with him other little ships.

37 And there arose a great storm of wind, and the waves beat into the ship, so that it was now full.

38 And he was in the hinder part of the ship, asleep on a pillow: and they awake him, and say unto him, Master, carest thou not that we perish?

39 And he arose, and rebuked the wind, and said unto the sea, Peace, be still. And the wind ceased, and there was a great calm.

40 And he said unto them, Why are ye so fearful? how is it that ye have no faith?

41 And they feared exceedingly, and said one to another, What manner of man is this, that even the wind and the sea obey him?

NOTES

Jesus Calms a Storm

Lesson Text: Mark 4:35-41

Related Scriptures: Psalm 107:23-32; Jonah 1:1-16; Matthew 8:23-27; Luke 8:22-25; Acts 27:13-44

TIME: between A.D. 26 and 30 PLACE: Sea of Galilee

GOLDEN TEXT—"And they feared exceedingly, and said one to another, What manner of man is this, that even the wind and the sea obey him?" (Mark 4:41).

Introduction

Over the last two weeks, we have seen God's overwhelming power. This week, we see Jesus display that same power to calm a violent storm and control the weather.

Only God has the power to control the raging sea, and Jesus therefore demonstrated His divinity in this passage. And yet, He also grew tired and needed sleep, demonstrating His real humanity. In response to His demonstration of power, the disciples marveled and wondered, "What manner of man is this, that even the wind and the sea obey him?" (Mark 4:41).

One implication of this passage is that Jesus is able to deliver us from the troubles of our lives. No matter how fiercely the metaphorical storms of life may rage around us, He is all-powerful and able to deliver us easily. At the same time, however, that is not the main point of the story. The main point is Jesus' identity as truly God and truly man. Every one of us must answer the disciples' question: Who is Jesus?

LESSON OUTLINE

1. **THE SETTING—Mark 4:35-36**
2. **THE STORM—Mark 4:37-38**
3. **JESUS' RESPONSE—Mark 4:39-40**
4. **THE DISCIPLES' RESPONSE—Mark 4:41**

Exposition: Verse by Verse

THE SETTING

MARK 4:35 And the same day, when the even was come, he saith unto them, Let us pass over unto the other side.

36 And when they had sent away the multitude, they took him even as he was in the ship. And there were also with him other little ships.

After a long day of teaching, Jesus told the disciples to go to the other side of the Sea of Galilee. Presumably, He did that in order to rest, as He did on other occasions with the disciples (cf. Mark 6:30-32). The long day had been exhausting. As a human being, Jesus had real physical needs for food, water, and sleep (cf. Matt. 4:2; 21:18). So did the disciples; they needed a break. (Tangentially, if even Jesus needed rest, why do some of us think that we don't?)

{This passage comes immediately after a series of parables (Mark 4:1-34). Jesus had been teaching about the kingdom of God, and now He was about to demonstrate its power.}[Q1] It seems probable that these were some of the parables Jesus had told just before getting into the boat, or perhaps from the boat. Would the disciples prove to be rocky ground or rich soil (cf. vss. 1-20)? Had they understood the secret of the kingdom of God (cf. vs. 11), and would they now see it grow (cf. vss. 26-32)?

{Sometimes, when the crowd was thick and crushing, Jesus would get into a boat and put off a little from the shore. That way, He would not be tightly surrounded by people and could be more easily seen and heard by a greater number of people. From there, He would preach to the people (Luke 5:1-11). That may have been the case here.}[Q2] After a long day of preaching (Mark 4:1-34) and perhaps also performing miracles, He was tired, and they headed for the other side of the sea.

The remark in verse 36 that other boats were with Him has no real bearing on this story, but it does have surprising importance for us. We never hear anything specific about the people who followed after Jesus and the apostles, what condition their boats were in, or even their names. They are not recorded interacting with Jesus during or after the storm. {Although this may therefore seem like a wasted line, it is actually quite helpful for us, precisely *because* it has no real relevance to the story. If you were making up a carefully crafted myth in the first century (cf. 2 Pet. 1:16), you would not throw in random, irrelevant details like this. But we say this sort of thing in passing all the time during everyday conversation when telling a story. This throwaway line about an incidental detail is the mark of a true eyewitness account, not a legend. It provides internal evidence that someone who was a real eyewitness (almost certainly Peter, according to church history) recounted this story to Mark, and he recorded it faithfully for us.}[Q3]

The Gospels present real historical events, not myths. The details that Jesus slept on a cushion and that He was specifically in the stern are similar to the mention of other boats; they do not deeply impact the narrative but are marks of real eyewitness testimony. (The fact that the disciples are often portrayed in a less-than-flattering way throughout all the Gospels is also a mark of authenticity.)

{The disciples did not get into this storm because they disobeyed Jesus. He did not command them to go in one direction only for them to flee the opposite way, as Jonah had centuries earlier. In fact, the disciples got into this storm precisely *because* they obeyed His command to cross over to the other side.}[Q4] Not all difficulties in life are the result of disobedience—in fact, some difficulties may come precisely *because* we obey God! But He is in control of even those difficult circumstances and has the power to bring us through them.

When we experience hardships, we sometimes meticulously examine our lives to see whether we have sinned somehow and are being disciplined. That is not inappropriate, because sometimes we are being disciplined. But sometimes, we are not. If we assume that every time someone has trouble they are experiencing God's discipline, we make the same mistake as Job's friends (cf. Job 4:1-32:1). Sometimes the difficulties we experience are because of our obedience, not our disobedience (cf. 1 Pet. 3:17). Did Jesus supernaturally know this storm was coming when He told the disciples to get in the boat? We don't know, but it is very possible He did. If so, He led them directly and intentionally into the storm to further reveal who He is.

THE STORM

37 And there arose a great storm of wind, and the waves beat into the ship, so that it was now full.

38 And he was in the hinder part of the ship, asleep on a pillow: and they awake him, and say unto him, Master, carest thou not that we perish?

A great storm suddenly arose on the sea, shaking the boat and frightening even the most experienced sailors of the group. Although not all of Jesus' apostles were former fishermen, a good number of them were. These were not inexperienced men scared of a small wind and a little rain. Some of them had spent years on this very sea, yet they were frightened by the power of the storm. Even with modern technology, ships can be battered by powerful storms. Imagine how terrifying it would have been in a first-century wooden vessel!

{Meanwhile, Jesus was fast asleep! This highlights Jesus' genuine humanity. He was completely exhausted! After a long day of preaching, He was worn out. He was not a tireless superhero. He truly experienced human weaknesses, and He needed rest.}[Q5]

It seems that the disciples waited for a while to wake Jesus. They did not wake Him when the clouds gathered. They did not wake Him when the wind picked up and the waters got a little rough. Only once the waves were filling the boat did they wake Jesus. They seemingly had not wanted to bother Him before, but now they needed Him. Perhaps before they thought that they could handle things themselves, but now they recognized that they were truly desperate. How often do we do the same thing, trying to handle things ourselves and only coming to God as a last resort when we are truly desperate?

When the disciples asked whether Jesus cared about them, they were questioning His character, not His power. {They seemed to believe that He could do something—that was the whole point of waking Him up, after all! It is not clear what they expected Jesus to do given their shock and fear when He did respond, and perhaps it was just nervous panic, but they seemingly expected Him to do *something*. Perhaps they thought He would call out to God in prayer, and they would be delivered.}[Q6]

JESUS' RESPONSE

39 And he arose, and rebuked the wind, and said unto the sea, Peace, be still. And the wind ceased, and there was a great calm.

40 And he said unto them, Why are ye so fearful? how is it that ye have no faith?

When Jesus woke, He stood up and rebuked the wind and the sea, and the storm died down immediately. It was not a gradual calming but a dramatic and sudden stillness. He did not repeatedly pray to the Lord about the weather as Elijah had done (1 Kgs. 18:41-46). Nor did He act in response to a command from God, as Moses had when parting the Red Sea (Ex. 14:16-21). That might have shown He was at least a true prophet, but this was far more dramatic. He did not perform some elaborate ceremony or ritual. He did not even pray! He simply commanded the storm, and it instantly obeyed Him.

The sudden storm had been frightening, but the eerie calm was even more terrifying. Before, their fear had been for their lives, but now their fear was the reverent realization of Jesus' tremendous power. The man in the boat was far more powerful than the storm that had previously frightened them. No wonder they were terrified as this suddenly dawned on them with startling clarity.

The disciples had seen Jesus miraculously heal many people and cast out demons already (Mark 1:29-34; 3:7-12), but this miracle had an epic scope to it. {Jesus had power that belonged to God alone. Only God could calm a storm (cf. Ps. 107:23-32).}[Q7]

The apostles had woken Jesus up because they rightly believed He could do something, but He still rebuked them for having no faith. They might have thought, *Wait a minute, we* do *have faith—that's why we woke you!* They seemed to believe that He had the power to do something. {But genuine faith involves more than just belief in Jesus' power. It also includes trust in His love.}[Q8] When we believe that God is all powerful but question God's care for us and doubt His love for us, we are not displaying true faith. We may believe that He has all the power in the world, but if we question His character, we are not showing genuine faith in Him. We must have belief in both His power and His goodness.

Faith also involves trusting God when He is seemingly doing nothing. Jesus had been asleep, and the storm had been raging. Yet if the disciples had deeply believed that Jesus was the Messiah, that He had a divine mission, and that God would not allow Him to drown in a boat, they could have had confidence, even though God appeared to be doing nothing. The faith-filled act may have still been for them to wake Jesus up and ask Him to help them, but they would have asked Him differently. Lest we be too hard on the disciples, we should remember that we can all too often question whether God really loves us when He allows difficulties in our lives.

After calming the storm, Jesus asked the disciples why they were afraid. When we have faith and a proper fear of God, we do not need to fear anyone or anything else. He rules over all of creation. He commands storms, demons, disease, and death. We do not need to fear other people (cf. Prov. 29:25). We do not need to fear circumstances. If God is for us, who can be against us? Nothing can separate us from His love (Rom. 8:31-39). The practical question is, What do we fear: God or circumstances? If we fear our circumstances, perhaps we need to spend more time reflecting on who God is—both the fact that He has all power and that He is love (1 John 4:8). He has the power to solve all the problems in our lives, and He loves and cares for us.

{Also, note that Jesus calmed the storm and saved them even though He rebuked them for having no faith.}[Q9] Even when our faith is weak and mixed with fear, He hears us. Even when we have doubts, He hears us. Even when we think He does not care, He hears us, and He acts. We do not need to waste time worrying whether our faith is strong enough before we come to Him for help. He will not turn us away just because our faith is weak. When we call out to Him, He will respond.

THE DISCIPLES' RESPONSE

MARK 4:41 And they feared exceedingly, and said one to another, What manner of man is this, that even the wind and the sea obey him?

{The disciples' question in verse 41 is the main point of the story.}[Q10] Who was this, who both needed sleep and could calm the storm with a word? While it is right to say that Jesus can calm the metaphorical storms in our lives, that is not the main point of this passage. The focus is on Jesus and

His identity. Perhaps Mark allows the question to hang unanswered in the narrative for rhetorical effect. He provides us with clear evidence, but we must reach the obvious conclusion ourselves. Everyone must answer the question: Who is Jesus?

Mark does not ultimately leave that question unanswered. This story provides clear evidence of Jesus' identity; indeed, all of Mark's Gospel demonstrates that Jesus is the Son of God (1:1), something that becomes increasingly clear throughout the book. From this specific story we see clearly that Jesus is a real man who gets tired and needs to rest. He is fully and truly human, with real needs and weaknesses. When Jesus took on humanity, He was made like us in every way, except that He never sinned (Heb. 2:17).

Jesus is also fully and truly God, able to command the winds and the waves. No one else possesses the power to control a storm. He did not need to plead with God to change the weather, as the prophet Elijah had. He did not act in response to God's command, as Moses had. He personally had the power to change the weather in an instant. He is not partly divine or part of the divine; He is completely God (Col. 2:9). He is fully human and fully divine.

As difficult as it is to comprehend how both these things can be true at once, we must affirm them both. The earliest heresies in the church usually denied that Jesus was truly human. Today false teachers are more likely to acknowledge His humanity but question His divinity. No credible historian questions Jesus' existence as a historical figure, but many deny that He is who He claimed to be. But if Jesus had not been God, He would not have been capable of redeeming us. If He had not been man, He could not represent us before God. We must affirm both Jesus' humanity and His divinity. There is no one like Him!

This account is primarily about who Jesus is. Before we allegorize this story and say that Jesus can guide us through the storms of our lives (which He can), we first need to answer the question the disciples asked. Who is this? Who do you say that Jesus is? We must accept that He is fully God and fully man to accept Him as He is.

Do you tend to forget either Jesus' divinity or His humanity in your daily life? If we forget His divinity, we will miss His authority and power. If we downplay His humanity, we will miss that He understands and sympathizes with our weakness. What effects might that have on our lives?

—Tom Greene

QUESTIONS

1. What happened immediately before this passage?
2. How did Jesus sometimes preach to crowds?
3. How is the detail that there were other boats helpful to us?
4. Why were the disciples caught in the storm?
5. What does Jesus falling asleep demonstrate?
6. Why did the disciples wake Jesus in the storm?
7. What did Jesus' calming of the storm demonstrate?
8. What two things does genuine faith involve?
9. How did Jesus respond to the disciples' lack of faith?
10. What is the main point of this story?

—Tom Greene

Preparing to Teach the Lesson

Today's lesson is one of the most popular events in the life of Christ. This account is in Matthew, Mark, and Luke (the Synoptic Gospels).

This miracle further explains God's omnipotence, showing that Jesus Christ has power over nature. As the Son of God, Jesus has power equal to the Father's.

TODAY'S AIM

Facts: to observe Jesus calming the storm.

Principle: to understand that Jesus has power over nature.

Application: to realize God is in control of every aspect of our lives.

INTRODUCING THE LESSON

This story shows us that the Lord isn't surprised or worried about anything. The disciples were anxious about the storm and worried for their lives, but Jesus slept peacefully.

DEVELOPING THE LESSON

1. Jesus crosses the sea with His disciples (Mark 4:35-36). Chapter 4 begins with Jesus teaching in parables. A parable uses a simple story to explain a deeper truth. When Jesus used parables, the hearer knew He was illustrating something with a story. Parables are not historical accounts of real people. They are stories. Sometimes Jesus would explain the meaning of a parable, other times He chose not to (cf. Matt. 13:10-17).

After teaching, Jesus decided to leave Galilee by crossing the sea to the area of the Gadarenes. Verse 35 tells us that it was His idea to leave that evening via boat. This is an interesting example of the Lord placing His followers in stressful situations to grow their faith. He knew the storm was coming that day, just as He knows about the storms in our lives.

In verse 36, we are told that Jesus was teaching from that same boat previously mentioned. The people gathered along the Galilean shore and the water helped carry His voice. It was like an amphitheater. Other boats went with them carrying other followers.

2. Jesus sleeps as a terrifying storm begins (Mark 4:37-38). The Sea of Galilee is quite large. It is surrounded by mountains, hills, and ravines with mighty winds that can funnel storms onto the lake. In the back of some of our Bibles, there are maps of this area of the world. It is about thirteen miles long and seven miles wide. This was the same lake some of the disciples had lived by when Jesus called them and upon which Jesus later walked on the water.

Verse 37 says a windstorm started suddenly and the boat began to fill with water. Jesus was in the stern (the back) of the boat, asleep on a cushion. We can imagine the extreme imagery: a horrible storm compared to a sleeping teacher. He showed the disciples (and us) that in times of stress, we should trust God. But in the heat of the moment, the disciples woke Him and asked if He cared if they died. They thought He did not care about their safety, but He was in control and at peace. This must have been a very bad storm to scare this group of men that included professional fishermen who had probably experienced severe weather on that same body of water.

It is interesting to compare this event to the story of Jonah who fell asleep on a boat during a storm and had to be awakened by others. In Jonah 1, we read that the sailors worried that they would die in the terrible storm, so they begged Jonah to pray to his God. Now,

Jesus Himself, Jonah's God, was also asleep on a boat in a storm.

3. Jesus calms the storm and chastises the disciples for their lack of faith (Mark 4:39-41). Jesus got up and rebuked the wind and told the waves, "Peace, be still" (vs. 39). The storm ended, and there was calm. The Lord has power over nature. This amazing power contained in the spoken words of Christ reminds us that He created the universe by speaking. Psalm 107:23-32 tells of God's amazing power to cause great storms and to calm them.

Jesus also took this opportunity to rebuke His disciples by asking, "Why are ye so fearful? how is it that ye have no faith?" (Mark 4:40). We see two interconnected things: fear and lack of faith. They should have trusted Him. This was near the beginning of their three-year apprenticeship with Christ, but they still should have known that God is our refuge and strength even when the waters roar (Ps. 46:1-3).

It is interesting to think about the situation. If we were in a boat with Jesus, would we be afraid of a storm? Many would probably answer "No!" But isn't the Lord with us every day, yet we experience fear? Is it possible to be in a situation of great stress and then choose faith over fear?

The response recorded here (and in Matthew and Luke) is interesting in a few ways. They did not immediately repent. Nor did they rejoice that Jesus saved them from drowning. Verse 41 says they were terrified and asked one another what kind of man Jesus is, that He can calm winds and waves. Of course, we know the answer: He is God! Multiple times in the Gospel of Mark, we see people amazed by the miracles of Jesus. Mark's Gospel proportionally records the most miracles of Jesus compared to the other three Gospels. These miracles indicated Jesus' identity as God's Son (Mark 1:1).

ILLUSTRATING THE LESSON

Jesus' disciples were afraid the storm would overtake them. Jesus was not afraid. He can calm any storm.

CONCLUDING THE LESSON

It makes sense that the Creator has complete control over His creation. This is one of multiple occasions on which the Lord showed His power over nature. How can this characteristic of God help you in your life? How do you respond to situations beyond your control? Do you pray big prayers? Do you trust Him to do even more than you could expect (cf. Eph. 3:20)?

Jesus rebuked the storm and His disciples. He was disappointed in their lack of faith. What does the Lord think about our faith? We know that the storms of life come. Do we trust the Lord to take care of us in the storm?

ANTICIPATING THE NEXT LESSON

Next week's Bible study picks up where this one leaves off. In Mark 5, Jesus and the disciples finish their boat trip by arriving at the area of the Gadarenes. Jesus is immediately met by a demon-possessed man. In our next lesson, we will explore the Lord's power over demons.

—Adam Clagg

PRACTICAL POINTS

1. Sometimes obeying Jesus will lead us into difficulty (Mark 4:35-37).
2. Jesus understands our needs, so we can pray confidently (vs. 38).
3. When difficulty comes, sometimes we doubt God's goodness. But even when we only have a little faith, Jesus answers prayer (vss. 38-39).
4. Jesus has power that belongs to God alone and is fully God (Mark 4:39; cf. John 8:58; Col. 1:15-20).
5. Doubting God's goodness shows we lack true faith, even if we believe in His power (Mark 4:40).
6. God is to be feared (Mark 4:41; cf. Deut. 10:12; Eccl. 12:13).

—Tom Greene

RESEARCH AND DISCUSSION

1. Do you tend to emphasize either Jesus' divinity or His humanity more than the other? Why is that?
2. How does it negatively impact our lives if we forget Jesus' humanity? What are some verses that clearly teach His humanity?
3. How does it negatively impact our lives if we forget Jesus' deity? What are some verses that clearly teach His deity?
4. If God still answers the prayers of those who have weak or no faith (Mark 4:40), what are we to make of calls to pray in faith, such as James 1:6-8?
5. What does a proper fear of God look like (cf. Ps. 130:3-5; Prov. 9:10)? How does this fit with 1 John 4:18?
6. If you don't fear God in your daily life, what can you do to help change that?

—Tom Greene

ILLUSTRATED HIGH POINTS

He saith unto them, let us pass over (Mark 4:35)

When Susan converted from Islam to Christianity in 2009, her father beat her, threatened to kill her, and locked her up. When the Ugandan police finally rescued her, she was severely malnourished. She will likely require crutches her whole life, but she has mostly recovered. Did Susan do something wrong to suffer this way? No, she did not. Sometimes our obedience to Jesus results in difficulty.

Master, carest thou not (vs. 38)

The famous musical *Les Miserables* opens in a harsh work camp. In response to one prisoner's prayer, the others sing "Sweet Jesus doesn't care." This illustrates how many feel in the face of disaster. But God *does* care. Joseph was imprisoned in Egypt so that good would come (Gen. 50:20). Jesus cried out on the cross, asking why God had abandoned Him (Matt. 27:46). But on the cross, He won the greatest victory the world has ever known. Even when it seems God does not care, He does.

What manner of man is this (Mark 4:41)

C.S. Lewis argued in *Mere Christianity* that Jesus must be a lunatic, a liar, or the Lord. If He was a lunatic or a liar, His followers would have realized that shortly after His death. However, they claimed to have seen Him risen from the dead, and they maintained this under torture and death. A few atheists try to add a fourth option: that Jesus was a made-up legend. But reliable secular sources mention Him, and no credible historian doubts Jesus' existence. There is only one possible conclusion: Jesus is who He said He is—the Lord!

—Tom Greene

Golden Text Illuminated

"And they feared exceedingly, and said one to another, What manner of man is this, that even the wind and the sea obey him?" (Mark 4:41).

The apostle Paul was right when he declared, "Great is the mystery of godliness: God was manifest in the flesh" (1 Tim. 3:16). The Council of Chalcedon stated in A.D. 451 that Jesus Christ is "perfect in Godhead and also perfect in manhood; truly God and truly man."

Great indeed is the mystery of godliness *and* the incarnation, and this mystery is on full display in Mark 4:35-41. With Jesus asleep in the stern of the boat as they traveled across the sea, "there arose a great storm of wind" (vs. 37). The waves crashed over the boat, filling it with water. The disciples—several of whom were professional fishermen and well acquainted with the sea—panicked and called to Christ: "Master, carest thou not that we perish?" (vs. 38). Then, calm, cool, and collected, Christ arose and silenced the winds with nothing but a spoken word, and at that moment, "the wind ceased, and there was a great calm" (vs. 39). In verse 40, Christ then rebuked them for their lack of faith: "Why are ye so fearful? how is it that ye have no faith?"

His reproach of their fear was right and appropriate. At this point in His ministry, the disciples had seen more than enough evidence of His deity to not respond in such a fearful manner. It was as if they had not seen His power at all! Their panic revealed that they did not yet understand the Master for whom they had forsaken all. The rebuke of Christ, however, brings us to our golden text in verse 41: "And they feared exceedingly, and said one to another, What manner of man is this, that even the wind and the sea obey him?"

This statement from verse 41 contains two principles that help us worship Christ rightly and trust Him more deeply.

Principle #1: The fear of the disciples is the faith they should have had. In the Greek, the disciples "feared a great fear," and yet, this great fear was *after* Jesus had calmed the storm! Thus, it was not a fear for their safety but the fear of majesty. He who had just rebuked the wind and the waves was none other than God in human flesh.

The response of fear by the disciples was one of worship and faith that may have dimly perceived that, as the Council of Chalcedon declares, Jesus Christ is "perfect in Godhead and also perfect in manhood; truly God and truly man." Faith in Christ and fear of Christ are intermingled and inseparable.

Principle #2: The question of the disciples contains the theology they should have had. Embedded in the question, "What manner of man is this, that even the wind and the sea obey him?" is the profound truth that Christ is matchless and supreme. Although fully man, He possesses the power to command the elements. He slept like any other man before the storm and yet calmed a storm *unlike* any other man. The disciples' amazement after Christ calmed the storm reveals why they should have trusted Him before He calmed the storm.

To apply this to our lives, we must search the Scriptures and meditate on the glory of Christ. The more we see His infinite power and matchless authority, the more we will fear Him and have unwavering faith in Him to do the impossible.

—Jerod A. Gilcher

Heart of the Lesson

Many of us marvel at great people from history and those today who perform incredible achievements. We stand in awe of the strongest man, the first man in space, the fastest runner in the world, the creator of some ingenious invention, and so on. There is in the human soul an inclination to marvel at greatness. We are this way because God made us to marvel at Him and stand in awe of His majestic glory and power.

What Jesus Christ did while on earth was incomparably greater than lifting heavy things, going to outer space, or inventing something. Rather, he opened blind eyes, cast out demons with a single word, healed diseases at a great distance, and raised the dead. Christ performed the supernatural—and in so doing, He proved that He is God and worthy of worship. One such moment came when Christ silenced a storm with a word.

1. Jesus calms a storm (Mark 4:35-40). After a teaching session, Jesus told the disciples to take Him to the other side of the Sea of Galilee in their boat, and they obeyed (vss. 35-36). A great storm arose while He slept, and the disciples were terrified (vss. 37-38). When they woke Jesus, He calmed the storm and then asked if they still had no faith (vss. 39-40).

2. The disciples respond (Mark 4:41). When the disciples saw what Jesus did, "they feared exceedingly, and said one to another, What manner of man is this, that even the wind and the sea obey Him?" (vs. 41). From that response to the unmistakable supremacy of Christ, we find several practical insights for our lives.

First, the supremacy of Christ warrants a response of fear. The Greek of verse 41 literally reads, "They were afraid with great fear." This was a fear that drove them not *away* from Christ but *to* Christ. It caused them to stand in awe and tremble before Him as supreme.

Believers must strive for that same trembling worship and awe of Christ. Such fear is not an *alternative* to trusting or loving Christ but describes the *quality* of our trust and love for Christ.

Second, the supremacy of Christ should provoke unparalleled admiration of Him. After witnessing the storm-calming power of Christ, the disciples asked, "What manner of man is this?" That question was an expression of admiration. Jesus exceeds all other men in history. He is incomparable, unrivaled, matchless, and supreme. He is not a Savior to be considered lightly or flippantly.

Third, the supremacy of Christ should provoke recognition of His deeds and achievements. After Jesus calmed the life-threatening storm, the disciples exclaimed that "even the wind and the sea obey Him." Christ's sovereign authority over the wind and sea produced great fear and admiration.

Genuine responses of worship and trust in Christ are not produced in a vacuum. Rather, true worship, trust, and awe of Christ are produced by the careful contemplation of His deeds and achievements. That is especially true of His sin-bearing death for sinners and grave-defying resurrection from the dead. When we fix our heart's gaze on the Word of God and meditate long on the saving deeds of Jesus Christ, our heart cannot remain long in an apathetic state. Instead, worship, trust, and joyful fear are awakened in our soul.

—Jerod A. Gilcher

World Missions

The missionary was sitting across from the state police official in the policeman's office. The security officer interrogated him and scrutinized his passport, leafing through it repeatedly and asking the same set of questions over and over. He was tired and had been fasting that day, and his hunger and thirst deepened as the time wore on. As the questions kept coming as to the purpose of his presence there, he felt as though he were in a storm of both spiritual and potentially legal pressure. He realized that, rather than just sitting concerned about his interrogation, he should pray and cry out to God for wisdom—and ask Jesus to *calm* the storm.

As he prayed in his mind and under his breath, he remembered that central to the Asian culture of the officers before him was the concept of hospitality. Eating or drinking together was indicative of being *family* on some level. Also, willingness to accept water from someone implied that one accepted that person without considerations of class or caste.

Noticing that one of the officers had brought what looked like a bottle of water from home, he requested to take a sip. Surprised, the officer very happily gave him the bottle. It was as if the storm had dissipated. From that moment on, the entire tone of the conversation changed, and what had been tense questioning gave way to friendly banter and questions in *both* directions. There was even an opportunity for the young man to share his testimony. He promised them a New Testament in the local language and later returned to bring it to them.

Psalm 107 presents a number of scenarios in which people found themselves faced with calamity. In some of the stanzas, the calamity faced is connected with their own sin and rebellion against God. In verses 23-32, however, the calamity of a deadly storm arose as they were simply going about their business on the sea. They had come to the end of their senses, and so they cried out to the Lord amid impending disaster. At the center of this passage are verses 27-28: "They reel to and fro, and stagger like a drunken man, and are at their wits' end. Then they cry unto the Lord in their trouble, and he bringeth them out of their distresses." Even in the midst of insurmountable circumstances, God had them in His capable hands.

Both Psalm 107 and the story above remind us of the account of Jesus calming a storm. Jesus and His disciples were caught in the midst of a frightening storm while out on the Sea of Galilee. Jesus was unfazed; in fact, he was asleep. The disciples cried out in fear and then finally woke Him, asking, "Master, carest thou not that we perish?" (Mark 4:38).

That question was also a kind of ironic echo of the words of the pagan sailors to the renegade prophet Jonah, who slept and sulked while the storm raged (Jonah 1:6). Jonah's response to the sailors' question was effectively, "Kill me now." By contrast, in response to the disciples' question, Jesus got up and rebuked the wind and waves, and they were calmed. In Jonah's case, the prophet was thrown overboard, and that resulted in the storm stopping and the pagan sailors turning to the Lord (vss. 15-16). In a similar way, Jesus' calming of the storm led His disciples to draw ever closer to understanding His true identity, and they exclaimed, "What manner of man is this, that even the wind and the sea obey him?" (Mark 4:41).

As we endure our own storms, may we cry out to Jesus, and may the answer he grants us not only draw us closer to Him but also open the eyes of others to Him.

—Matthew Friedman

The Jewish Aspect

In first-century Judea, Jews understood that only God could control the weather. Not only was this known from the Old Testament, but non-canonical writings also affirmed it. For example, 2 Maccabees 9:8 says that the tyrant Antiochus IV Epiphanes believed he could command the waves of the sea, and the book lists other blasphemous boasts he made. However, God struck him down with an excruciating sickness, and he acknowledged before his death that mortals should not think they are equal to God. The point was clear: only God can control the weather, and claiming otherwise was blasphemous.

In the Old Testament it was also clear that God controls the weather (Pss. 18:15; 65:5-7). No one else has that power (89:8-9). God created the seas and placed limits on them (Gen. 1:9), and He rebuked them (Isa. 50:2; Nah. 1:4). He demonstrated this power dramatically by drying the Red Sea for Israel when they escaped Egypt and then using it to drown the Egyptians (Ex. 14:21-31; Ps. 106:9-11). The Lord alone has power over the sea.

It is against this backdrop that we understand the apostles' question about who Jesus could be. The answer is clear: God. Only God has power over the winds and the waves. No mere man can control the weather. Yet this, together with Jesus' clear humanity, puzzled the disciples. The disciples knew that there was only one God. They had seen Jesus asleep on a cushion, exhausted from a long day. He was clearly a man. Yet He possessed power that belonged to God alone. How could both things be true? How could Jesus be both God and human?

Jesus Himself later hinted at this issue when He asked how the scribes could say that the Christ was the son of David (cf. Mark 12:35-37). The scribes rightly recognized that Psalm 110 was about the Christ, the Son of David. Jesus did not deny this. Psalm 110 is a messianic psalm, and the Son of David was David's physical descendant. But Jesus pointed out that David called his descendant his Lord. How could David be a servant of the Christ if the Christ was merely a man who had not even been born when David wrote Psalm 110? The answer, though the Pharisees did not accept it, was that although the Christ was a man, He was also far more than that. David's Son was also David's Lord.

Psalm 107:23-32 feels like it was written about this week's passage. The disciples cried to the Lord in their distress, and He delivered them. He calmed the sea and brought them safely to their destination. Was there a separate context that the psalmist had in mind when he originally wrote this? Very likely. Yet Jesus fulfilled it in a truly striking way.

Importantly, Psalm 107 attributes these miraculous actions to the Lord. This is not the generic title "lord" that might be applied to human rulers. Psalm 107 attributes these miracles to "Yahweh." If Yahweh, the Creator and Ruler of all, performed the miracles of Psalm 107:23-32, and if Jesus performed these miracles, the conclusion is clear: Jesus is God, the Creator and Ruler of all.

This background helps explain the disciples' astonishment and answer the disciples' question: "What manner of man is this, that even the wind and the sea obey him?" (Mark 4:41). Jesus is fully God and fully man.

—Tom Greene

Guiding the Superintendent

The first half of Mark (1:1-8:26) answers the question, Who is Jesus? while the second half (8:27-16:20) answers the question, What is Jesus' mission? Therefore, Mark 4:35-41 contributes to our understanding of Jesus' identity.

DEVOTIONAL OUTLINE

1. Setting: Jesus travels across the lake (Mark 4:35-36). A huge crowd had gathered to hear Jesus. When evening came, Jesus was tired and wanted to cross the sea.

2. Conflict: Jesus sleeps during a deadly storm (Mark 4:37-38). Since only God can tell creation what to do, Mark 4:35-41 clearly teaches that Jesus is God. Paradoxically, and in keeping with the historic Christian confession that Jesus is both fully God and fully human, the text also teaches the humanity of the Lord Jesus "asleep on a pillow" (vs. 38). He was tired. God does not need sleep (Ps. 121:3), but in Christ divinity and humanity reside in one Person.

3. Resolution: Jesus calms the storm (Mark 4:39). Mark 4:35-41 shows Jesus' identity through His actions. The Old Testament provides the background for the narrative. In the Old Testament, only the Lord has authority over the status of the sea. In Jonah, the Lord started and stopped a sea storm (Jonah 1:4, 15) because He "made the sea" (vs. 9). Even more directly, Psalm 107:29 declares that the Lord "maketh the storm a calm, so that the waves thereof are still."

Mark showed that Jesus is God by attributing to Him an action that only God can do. For Jesus to do this by speaking (Mark 4:39) demonstrates the word-based authority over creation shown with God in Genesis 1. Jesus' power demonstrates that He is one being with the Father and Spirit.

4. Result: Jesus challenges the disciples' faith (Mark 4:40-41). The disciples had followed Jesus since the beginning of His ministry and had witnessed Him healing people. So why did Jesus say that the disciples had "no faith" (vs. 40)? D. A. Carson offers a plausible explanation: "They lacked faith not so much in his ability to save them as in Jesus as Messiah, whose life could not be lost in a storm" (*Expositor's Bible Commentary: Matthew*, Zondervan). The disciples' question revealed they did not previously have that kind of faith.

Jesus' challenge of the disciples' faith also parallels God's challenge of the Israelites in last week's passage (Ex. 14:10-22). As the Israelites cried out to God in desperation at the Red Sea, so the disciples cried out to Jesus in desperation on the Sea of Galilee. As God rebuked the Israelites for crying out, so Jesus rebuked the disciples. It is never wrong for God's people to cry out in faith, but in both cases God recognized faithlessness.

The primary application of today's text is to counteract deficient faith by trusting that the nature of Jesus guarantees that nothing will stop Him from saving believers and restoring the world. From this we can learn to be confident in our prayers. He wants us to cast our anxieties on Him because we trust Him with those anxieties.

CHILDREN'S CORNER

As you teach children, remember that they can also teach you important lessons. Their faith often exhibits a type of trust that evades adults. Jesus said we need to be like humble children to enter the kingdom of heaven. Children readily believe and trust Jesus as they take Him at His word. Jesus has power over every part of our lives.

—Matthew Swale

SCRIPTURE LESSON TEXT

MARK 5:1 And they came over unto the other side of the sea, into the country of the Gadarenes.

2 And when he was come out of the ship, immediately there met him out of the tombs a man with an unclean spirit,

3 Who had *his* dwelling among the tombs; and no man could bind him, no, not with chains:

4 Because that he had been often bound with fetters and chains, and the chains had been plucked asunder by him, and the fetters broken in pieces: neither could any *man* tame him.

5 And always, night and day, he was in the mountains, and in the tombs, crying, and cutting himself with stones.

6 But when he saw Jesus afar off, he ran and worshipped him,

7 And cried with a loud voice, and said, What have I to do with thee, Jesus, *thou* Son of the most high God? I adjure thee by God, that thou torment me not.

8 For he said unto him, Come out of the man, *thou* unclean spirit.

9 And he asked him, What *is* thy name? And he answered, saying, My name *is* Legion: for we are many.

10 And he besought him much that he would not send them away out of the country.

11 Now there was there nigh unto the mountains a great herd of swine feeding.

12 And all the devils besought him, saying, Send us into the swine, that we may enter into them.

13 And forthwith Jesus gave them leave. And the unclean spirits went out, and entered into the swine: and the herd ran violently down a steep place into the sea, (they were about two thousand;) and were choked in the sea.

14 And they that fed the swine fled, and told *it* in the city, and in the country. And they went out to see what it was that was done.

15 And they come to Jesus, and see him that was possessed with the devil, and had the legion, sitting, and clothed, and in his right mind: and they were afraid.

16 And they that saw *it* told them how it befell to him that was possessed with the devil, and *also* concerning the swine.

17 And they began to pray him to depart out of their coasts.

18 And when he was come into the ship, he that had been possessed with the devil prayed him that he might be with him.

19 Howbeit Jesus suffered him not, but saith unto him, Go home to thy friends, and tell them how great things the Lord hath done for thee, and hath had compassion on thee.

20 And he departed, and began to publish in Decapolis how great things Jesus had done for him: and all *men* did marvel.

NOTES

Jesus Casts Out Legion

Lesson Text: Mark 5:1-20

Related Scriptures: Matthew 8:28-34;
Mark 3:22-27; Luke 4:16-21; 5:1-8; 8:26-39

TIME: between A.D. 26 and 30

PLACE: territory of Gadara

GOLDEN TEXT—"Howbeit Jesus suffered him not, but saith unto him, Go home to thy friends, and tell them how great things the Lord hath done for thee, and hath had compassion on thee" (Mark 5:19).

Introduction

This week's lesson picks up right where last week's left off. Having demonstrated His power over creation by calming a storm in Mark 4, Jesus was next confronted by a violent, demon-possessed man. This man was not merely possessed by a single demon but rather by an intimidating legion. Would such an intimidating adversary be able to resist Jesus? The text does not even entertain the idea. Jesus easily overcame them by simply ordering them out.

By easily casting out the legion of demons, Jesus demonstrated that He rules over not only the natural but also the supernatural. No matter whether our problems today are natural or supernatural, Jesus can take care of us as well. His power is unmatched, and He uses it both to protect His followers from danger (4:35-41) and to save spiritually oppressed people (5:1-20). No matter the person and no matter the circumstances, Jesus is able to deliver anyone.

LESSON OUTLINE

1. **THE SETTING—Mark 5:1-5**
2. **THE CONFLICT—Mark 5:6-13**
3. **THE FALLOUT—Mark 5:14-20**

Exposition: Verse by Verse

THE SETTING

MARK 5:1 And they came over unto the other side of the sea, into the country of the Gadarenes.

2 And when he was come out of the ship, immediately there met him bound with fetters and chains, and the chains had been plucked asunder by him, and the fetters broken in pieces: neither could any man tame him.

3 Who had his dwelling among the tombs; and no man could bind him, no, not with chains:

4 Because that he had been often bound with fetters and chains, and the chains had been plucked asunder

by him, and the fetters broken in pieces: neither could any man tame him.

5 And always, night and day, he was in the mountains, and in the tombs, crying, and cutting himself with stones.

Meeting the demoniac (Mark 5:1-2). {There is no conflict between the various Gospel accounts of this miracle happening in the land of the Gergesenes or the land of the Gadarenes. Both phrases refer to the same Gentile area. This story took place in the small town of Gergasa by the sea. The town was in the general region associated with Gadara, the larger city that the whole region would have been associated with.}[Q1] This might be comparable to telling someone living in another state "I'm from Cleveland" but telling someone local that you are from Middleburg Heights, a suburb only someone from Ohio would recognize. In neither case are you being deceptive; you are just more specific for the person who knows the area.

Description of the demoniac (Mark 5:3-5). The demon-possessed man was miserable and constantly abused by unclean spirits. He cut himself (vs. 5) and lived in a graveyard, which would have rendered him ceremonially unclean. It also would have provided him little shelter, and He was undoubtedly exposed to the elements. He was an outcast from society and isolated from everyone but the demons who tormented him. It was a miserable experience physically, emotionally, and spiritually.

{The term "unclean spirit" used in the passage is synonymous with "devil" (cf. vs. 16). We should not waste time trying to draw nuanced distinctions between unclean spirits and devils, given that the book of Mark uses both terms interchangeably (cf. vss. 2, 12).}[Q2]

Day and night the man cried out among the tombs. That does not mean that he never slept but rather that the unclean spirits would afflict him at any time of day. {The afflicted man could not be restrained. He had unnatural strength. He was able to break chains. Demons can confer supernatural strength.}[Q3] Society could not tame him. The wording of the Greek text in verse 3 *might* imply that at one time he could be bound, but now he no longer could because he was getting worse. Either way, he was able to break chains with demonic fury, and there was nothing anyone could do. As far as anyone could tell, he was beyond help.

THE CONFLICT

6 But when he saw Jesus afar off, he ran and worshipped him,

7 And cried with a loud voice, and said, What have I to do with thee, Jesus, thou Son of the most high God? I adjure thee by God, that thou torment me not.

8 For he said unto him, Come out of the man, thou unclean spirit.

9 And he asked him, What is thy name? And he answered, saying, My name is Legion: for we are many.

10 And he besought him much that he would not send them away out of the country.

11 Now there was there nigh unto the mountains a great herd of swine feeding.

12 And all the devils besought him, saying, Send us into the swine, that we may enter into them.

13 And forthwith Jesus gave them leave. And the unclean spirits went out, and entered into the swine: and the herd ran violently down a steep place into the sea, (they were about two thousand;) and were choked in the sea.

Demons (Mark 5:6-9). Seeing Jesus from afar, the man ran toward Him. Once the man got closer, the demons recognized who Jesus was. This is in sharp contrast to the disciples, who wondered about Jesus' identity in the preceding chapter. That was not the only time that demons recognized Jesus (cf. 1:21-28). Although many people failed to recognize who Jesus was, demons immediately recognized Him and knew that He had power over them. Despite knowing *about* Jesus, they remained His enemies. Knowing *about* Jesus is not enough.

The man ran up to Jesus, worshipped Him, and begged Jesus not to torment him. His simultaneous attraction to and repulsion from Jesus is striking, and it is difficult to tell how much this man was in control of his actions and how much the demons were.

{Usually, Jesus is recorded as simply casting demons out rather than talking to them at length.}[Q4] This story is not meant to be a template for modern-day exorcisms, as some Christians seem to assume when they ask demons to name themselves. This story is an exception, not a rule.

The scope of this exorcism was greater than any other recorded in the Gospels. Jesus cast seven demons out of Mary Magdalene (Luke 8:2) but not this many. Matthew 12:43-45 shows that it is worse to be inhabited by many evil spirits than just by one.

{We do not know how many demons this man had. The size of a Roman legion at the time was roughly six thousand men if both infantry and cavalry were counted. However, demons are liars, and even if Jesus compelled them to speak truthfully, they only declared that they were many, not that they were the exact count of a Roman legion.}[Q5] The exact count is not the point. The fact that they could drive the herd of pigs down into the sea does seem to indicate that it was a large number, however. Their vast numbers highlight the tremendous power of Jesus in easily overcoming a legion of demons.

{When the demons encountered Jesus, they knew multiple things. First, they knew His identity. Second, they knew that He had power over them, so they appealed to Him not to torment them. Third, they knew that He would one day judge them.}[Q6] Matthew recorded that they begged not to be tormented "before the time," and Luke added that they begged not to be cast into the abyss (cf. Matt. 8:29; Luke 8:31). Demons know they are doomed and have a limited time before they are finally judged (cf. Rev. 12:12). Demons are powerful, but they are powerless before God. Jesus has infinitely more power than a legion of demons, who were immediately reduced to groveling. That dramatically highlighted Jesus' power. Not only does He have total power over creation, as demonstrated by calming the storm, but He also has power over the supernatural.

Pigs (Mark 5:10-13). The demons begged to be sent into the pigs. Surprisingly, Jesus granted their request, and the pigs rushed into the sea and drowned. What was the demons' motivation, and why did Jesus grant them their request? Sincere Christians have proposed a variety of explanations. Since the Gospel writers do not clearly provide the answer, we will survey some of the explanations without picking one. We should study the passage and try to come to a correct understanding of it and be charitable toward others who come to a different understanding.

{It is possible the demons were trying to stir up trouble for Jesus and hoped their actions would result in Him being asked to leave the region. Killing two thousand pigs could cause serious problems for the local economy. Alternatively, perhaps the demons simply liked death and destruction and were violently expressing frustration at being cast out of the man by maliciously killing the pigs. Both of these explanations assume that the demons intentionally drove the pigs into the sea.

Since demons, however, do not seem to like being without a host (cf. Matt. 12:43-45), some Christians think that they were not intending to destroy the herd immediately. In this view, Jesus was judging the demons, and although He allowed them into the pigs, either the pigs preferred to drown themselves rather than be possessed by demons, or Jesus Himself drowned the pigs as judgment upon the demons. While Jesus did curse the fig tree (cf. Mark 11:12-25), there are no other recorded miracles of Jesus that are destructive. Therefore, it seems unlikely that Jesus drove the pigs into the sea.}[Q7]

Whether Jesus allowed the demons to drown the pigs or judged them after allowing them into the herd, we should address Jesus' motivation. Why would He allow the pigs to die? Several ideas have been proposed. {First, the death of the herd dramatically revealed what Jesus was dealing with. It is one thing to say Jesus cast many demons out of a man. It is another to see a herd of two thousand pigs wildly trample down a cliff and drown. It highlighted how many demons there were and how great Jesus' power is. Second, upon seeing the pigs drown, those tending the pigs went back to town and reported all that had happened (5:14-16). That caused Jesus' actions to be more widely known in a way that might not have happened if Jesus had simply cast the demons out. Third, pigs were unclean for Jews. Although it was a Gentile region, some wonder whether there were Jews who helped raise these pigs or ate them. By removing this potential source of defilement, Jesus could have been merciful in preventing some Jews from sinning.}[Q8]

Although we do not know with certainty why Jesus allowed the demons to enter the pigs, we clearly see that one man was worth more than thousands of pigs. Further, this miracle brought tremendous attention to Jesus' power and His compassion on the man who had been demon-possessed.

THE FALLOUT

14 And they that fed the swine fled, and told it in the city, and in the country. And they went out to see what it was that was done.

15 And they come to Jesus, and see him that was possessed with the devil, and had the legion, sitting, and clothed, and in his right mind: and they were afraid.

16 And they that saw it told them how it befell to him that was possessed with the devil, and also concerning the swine.

17 And they began to pray him to depart out of their coasts.

18 And when he was come into the ship, he that had been possessed with the devil prayed him that he might be with him.

19 Howbeit Jesus suffered him not, but saith unto him, Go home to thy friends, and tell them how great things the Lord hath done for thee, and hath had compassion on thee.

20 And he departed, and began to publish in Decapolis how great things Jesus had done for him: and all men did marvel.

The response of the people (Mark 5:14-17). The people were frightened when they saw the man in his right mind (vs. 15). This man had been uncontrollable and terrifying, but he sat meekly at Jesus' feet. Clearly, Jesus had far greater power than the legion of demons who had previously made this man impossible to overcome!

It is not recorded that any people were glad he had recovered. Rather, they were simply terrified of Jesus! Perhaps the people valued money rather than this man being healed, and the loss of two thousand pigs was a huge blow. {However, Luke gave a different motivation for the people asking Jesus to leave: they were seized with great fear (cf. Luke 8:36-37).}[Q9] This is likely comparable to the great fear the disciples had after Jesus calmed the storm in Mark 4. They were in awe and terror of Jesus and His unrivaled power.

Rather than asking Jesus to do further miracles, they asked Him to leave, and He obliged. It is the same in our lives. Tragically, if we ask Jesus to leave us alone, He will often do so.

The response of the man and of Jesus (Mark 5:18-20). Jesus granted the request of the demons to send them into the pigs. He granted the request of the people to leave. Surprisingly, the only request He did not grant was that of the man to follow Him! Instead, He told the man to proclaim what the Lord had done for him. In response, the man obeyed and proclaimed what *Jesus* had done for him. It is clear that what Jesus does and what the Lord does are inseparable. Taken together with the fact that Jesus calmed the sea (something only God could do) and drove out a legion of demons, Mark was making it increasingly clear that Jesus is the Lord. Mark began his Gospel by calling Jesus "the Son of God" (1:1), and he continued to pile up evidence that supported claim. Jesus does what the Lord alone can do.

The man went throughout the Decapolis declaring what Jesus had done, and we see that this man was probably a Gentile, given his home was in Gentile country. {His testimony caused everyone to marvel, and when Jesus later returned, a crowd was ready to bring people to Him (cf. 7:31-37). This man was an effective witness who prepared the area for when Jesus returned.}[Q10] A man who had once been considered a lost cause proved an effective witness for Christ. If there are people you consider hopeless, do not give up. God may have plans for them!

After crossing the sea during a furious storm and healing the man with unclean spirits, Jesus got back into the boat and went to the other side (5:21). Jesus crossed the sea and passed through a storm to teach the disciples about who He is and to reach this man. Jesus cares deeply about individuals, not just crowds.

—Tom Greene

QUESTIONS

1. Do the Gospel writers contradict each other on where this story took place?
2. What is the difference between unclean spirits and devils?
3. Why could the man not be restrained previously?
4. What was unusual about Jesus casting out these demons?
5. Do we know how many demons this man had?
6. What three things did the demons immediately know about Jesus when they met Him?
7. Why *might* the demons have driven the pigs into the sea?
8. Why *might* Jesus have allowed the demons to drive the pigs into the sea?
9. Why did the people ask Jesus to leave, according to Luke?
10. How effective of a witness was the demon-possessed man?

—Tom Greene

Preparing to Teach the Lesson

Spiritual warfare can be a difficult subject to teach on. Using events from the life of Christ can help learners empathize with those oppressed by the devil. This account shows a life completely changed by the power of Christ.

TODAY'S AIM

Facts: to observe Jesus' power over demons.

Principle: to realize the Lord has authority over the supernatural.

Application: to live knowing that Jesus can set us free from all evil.

INTRODUCING THE LESSON

Throughout the Bible, we see Satan deceiving and harming people. The devil hates God and all who follow Him. The Bible describes him as an accuser, a deceiver, and a thief. Jesus said, "The thief cometh not, but for to steal, and to kill, and to destroy: I am come that they might have life, and that they might have it more abundantly" (John 10:10). In our lesson we will read about a demon-possessed man whom Jesus delivered. The Lord has authority over everything spiritual and supernatural.

DEVELOPING THE LESSON

1. The oppressed man approaches (Mark 5:1-5). After Jesus calmed the waters in Mark 4, He arrived on the other side of the Sea of Galilee in the area of the Gadarenes. The residents here were Gentiles (not Jewish). As Jesus left the ship, a demon-possessed man ran straight to Him.

We see several ways evil spirits had attempted to ruin this man's life. The man was homeless and lived in the tombs. People had tried to bind him with chains but were unsuccessful. These attempts to bind him could have been ways to keep him from harming himself and others. The people from the area (possibly friends and family) had chained him hand and foot, but he broke the fetters. No one could tame him.

This demon-possessed man was not just homeless; he roamed the mountains and tombs day and night, crying out and cutting himself with stones. It is terrible to see how the devil can destroy a person's life. We see similar things today. Not all mental and emotional illness is demon possession, but we know that all sickness came into the world because Adam and Eve sinned. We inherit a sinful nature and bodies that fail us.

When we read about this man or discuss others who are oppressed by the devil, we find hope in Scripture. Jesus came to bring deliverance! Christ Himself is the fulfillment of Isaiah's prophecy in Isaiah 61:1-2 and 58:6. Jesus read this scroll in Luke 4, declaring that He came to bring good news to the poor and heal the brokenhearted. Jesus came to preach deliverance to the captives, give sight to the blind, and set the oppressed free!

2. The demons encounter Jesus (Mark 5:6-13). When the man saw Jesus, he ran to him and fell to his knees in submission (not worship). He cried in a loud voice, asking the Lord to leave him alone. The demons inside of the man knew exactly who Jesus is. The demons called Him the "Son of the most high God" (vs. 7). This is an interesting contrast to the disciples' reaction to the calming of the storm in the previous chapter. They asked who this man was who commanded the wind and waves. The demoniac answered clearly. He is the Son of the Most High God.

The man begged in God's name that Jesus would not torture him. Of course, Jesus knew this was the demons speaking, not the man. He commanded the unclean spirits to come out of the man.

Then Jesus did something here that is abnormal compared to His other confrontation with demons. After telling the spirits to leave the man, He asked for their name. The demons' response is something that would bring fear to others. They said that their name was "Legion" (vs. 9). Instead of a name, they gave a number. In the Roman military, a large unit of over five thousand men was called a legion. This man had many demons living inside him.

Then the demons begged Jesus not to send them out of the area. They enjoyed destroying this man, bringing fear throughout the area, killing the man's relationships, and more. Verse 11 gives a detail that reminds us this was not a Jewish area: there was a large herd of about two thousand pigs on a nearby hillside. The demons begged Jesus to send them into the pigs. He allowed them to leave the man and enter the pigs. The pigs all ran to the steep bank and drowned in the same water that Jesus had previously calmed.

3. The community hears about Jesus and responds (Mark 5:14-20). Just as in our communities today, strange stories travel quickly. Those who took care of the large group of pigs ran back to the town and countryside. That brought a huge crowd to Jesus. They found Jesus and the man who was formerly demon-possessed. He was in his right mind, clothed, and sitting with Jesus. Those who witnessed the event told the story, and those from the town began to plead with Jesus to leave. This could have been a financially motivated request, since two thousand of their pigs had just died.

In verse 18, we read that the formerly demon-possessed man tried to join Jesus as the Lord was getting into the boat. Then we come to our golden text in verse 19: "Howbeit Jesus suffered him not, but saith unto him, Go home to thy friends, and tell them how great things the Lord hath done for thee, and hath had compassion on thee." We see a few amazing things in this verse. The man was no longer homeless living in the tombs. He was told to go home to his friends. The Lord can restore broken relationships! The man became an evangelist by telling everyone what God had done for Him. The man obeyed, and many people in the Decapolis were amazed.

ILLUSTRATING THE LESSON

All who trust in Jesus have been set free. They are no longer slaves to sin, and death is not a threat to them anymore.

CONCLUDING THE LESSON

Not only does the Lord have all power over everything, both the natural and the supernatural, but He also has mercy and compassion. We can bring our problems to Him no matter what they are.

ANTICIPATING THE NEXT LESSON

In our final lesson of the quarter, we will spend time in Isaiah 40 exploring the question, Who is like God?

—Adam Clagg

PRACTICAL POINTS

1. Jesus can help those who are otherwise hopeless (Mark 5:1-5).
2. Remember that demons are real and affect the world (vss. 6-9).
3. People are more important than animals or financial considerations (vss. 10-13).
4. Sometimes when people see the power of God, they reject Him. If we share the gospel and someone does not listen, that does not necessarily mean we have done something wrong (vss. 14-17).
5. Jesus does not always call us to what we would like to do (vss. 18-19).
6. Jesus calls us to share what He has done with our friends and family (vss. 18-20).

—Tom Greene

RESEARCH AND DISCUSSION

1. Do you think unclean spirits were more active during the New Testament period than today? Why or why not?
2. Why did the demons beg Jesus not to torment them (Mark 5:7)? (Refer to Matthew 8 and Luke 8 if needed.)
3. How is this encounter different from other examples in the Bible of Jesus and others casting out demons?
4. Why do you think Jesus allowed the demons to go into the pigs, and why did the pigs drown (Mark 5:13)?
5. Jesus crossed the Sea of Galilee, performed this miracle, and then crossed back over the sea again. What does that tell us about Jesus, and what does it tell us about this miracle?
6. Why do you think Mark included this story in his Gospel?

—Tom Greene

ILLUSTRATED HIGH POINTS

Into the country of the Gadarenes (Mark 5:1)

"I'm from Chicago." "Oh, I used to live there! Where in Chicago?" "I'm from Naperville." If you heard this, you would not accuse the first speaker of lying, even though Naperville is outside of Chicago's city limits. When we talk to someone from out of town, we might say we are from a large city nearby but be more specific with someone who knows the area. Matthew placed this story in the country of the Gergesenes, and Mark identified it with the Gadarenes. That is no contradiction—this was Gentile country. Writing mostly to Gentiles, Mark used the name of the smaller town, while Matthew named the larger city for his mostly Jewish audience.

My name is Legion: for we are many (vs. 9)

Have you ever seen a colony of bats erupt out of a cave at twilight? Certain types of bats form colonies that can number in the millions, and many find watching them emerge in force to be unnerving. We do not know exactly how many demons were in this man, but a Roman legion was over six thousand soldiers, and the demons drove a huge herd of pigs into the sea. That is far worse than a colony of bats! Despite the demons' massive numbers, Jesus has far greater strength than any legion of demons.

Go home to thy friends (vs. 19)

Mission trips can stir our imagination. But what about sharing the Gospel with our neighbors? We do not need to cross oceans to find people in need. Jesus often calls us to go to our friends and family to tell them about the great things He has done. It may not seem glamorous, but the Lord will use this to bear fruit (cf. 7:31-37).

—Tom Greene

Golden Text Illuminated

"Howbeit Jesus suffered him not, but saith unto him, Go home to thy friends, and tell them how great things the Lord hath done for thee, and hath had compassion on thee" (Mark 5:19).

During His earthly ministry, Christ displayed supreme power and control over every realm. Sickness (cf. Mark 1:31); disease (cf. vss. 40-43); physical deformities and incurable paralysis (cf. 3:1-6; John 5:8-9); blindness (cf. John 9:1-7); deafness (cf. Mark 7:31-37); the molecular structure of water (cf. John 2:1-11); the instantaneous production of food (cf. Matt. 14:13-21); storms, the weather, and the sea (cf. Luke 8:22-25); and on and on it goes. Over every aspect of life, Christ shows Himself supreme and sovereign. The purpose of this display, however, needs to be understood. The purpose was not so much to win a large following of disciples but to prove His identity as the messianic King. With each realm over which Christ showed Himself the King, He supplied a sample and a preview of what His future reign and kingdom will be like. Christ demonstrated through His sovereign power that He will bring the planet back to its pre-Fall, paradise conditions when He comes again to establish His kingdom.

One of the other realms over which Christ displayed His sovereign power was the spirit world. He could resist Satan's temptations (cf. Matt. 4:1-11), and He could make the most stubborn and powerful demons cry out in fear and beg for His mercy. One example is the passage in which our golden text is found.

Christ and His disciples arrived at the country of the Gadarenes, which was haunted by a violent, demon-possessed man who could not be subdued (cf. 5:3-4). When Christ walked onto the shore, however, the man with the unclean spirit ran to Christ, bowed down before Him, and pled with Him to spare him from torment (vss. 6-7). Moments later, Jesus removed the demons with ease, displaying His supremacy over the spirit world and restoring a once-troubled soul from eternal destruction. However, when the man asked to accompany Christ on His journey, He refused and said instead, "Go home to thy friends, and tell them how great things the Lord hath done for thee, and hath had compassion on thee" (vs. 19). This scene has powerful implications for our lives today.

First, Christ still has full dominion over the spirit world, even though He is not physically present on earth. We might be frightened at the thought of demons and their attacks, but they still tremble in fear at the Son of God. In Christ, neither Satan nor demons pose any threat at all to our souls.

Second, Christ's compassion for the man reminds us that Christ is not just the supreme authority; He is also a Savior of infinite compassion. He knows and cares about the afflictions we face and will always supply all that we need to endure for the glory of His name.

Third, this scene gives a glimpse of what all the earth will be like in the kingdom of the Son. In that day, all rebels will be subdued, all demonic activity will be down to zero, the nations will be redeemed, the curse of sin will be broken, and Christ will reign. These realities give us courage and joy to persevere through the terrors of a fallen world, knowing that the best is yet to come.

—Jerod A. Gilcher

Heart of the Lesson

For many, fear of the unknown is the greatest fear of all. Yet throughout the Gospels, we see that Jesus Christ has power over the unknown and the unseen. Jesus Christ rules over the things in life we cannot control *as well as* the things in life we cannot see (cf. Col. 1:16), and He does so with supreme, victorious power.

In Mark 5:1-20, Christ encountered a violent man who had been possessed by many demons for a long time. When Christ asked the name of the demon inhabiting the man, the reply was, "Legion: for we are many" (vs. 9). In those days a Roman legion had roughly five thousand soldiers, so this man was potentially controlled by thousands of unseen soldiers of Satan. He could not be bound, tamed, or controlled. The forces of evil inside him were greater than that of human beings.

This man is a picture of our lives today. We are jostled by life and afraid of the unknown. We cannot control the future, we struggle with sin, and the devil seeks our destruction by trying to break our faith. Those factors are enough to drive us to despair, and yet, in Mark 5:1-20, three realities of Christ give us triumphant comfort in the face of the unknown and unseen.

1. The deity of Jesus Christ. Jesus is God. In the scene with the demon-possessed man, we clearly see the deity of Christ. The demons had no choice but to declare His identity as God: "What have I to do with thee, Jesus, thou Son of the most high God?" (Mark 5:7). To be the "Son" of the Most High does not make Jesus less than God but rather clarifies which Person of the Trinity He is. He is God the Son, the Second Person of the Trinity.

In verse 19, after removing the legion of demons from the man, Jesus instructed him, "Go home to thy friends, and tell them how great things *the Lord* hath done for thee" (emphasis added). The man then proceeded to declare what "great things *Jesus* had done for him" (vs. 20; emphasis added). The healed man recognized that what Jesus did, the Lord did! What fear do we need to have of the unseen or unknown? Jesus Christ, God the Son, has supreme power over all the terrors of Satan and this fallen world.

2. The supremacy of Jesus Christ. Satan is not Jesus' equal. There are no beings Jesus did not create and does not control (cf. Col. 1:16). When the possessed man saw Christ, he ran to Him and kneeled in submission (Mark 5:6); the demons knew that Christ had the power to torment them (vs. 7) and that they had to go where Christ commanded (vss. 12-13). Christ easily wrenched the tormented man free from the demons that controlled him and made him an eager and joyful disciple (vss. 18-20).

We need not fear the unseen or unknown. Jesus Christ, the great Tormentor of demons and the Lord of all creation, has all authority in heaven and earth, and everything must do what He commands. We can take comfort in knowing that nothing happens in our lives apart from Christ. He will surely supply the grace we need to endure.

3. The compassion of Jesus Christ. Before leaving, Christ instructed the healed man to tell others how the Lord had "compassion" on him (vs. 19). What a great comfort to us! Jesus is not just the supreme authority but a Savior of infinite compassion. He knows and cares about the afflictions we face, and He will always supply all that we need to endure for the glory of His name.

—Jerod A. Gilcher

World Missions

The visiting missionary had been asked to preach in a church in Bolivia. He had come to the nation to train Bolivians and others from across Latin America to serve cross-culturally among some of the most unreached peoples in the world. As the service was about to begin, he saw a line of about fifteen young men enter the sanctuary, and one of the elders explained to him that these young men were from a local branch of the remarkable Teen Challenge program. Of their own initiative, they had come seeking to be set free from alcohol and drugs. It would be enough if they could just turn the corner to freedom and to living some sort of productive lives.

The missionary smiled as he heard this. Many years ago, he too had been set free from alcohol and drugs. He had realized early on that God had not just set him free for his own sake but to be used by God to help others to experience the same freedom he had found in Jesus.

As he looked at his sermon notes, which challenged Christians to be available to God for missions, he realized that the message was not just for mature Christians but also for those who were still struggling as much as the teens who had just walked in the door. He had been set free so he could reach out to those who had never heard the gospel in a way they could understand. These young men could receive the same challenge. Even though they were just starting out on their journey to freedom, they could begin preparing for God to powerfully use them *in any ministry and in any place where it pleased God to send them.*

Mark 5:1-20 relates Jesus' confrontation of a man inhabited by a "legion" of demons. This was a man whose own pagan society had completely given up on him, for it says that "no man could bind him," not even with a chain, "neither could any man tame him" (vss. 3, 4). It was an impossible situation! He had been left to his own devices, to live in the cemetery outside of town, for not only had everyone given up on attempting to help him, but they were terrified of him.

As it turned out, however, there *was* someone who could help—the One who possessed the power of God against the demonic. He came to this hopeless man and cast out the legion of demons into the herd of pigs nearby. Jesus set the man free from his affliction and so brought order and peace into a situation of utter bondage and chaos.

What was he to do after he had been set free from demonic bondage? He expressed that he wanted to go with Jesus and His disciples, to follow along with them. We see, however, that Jesus had other plans for him. Jesus told him, "Go home to thy friends, and tell them how great things the Lord hath done for thee, and hath had compassion on thee" (vs. 19). So the man did as he was commanded and told the people of his town how much *Jesus* had done for him. Jesus sent him out as a *missionary* to reach out to his own people and prepare the way for the gospel. It seems he was effective (cf. Mark 7:31-35).

As the missionary from our earlier story began to preach, the song "Man of the Tombs" by Christian artist Bob Bennett came into his mind—a song that interprets and applies Mark 5. The missionary thought of how God could very well be preparing the young men in the congregation before him for missionary work, just as He had prepared the man with the legion of demons.

—*Matthew Friedman*

The Jewish Aspect

Sometimes atheists will try to raise this passage and the parallel accounts in Matthew 8 and Luke 8 as supposed evidence of contradictions in the Bible. Where did Jesus and the disciples land? Was it in the region of the Gergesenes or the Gadarenes? Gergasa, Gerasa, and Gadara were all cities. But Gadara was about six miles from the Sea of Galilee, and Gerasa was about twenty-five miles from the Sea of Galilee. It seems obvious that this miracle took place right next to the sea. But why the different readings?

This superficial difficulty can be dealt with easily, and all the differing statements are true. This story took place near the small town of Gergasa by the Sea of Galilee. This town was in the general region associated with Gadara, which was the larger city that the whole region would have been associated with. Professional sports teams may claim the name of a metropolis even though their stadium is technically located in a nearby suburb. There is no reason for us to be concerned about this supposed contradiction between Mark and the other Gospels.

Another issue that critics frequently raise is that Matthew recorded that there were two demon-possessed men (cf. Matt. 8:28-34) while Mark and Luke (cf. Luke 8:26-39) both mentioned only one. Many Christians answer this objection by pointing out that neither Mark nor Luke said that there was *only* one demon-possessed man. This is comparable to the answer to objections about the differences between the number of women named at the resurrection by the various Gospels or the number of angels present at Jesus' tomb.

In Mark 16:1-5, Mary Magdalene went with two other women to the tomb. When they entered the tomb, they saw a young man dressed in white (probably an angel). In John 20:1-12, only Mary Magdalene is mentioned as going to the tomb. When she saw that the stone was rolled away, she ran to tell the disciples. She said, "They have taken away the Lord out of the sepulchre, and we know not where they have laid him." Notice that she said "we," even though she was the only one mentioned by John as going to the tomb. Later, when Mary and some of the disciples went to the tomb, Mary saw two angels in white sitting where Jesus' body had lain (vss. 11-12). Just because someone was not mentioned does not mean that the person was not present. In a few instances, Matthew lists pairs when other Gospel accounts only list one (cf. Matt. 20:29-34; Mark 10:46-52).

In Jesus' day, the tenth Roman legion occupied Judea. They had multiple symbols, one of which was a boar flag. Romans were often compared to swine. Some scholars have made much of the fact that Jesus drove out this "Legion" into a herd of pigs that drowned. They argue that in the first century, hearers of this story would have instantly recognized it as being loaded with political language and as a claim that Jesus could drive out Rome (Dormandy, "The Expulsion of Legion, A Political Reading of Mark 5:1-20," *Expository Times*). Some argue that the parable might also be an echo of Moses leading Israel out of Egypt and of the Red Sea swallowing the Egyptian army (cf. Ex. 14). Not everyone agrees, but either way, anti-Roman rhetoric is not the main point of the story. The authority of Jesus over demons is the main point, and *perhaps* His authority over earthly authorities is implied as well.

—Tom Greene

Guiding the Superintendent

Where would you last expect to hear a testimony of Christ's life-changing power? Christ has power there! Where does Satan seem to have the firmest grasp on people's lives and affections? Jesus went to such a place in today's text.

DEVOTIONAL OUTLINE

1. Setting: Jesus enters a Gentile region (Mark 5:1-2). Jesus entered a pig-farming Gentile region of Gadarenes, home to a legion of demons. Most Jews would have avoided such a place, but Jesus was not afraid to enter enemy territory. What great lengths our Lord goes to in His mission to save the lost!

2. Conflict: Jesus encounters a demon-possessed man (Mark 5:3-7). The demons resided in a man. No one could bind the man, because he broke any chain. But when he saw Jesus, he bowed down and begged Him not to torment him. The demon-possessed man provided affirmation of Christ's omnipotence by showing that demons know of His power over them (cf. Matt. 8:29).

3. Resolution: Jesus authoritatively commands the demons to leave the man (Mark 5:8-13). The turning point in the plot is Jesus' command for the demons to "come out" (vs. 8). Elsewhere, Jesus explained: "But if I cast out devils by the Spirit of God, then the kingdom of God is come unto you" (Matt. 12:28). In the demons' request, they acknowledged they cannot do anything without Jesus' permission (cf. Job 1:6-12). Jesus' power over demons relates to His destroying "him that had the power of death, that is, the devil" (Heb. 2:14).

Together with the previous section, this narrative contributes to the overarching question of Mark 1:1—8:26: Who is Jesus? Mark 5:1-20 answers that Jesus is the omnipotent Lord with authority over all spiritual beings.

4. Result: contrasting responses to the revelation of Jesus' authority (Mark 5:14-20). The townspeople reacted with fear and pleaded for Jesus to leave their region. The proper response, by contrast, was the man desiring to leave everything and follow Jesus (5:18; cf. 1:17). Surprisingly, Jesus, who often told recipients of miracles not to testify (cf. 1:44; 3:12), told the man to proclaim in his hometown everything God had done for Him (5:19).

Why was this man to testify, while others were told not to do so? One possible reason is that the Gentiles did not equate messianic status with a conquering political ruler. The man's testimony would not be heard with misguided messianic expectations but could be marveled at for what it was: evidence that the omnipotent Lord had come to change lives.

Because demon possession is less common in many cultures today than it was during Jesus' ministry, we can sometimes have trouble applying this kind of passage to our lives. One approach is to recognize that idolatry brings about the same end result as demon possession: the complete destruction of a human being (cf. 1 Tim. 6:9). We are often like the townspeople, thinking more about the inconvenience of offering our possessions for God's work than the opportunity to partner in gospel work among the lost.

CHILDREN'S CORNER

Ask the children if they could think of anything more wonderful than seeing Jesus. Tell them how nothing can compare with the life change that results from knowing Jesus. No toy or game, no amount of money can compare with the gift of grace that we have in Christ. The formerly demon-possessed man recognized that, but the townspeople did not.

—Matthew Swale

LESSON 13 NOVEMBER 30, 2025

SCRIPTURE LESSON TEXT

ISA. 40:12 Who hath measured the waters in the hollow of his hand, and meted out heaven with the span, and comprehended the dust of the earth in a measure, and weighed the mountains in scales, and the hills in a balance?

13 Who hath directed the Spirit of the LORD, or *being* his counsellor hath taught him?

14 With whom took he counsel, and *who* instructed him, and taught him in the path of judgment, and taught him knowledge, and shewed to him the way of understanding?

15 Behold, the nations *are* as a drop of a bucket, and are counted as the small dust of the balance: behold, he taketh up the isles as a very little thing.

16 And Lebanon *is* not sufficient to burn, nor the beasts thereof sufficient for a burnt offering.

17 All nations before him *are* as nothing; and they are counted to him less than nothing, and vanity.

NOTES

Who Is like God?

Lesson Text: Isaiah 40:12-17

Related Scriptures: Psalm 33:8-17; Isaiah 41:21-29; Jeremiah 10:1-25; Daniel 4:28-37; Revelation 15:2-4

TIME: about 700-695 B.C. PLACE: Jerusalem

GOLDEN TEXT—"All nations before him are as nothing; and they are counted to him less than nothing, and vanity" (Isaiah 40:17).

Introduction

Many Christians are familiar with Isaiah 40. After thirty-nine chapters of impending judgment and destruction—with only brief respites of hope—the prophet delivered a new message for those who would be exiled in Babylon. One day, the exile would end and give way to freedom. Most popular are the opening verses, which anticipate John the Baptist (Isa. 40:1-3; cf. Matt. 3:3), and the concluding assurance of renewed strength (Isa. 40:29-31). Between these passages lies a series of poetic remarks on God's character.

Verses 12-17 form a coherent unit, which further divides in two. The opening verses (vss. 12-14) contain three sets of rhetorical questions, and the latter portion contains three sets of statements. The opening questions attend to cosmic dimensions, surveying the known world and God's counsel. The subsequent verses (vss. 15-17) shift from cosmology to politics, but the theological force remains. God is unmatched in power and wisdom; nothing compares with Him.

LESSON OUTLINE

1. **QUESTIONS WITHOUT ANSWERS—Isa. 40:12-14**
2. **STATEMENTS WITHOUT RESPONSES—Isa. 40:15-17**

Exposition: Verse by Verse

QUESTIONS WITHOUT ANSWERS

ISA. 40:12 Who hath measured the waters in the hollow of his hand, and meted out heaven with the span, and comprehended the dust of the earth in a measure, and weighed the mountains in scales, and the hills in a balance?

13 Who hath directed the Spirit of the LORD, or being his counsellor hath taught him?

14 With whom took he counsel, and who instructed him, and taught him in the path of judgment, and taught him knowledge, and shewed to him the way of understanding?

The passage's opening questions assume a cosmic focus. Attending to God's universal dominion, will, and knowledge, verses 12-14 invoke images of the Creation in Genesis 1. The prophet's questions were rhetorical—he did not need to provide an answer. To Isaiah and his audience, the response to each was clear. Only the God of Israel enjoys dominion; no one can access His will or knowledge.

The first set (Isa. 40:12). The first set of questions explored the expanse of the created order. Using parallel questions, Isaiah asked who had measured the great dimensions of the cosmos. By offering contrasting elements of the creation, the prophet effectively considered the universe's totality. His questions ranged from the water to the sky and from the earth's dust to the mountains. All creation is under God's dominion.

Underlying verse 12's cosmic survey is a theology of the Creation. {Recalling the order of Genesis 1, Isaiah progressed from the waters (Gen. 1:2-6) to the sky (vss. 7-8) to the earth (vs. 9).}[Q1] As we saw in lesson 1, the Old Testament offers a story of the Creation distinct from the creation myths of the ancient Near East.

The force of this contrast was most impactful in times of oppression and captivity. Many believed that military conquest reflected the superiority of the victor's gods over the gods of the defeated. The Jews exiting seventy years of exile bore the burden of that ancient theology. Many undoubtedly wrestled with the notion that Babylon's Marduk was greater than Israel's Yahweh. Isaiah, however, left no room for that. In his message of hope, the prophet dismantled a familiar Babylonian prayer to emphasize Yahweh's sole dominion.

Those seasoned by exile were familiar with the myths that shaped Babylon's religious life. Thus, Isaiah's allusion to its texts would have struck a chord with the ancient audience. Each year, the Babylonians recited their New Year Festival prayer to Marduk and other gods. In it they asked, "Who measures the water of the sea?" To this they answered, "Marduk." The question also reflected the Babylonian creation myth *Enuma Elish*. In it, Marduk proclaimed that he "measured the shape of Apsu," the freshwater deity.

In similar words, Isaiah asked who measured the waters in his hand. Although this echo may appear at first to equate Yahweh with Marduk, the text does just the opposite. To each question in the passage, the implied answer is "no one." Only Yahweh exercises dominion and counsel. {Isaiah's Babylonian-style question, then, delivered a theological punch to Israel's enemy. Marduk is nothing.}[Q2] No one is comparable to God, including the assemblies of gods revered by surrounding people groups.

Continuing his theological assault of Judah's captors, the prophet asked who had meted, or measured, the sky. Once again, those familiar with Babylon's religious life understood. Here, "meted" is more than the assessment of an item's dimensions. It denotes directing, determining, and ordering. The Babylonian Empire was fascinated by the night sky for that reason. Their astrologers sought to uncover the fate of individuals and empires. They believed the sky revealed destinies.

Interacting with that religious background, Isaiah articulated a different view: {Humanity is not subject to the sky's destiny. The sky is subject to God. Yahweh alone knows and directs the future.}[Q3]

Beyond its refutation of Babylonian theology, verse 12 introduced a second dimension of creation theology. God is the architect of the universe, using measuring instruments and techniques. In each question, Isaiah described God's trivial means of evaluation. The great expanse of the world is minute to Him. The waters fit in the cup of His hand. The span from His thumb to pinky finger contains the sky. He measures the mountains and hills on scales.

God's role as architect is also evident in two other Old Testament Creation accounts. In the divine speeches of Job 38 through 41, God described how He created all things. He laid the earth's foundation (38:4), fixed its dimensions and measured it (vs. 5), closed the sea behind doors (vs. 8), and set its limit (vs. 11). His acts were not spontaneous or miscalculated. As an architect meticulously designs structures on the blueprint, God created the cosmos with precision.

Likewise, Isaiah 40:12's set of rhetorical questions echoes Proverbs 8:22-31. {There, Wisdom personified describes her experience of the Creation. She was a spectator to God's craftsmanship, watching Him construct the cosmos.}[Q4] She watched God set up the sky on columns (Prov. 8:27-28*a*), confine the waters (vss. 28*b*-29*a*), and create the foundations of the earth (vs. 29*b*). Her presence at Creation, however, was not arbitrary or irrelevant. By noting Wisdom's place at the beginning, the text emphasizes the wisdom and purpose that motivated God's creative act. This resonates with both the wisdom orientation of Isaiah 40 through 55 and the questions that followed.

The second set (Isa. 40:13). With Wisdom's view of Creation in mind, the prophet presented the next series of questions. These concern God's will. Unlike the previous verse, verse 13 offers only two questions, succinctly driving the poem forward. They focus on God's Spirit and His counsel, respectively.

Verse 13 asked who has "directed" God's Spirit. Here, Isaiah's point is clear: no one is above God's Spirit. But the word is more nuanced than a cursory reading suggests. This is the same verb used in verse 12, which asked who "meted out" the sky.

As discussed earlier, Babylonian religion was fond of astrology, understanding the night sky to disclose destinies. Yet, as Isaiah retorted, God directs the movements of the sky. He alone understands our fate. In verse 13, Isaiah completed his refutation of Babylonian astrology. While the supposed source of fates follows God's directions, no one directs God's Spirit. {He is unmatched, free from outside manipulation. His Spirit is self-directing; no one directs, determines, or measures it.}[Q5]

Verse 13's second question emphasized that point. No one can counsel God. The religious milieu of Isaiah's day imagined a council of divine beings, with the lower deities advising the chief god. This is not so with Yahweh. He is the sole God of the cosmos, and no one directs Him in counsel. As Psalm 82 pointedly puts it, the so-called gods of the nations are mortals destined to die (vs. 7). Like Marduk, they are nothing.

The third set (Isa. 40:14). The final set of questions picked up where verse 13 left off. Emphasizing his previous point, the prophet asked from whom God seeks counsel. The answer, of course, is no one. No one advises Him (vs. 13), and He seeks no one's advice (vs. 14). The supposed counselors of deities have neither knowledge nor understanding. They stumble in the darkness (Ps. 82:5).

Isaiah continued this stream of thought in the subsequent questions, surfacing the Proverbial themes submerged in the text. In parallel fashion, the prophet questioned who can give God understanding or teach Him justice, knowledge, or wisdom. With the force of the previous verses mounting, the answer nearly explodes off the page. No one. The God who meticulously measures the expanse of the cosmos and created all things with Wisdom beside Him needs no teacher. No one knows the cosmos like its Creator. No one directs or informs the mind of God.

STATEMENTS WITHOUT RESPONSES

15 Behold, the nations are as a drop of a bucket, and are counted as the small dust of the balance: behold, he taketh up the isles as a very little thing.

16 And Lebanon is not sufficient to burn, nor the beasts thereof sufficient for a burnt offering.

17 All nations before him are as nothing; and they are counted to him less than nothing, and vanity.

Despite the stylistic shift in the next three verses, the prophet drove his theological principle forward. Here, Isaiah turned from the grandeur of the cosmos and God's counsel to the political landscape. He began and ended with general statements and narrowed in on a particular location in between. {Isaiah's discussion of Lebanon should serve as a model that we can apply to any nation.}[Q6]

The first set (Isa. 40:15). Continuing with the measurement imagery introduced in verse 12, Isaiah assessed the gravity of the nations. Undoubtedly, a people retreating from years of Babylonian exile felt they had a sufficient grasp of the weight of the nations. Assyria, Babylon, and now Persia were massive tyrants. Their weight was crushing.

Yet seemingly immense things are minute to God. If the waters fit in His hand and the mountains rest on His balances, how much smaller must the nations be to Him? He reckons them a drop of water in a bucket and dust on a scale. All the nations—from small city-states to domineering empires—are like specks of dust or a drop of water to God.

Similarly, Isaiah looked toward the isles. These distant bodies of land were the poetic counterpart to the nations. The political coalitions that roamed the land were dust to God. Likewise, the outermost regions of the continent, residing along the edge of the known world, were fine dust to God. No nation, near or far, bears weight before God.

When we consider Israel's history, verse 15's significance quickly grows apparent. As the Old Testament recounted, God's people experienced several waves of imposing might. {Already, Israel had suffered enslavement in Egypt, periods of Canaanite submission, Assyrian deportation, and Babylonian exile. Before the returning Jews stood a coming span of imperial dominance. Babylon gave way to Persia. Persia gave way to Greece. Greece gave way to Rome.}[Q7] Certainly, the weight of the nations felt heavy. Yet they are frivolous to God. They have no sway or power over Him. Instead, they yield to Him.

The second set (Isa. 40:16). After establishing the state of the nations before God, the prophet turned to one region in particular: Lebanon.

Lebanon was Israel's northern neighbor, residing along the coast of the Mediterranean Sea. Lebanon did not host a kingdom that warred against Israel. Instead, it was passed between kingdoms and empires. It was even briefly under Israelite control during Solomon's reign (cf. 1 Kgs. 9:19).

Due to fortuitous weather and agricultural conditions, the coastal mountain region was replete with wildlife, copper, iron, and wine. Its forests yielded pine, fire, cypress, and cedar trees. That wealth of timber drew nations throughout the ancient Near East to the region. Even the conquering empire Assyria demanded timber from it.

The sudden shift from a larger focus to a smaller one is neither accidental nor insignificant. The prophet used the famed northern region to construct a powerful argument. If even great Lebanon was insufficient, how much less so were the other regions? Lebanon's wealth and abundance only emphasized God's greatness.

The Old Testament largely discussed Lebanon favorably, as its proliferation of timber and wildlife proved valuable to Israel and Judah. Yet even its abundance of wood and wildlife fell short. {The surplus of its forests could not supply enough wood for sacrificial fires. That was true of its animals as well.}[Q8]

An important detail intensifies the line. Isaiah did not write that Lebanon's clean and ceremonial animals were not enough. He proclaimed that all beasts—appropriate or inappropriate for Levitical sacrifice—were not enough. That latter category, which far outnumbers the former, would not satisfy God. Lebanon simply was not big enough.

Although the prophet's driving point in verse 16 was the northern region's lack before the infinite God, his example recalls a peripheral point. In Psalm 50, God declared that every animal of the forest and the wildlife of a thousand mountains are His (vs. 10). {No animal sacrifice, even if it drained Lebanon of its wildlife, is sufficient. Instead, we are to offer a sacrifice of thanksgiving (vs. 14), praising the Architect of the cosmos for all He has done.}[Q9]

The third set (Isa. 40:17). Concluding the section, Isaiah returned to his dismissal of the nations. Whereas verse 15 regarded them as nearly nothing—mere droplets and dust—verse 17 states that they are less than nothing. Unlike the Creation narratives that Isaiah echoed in the previous lines, verse 17 described nations that had descended from ordered creation to chaos. Their description descended from resembling nothing to resembling less than nothing.

{The nations' final descriptor, "vanity," also means chaotic formlessness and fits firmly in the Creation theology Isaiah composed throughout. The idea of formlessness first appears in the second verse of the Bible, where it describes the pre-ordered state of the cosmos.}[Q10] Before God spoke, the universe was chaotic and formless. And the nations appear chaotic and formless in comparison to the Architect, who orders all things. The universe and all that inhabit it pale in comparison to the Creator of the cosmos.

—Andrew Rudolf

QUESTIONS

1. How does Isaiah imitate Genesis 1?
2. Why did Isaiah use language from a familiar Babylonian prayer?
3. How did the prophet express a view of the night sky different from Babylon's?
4. According to Proverbs 8, who watched God create the cosmos?
5. What does the word choice in Isaiah 40:13 suggest about God's Spirit?
6. How is Isaiah's mention of Lebanon applicable today?
7. How does Israel's history magnify God's might over the nations?
8. Which resources of Lebanon fell short before God?
9. What sacrifices does God ask of us?
10. What does the word "vanity" recall in verse 17?

—Andrew Rudolf

Preparing to Teach the Lesson

This week, we will conclude the quarter with a focus on God's greatness and sovereignty.

TODAY'S AIM

Facts: to explore what the Bible says about the greatness of God.

Principle: to understand that nothing and no one can compare to God.

Application: to submit to our sovereign Savior.

INTRODUCING THE LESSON

If we explored the entire universe throughout all history, we would never find anyone who can compare to the Lord. He is great in every way and in complete control of every aspect of His creation. Isaiah 40:12-17 is a longer description of verse 9's statement, "Behold your God!"

DEVELOPING THE LESSON

1. Creation points to God's greatness (Isa. 40:12-14). Our text begins with rhetorical questions. Teachers use rhetorical questions to help learners grasp a topic. The questions are not meant to be answered because the answer is obvious: no one. Using these questions, the prophet Isaiah described the Lord's awesome power and unlimited wisdom in the act of creation and in ruling all creation.

In verse 12, the prophet asked who has measured the waters in the hollow of his hand. It is amazing to picture all the water of the world easily fitting in the cupped hand of God. The prophet continued by asking who has measured the heavens. Then we are asked who has held the dust of the earth. Who has weighed the mountains or put the hills on a balance? Of course, none of us could attempt such a feat, but God could without any difficulty.

Comparing the Lord to an architect and contractor, verse 13 asks who advised Him. Those who build things typically go through an apprenticeship. God did not need that process. He did not need advice on the "job site" of creation. He did not need someone to teach or counsel Him about what to do.

The reference to the Spirit reminds us of the Holy Spirit's role in Creation (cf. Gen. 1:2). Isaiah 40:13 is quoted by Paul in Romans 11:34 and 1 Corinthians 2:16.

The Lord has perfect judgment. He is always right and fair, and He does not need someone to counsel Him. God has all knowledge. He understands everything in the universe, and no one had to show Him. How could anyone come close to comparing with Him?

Jeremiah 10 shares an interesting contrast between the Creator God and the idols that people create with their hands. How ridiculous it is to compare the Lord to idols that were made with the wood, silver, and gold that He created! These idols cannot speak. They cannot walk, so they must be carried.

In Isaiah 41:21-29, the Lord invited the idols to defend themselves and prove that they are gods by explaining ancient mysteries or prophesying the future. They were invited to do something . . . anything, good or evil! Since the false gods cannot do anything, Yahweh declared that they are less than nothing and worthless. They cannot defend themselves, and they cannot defend those who worship them.

2. The universe revolves around God, not us (Isa. 40:15-17). People tend to focus on themselves. Some people are involved in the lives of others. We know humanity is important to God, and He loved us so much that He gave His one and only Son for our salvation. But in comparison to God, we are nothing. Verses 15-17 use dramatic language to remind us of that fact.

Look at the illustrations used by God's prophet: the nations of the world are like a drop in a bucket. That is easy to visualize. Think of all the nations and rulers of the world who think they are amazing. In comparison to God, they all are just one drop of water in an empty bucket. Would you even take the time to bother drying one little drop of water in a bucket?

Isaiah also compared the nations to dust on a set of scales. Even when we are weighing something valuable, a little bit of dust does not make much difference. Even the beautiful islands of the world are not counted as important.

Lebanon was known for its amazing trees. The cedars of Lebanon are mentioned in multiple places in the Bible. Psalm 92:12 says, "The righteous . . . shall grow like a cedar in Lebanon." Yet Isaiah 40:16 says that Lebanon's trees were not sufficient to burn as fuel for an offering. Even the animals found in the mountains of Lebanon are not sufficient for a burnt offering to God.

Verse 17 makes it clear that we should never compare the nations of the world to God. All the nations before Him are as nothing. They are counted (or regarded) by God as less than nothing.

Psalm 33:8 says that all the earth should fear the Lord. Every inhabitant of the world should stand in awe. Verse 12 adds: "Blessed is the nation whose God is the Lord; and the people whom he hath chosen for his own inheritance."

Whenever a monarch, president, governor, or mayor thinks he or she is like God, or whenever we are tempted to fear political leaders unduly, we should read Daniel 4:28-37 and be reminded of how God humbled King Nebuchadnezzar. The powerful king of Babylon believed he had created his nation by his own mighty power, so God taught him a lesson in humility.

The king lost his mind and began eating grass as an ox would. He lived outside and was covered in dew. His hair grew like an eagle's feathers and his nails like birds' claws. But that humiliation taught Him to honor and respect the Lord God. He praised the Most High. When he publicly acknowledged the true King of the universe, his mind and body were restored to him, and later his reign was as well.

ILLUSTRATING THE LESSON

We submit to the sovereign Ruler of the cosmos.

CONCLUDING THE LESSON

God is great and mighty, ruling even over those who do not believe in Him. He is completely self-sufficient, and no power is worth comparing to Him. We should willingly worship, serve, and submit to the great and powerful God of the Bible—Yahweh.

ANTICIPATING THE NEXT LESSON

Next week we begin a new quarter. The theme is "God, the Holy One." We will study His holy presence, His holy house, and His holy expectation.

—Adam Clagg

PRACTICAL POINTS

1. In the face of challenges, we should remember that God holds the world in His hand (Isa. 40:12).
2. We can never try to manipulate God. Instead, we should rest in the comfort that what God has planned will come to pass (vs. 13).
3. God is the source of wisdom. We should seek His guidance in all that we do (vs. 14).
4. When we are burdened by politics, we can rest assured that God is greater than the nations (vs. 15).
5. God is far greater than anything the world can offer (vs. 16).
6. No obstacle can ever stand in God's way. He counts even the nations as nothing (vs. 17).

—Andrew Rudolf

RESEARCH AND DISCUSSION

1. If even the cosmos is minute to God (Isa. 40:12), how can God be personal with us (cf. John 1:14)?
2. Isaiah stated that no one can understand God's mind (Isa. 40:13). How, then, can Christians know God's will in their lives? How has God revealed Himself to us?
3. All the animals of Lebanon were insufficient for sacrifice (Isa. 40:16). What implications does that have for sacrifice (cf. Hos. 6:6)? What does that say about the gravity of Christ's sacrifice (cf. Heb. 10)?
4. If God counts the nations as nothing (Isa. 40:15, 17), does He care about the political affairs of the world (cf. Gen. 12:2-3)? How should Christians approach governments and their nations (cf. Rom. 13:1-7)?

—Andrew Rudolf

ILLUSTRATED HIGH POINTS

Weighed the mountains in scales (Isa. 40:12)

Scientists cannot be sure how much mountains weigh. They can estimate based on the size and the types of rock they think are inside, but without knowing the exact composition of a mountain (which no one can), it is only an estimate. Scientists estimate that Mount Everest weighs 357 trillion pounds. That is *far* more than the weight of every human being on earth added together! But what we can only estimate and find staggeringly large, God considers dust!

Who instructed him (vs. 14)

Isaiah made it clear that no one can match God's mind. He is the infinite Creator. We can never fully understand Him or His ways. Augustine put it this way: "To touch God a little with our mind is a great blessing, to grasp him is impossible." Praise God that through Christ we can grasp Him even a little!

And Lebanon is not sufficient to burn (vs. 16)

Scientists estimate that the earth is home to over 3.04 trillion trees! That is over 400 trees per person. Today some of the countries with the highest density of trees are Sweden, Taiwan, Slovenia, and French Guiana. In the ancient Near East, however, Lebanon won the prize.

The coastal mountain region was replete with wildlife, copper, iron, and wine. Its forests yielded pine, fir, cypress, and cedar trees. That wealth of timber drew nations throughout the Near East. Cedar from the region was the primary building material of Solomon's temple.

Yet even that mighty forest and its beasts could not offer enough burnt offerings to the Lord, who is infinitely greater than we can imagine!

—Andrew Rudolf

Golden Text Illuminated

"All nations before Him are as nothing; and they are counted to Him less than nothing, and vanity" (Isaiah 40:17).

Facing the worst crisis in their nation's history, Judah had the reality of exile coming in their future. After decades of Judah's unfaithfulness and idolatry, the prophet Isaiah declared certain doom and destruction for the people of God. Sure enough, around 120 years later, in 586 B.C., the armies of Babylon invaded the land, stormed the gates, leveled Jerusalem to the ground, and took the people captive.

Catastrophic though this was, it was not the end of Judah as a nation. God had made irrevocable promises for a hope, a future, a kingdom, and a prominent role in the world as God's blessing to the nations (cf. Gen. 12:3; Deut. 7:6). The question is: how could the nation go from here to there? How could they go from being scattered in captivity to being restored to royalty? Normally in the ancient Near East, nations did not recover from exile—they simply became extinct!

How could Judah have the assurance that God not only makes promises but keeps them? What could sustain their souls that were grim with despair and give them assurance their future was secure? There was but one answer: the matchless supremacy of an incomparable God. That is the point of Isaiah 40. It is a densely packed theological display of the majesty of God, but it is not theology for no purpose! It is the kind of theology that reinforces the heart with bulletproof steel, that calibrates the soul, and that supplies undaunted courage to face the terrors of a fallen world.

In our golden text, we see God's utter transcendence and supremacy over the nations of the world. Isaiah declared, "All nations before him are as nothing; and they are counted to him less than nothing, and vanity." This text is staggering news for us today, and it supplies us with two badly needed insights to face a world that is filled with terror.

1. The chaos and rage of the nations poses no challenge to God's supremacy. In declaring that the nations are as "nothing" to God, Isaiah did not mean He does not love the world but that, compared to who He is in His limitless perfections, it is as if the nations do not even exist. Although they rebel and seek to thwart His plan, they change nothing about His fundamental nature as God. At the end of the day, the nations could be here or *not* be here, and it would change nothing about God's perfections.

2. The chaos and rage of the nations poses no challenge to God's plan. While the rage of the nations might create a feeling of insecurity in *our* hearts, the Holy One has no such response (cf. Ps. 2). Despite the world's best efforts to hinder what God has decreed, His plan will always be "Plan A." The underlying point of Isaiah 40:17 (and all of Isaiah 40) is that who God is in His own majesty is the reason we *know* that everything is part of a good plan. The greatest proof that God will fulfill His plan is God Himself. The supremacy of God is our certainty for the future!

Therefore, as God's people, we pray for the nations, and we preach to the nations, knowing that because God is who He is, our praying and preaching are not in vain.

—Jerod A. Gilcher

Heart of the Lesson

Every question on a test requires an answer. But there are some questions for which the only answer is silence. Those are the kinds of questions Isaiah asked in chapter 40 about the supremacy of God.

In verse 1 God declared future comfort coming for His people Israel. The proof that God could make good on His promise of comfort was a riveting display of His matchless supremacy. Isaiah asked a series of rhetorical questions designed to drive home to Israel (and to us!) just how matchless God really is. The more we come to grips with who God is in His absolute supremacy, the more we will experience spiritual comfort in our lives.

Question 1 (Isa. 40:12*a*). "Who hath measured the waters in the hollow of his hand?" The implied answer to that question, of course, is God alone. The point is not that God has hands, let alone a giant hand in which He literally measures the volume of the oceans. Rather, the point is that the seas and oceans of the world—massive, dangerous, and unable to be tamed by humans—are ruled with ease by the greatness of God's power.

Question 2 (Isa. 40:12*b*). Who "meted out heaven with the span"? Again, the obvious answer is God, and the point is not that He has a hand or has to measure anything but rather that the endless stretches of space that not even NASA will ever see belong to Him. There is nowhere He does not rule and have dominion.

Question 3 (Isa. 40:12*c*). Who "comprehended the dust of the earth in a measure"? Answer? God, and God alone. It is not as if God has scales or a balance with which He weighs anything. Instead, the question means that God alone has authority over creation, down to the tiniest particle, because He alone created it.

Question 4 (Isa. 40:12*d*). Who "weighed the mountains in scales, and the hills in a balance?" God has no need to weigh anything, since He already knows all things, but the point is clear: the towering mountains and peaks that rightly take our breath away are but tiny glimpses of the God who made them. Our God is invincible and worthy of trust.

Question 5 (Isa. 40:13). "Who hath directed the Spirit of the Lord, or being His counsellor hath taught him?" Who has the power to control the Holy Spirit or make Him do something the Father has not sent Him to do? Silence is the right answer.

Question 6 (Isa. 40:14). "With whom took he counsel, and who instructed him, and taught him in the path of judgment, and taught Him knowledge, and shewed to him the way of understanding?" The only way to answer those questions is to leave the answer blank. No one has ever done those things for God, because He has infinite and immediate knowledge of all things forever.

The incomparability of God (Isa. 40:15-17). By now, Isaiah's purpose is clear: to overwhelm us with the matchless supremacy of God. In comparison to God, all the nations of the world are as nothing (vss. 15-17).

Isaiah 40 exists partly to explain where comfort in a fallen world comes from. Until we can say with absolute confidence, "There is no one like God!" we will always be plagued by the fears and dangers of life. But the cure to crippling fear is the unshakable comfort that comes when the supremacy of God moves us to silence and awe.

—Jerod A. Gilcher

World Missions

In 1818, two renowned English poets, Percy Bysshe Shelley and Horace Smith, both published poems entitled "Ozymandias." Both poems were inspired by the discovery and eventual transport to England from Egypt of a large sculpture of the bust of the great Egyptian Pharaoh Ramesses II. (Ozymandias is the Greek version of his name.)

In Shelley's more famous poem, he narrates a traveler's discovery of a derelict, damaged statue amid ruins in the desert. His concluding lines have stood as a kind of warning concerning the folly of pride:

> "My name is Ozymandias, King of Kings;
> Look on my Works, ye Mighty, and despair!"
> Nothing beside remains. Round the decay
> Of that colossal Wreck, boundless and bare
> The lone and level sands stretch far away.

Ramesses II was surely a remarkable king and one of the great builders of ancient Egypt. I have seen the impressive bust of Ramesses that inspired the poem, along with the many statues, temples, and other art and architecture left behind by Ramesses.

Although there are multiple viewpoints concerning this, Ramesses II is considered by some scholars to have possibly been the pharaoh during the Israelites' exodus, which we read about a few weeks ago. Pharaoh oppressed the Israelites and mocked their God when challenged by Moses to let God's people go. Certainly, Ramesses II built many remarkable public works with the aim of glorifying himself, but unlike the works of God, many of his works eventually crumbled and fell.

A number of years ago, I was in Delhi, India. There are many ancient monuments there built by various kingdoms and dynasties, and some are in a better state of preservation than others. At a major traffic circle in New Delhi is an ancient mausoleum, built in the fourteenth century. It was once a stately building, erected in celebration of the life of a great ruler and military leader with a lofty title. Yet now, that tomb stands neglected, covered with graffiti and marooned on a traffic island in a busy part of the city.

Many of us are "news junkies," constantly checking our screens or phones for the latest update on the news of the day. It is easy, and in a way understandable, to be drawn in by those updates and the endless waves of terribly negative news from around the world. All too often we are tempted to respond with fear or anger. A better approach would be to take the news as fuel for prayer.

The Scriptures help give us the proper perspective on world events and what is going on among the nations. Isaiah notes that "the nations are as a drop of a bucket, and are counted as the small dust of the balance," because before God, the nations are "as nothing" (Isa. 40:15, 17). The psalmist similarly reminds us that "the counsel of the Lord standeth for ever, the thoughts of his heart to all generations (Ps. 33:11).

God reigns supreme, and God's purposes will be fulfilled in His church, among His people, and among the nations in His mission. We remember that missions itself is first and foremost the work of God—the work of proclamation and service that He is already doing and in which He invites us to join Him.

—Matthew Friedman

The Jewish Aspect

One notable difference between the practice of Judaism and Christianity is the religions' attitude toward missions. Although missions are central to the process of discipleship and the life of the church, few Jews focus on sharing their faith with others.

The diminution of the nations in our passage delivered a message Isaiah's audience desperately needed. Yet when we break through the text's original setting and attempt to generalize the text, pressing questions emerge. What does the Hebrew Bible say about its readers' attitude toward the nations?

Even in the book of Isaiah, the attitude toward the nations is not monolithic. In some places, the prophet spoke harshly against them. Isaiah 34 contains a long rebuke of the nations, identifying God's rage and desire to destroy them (vs. 2). Even the latter portion of Isaiah—a section dominated by encouragement and hope—compares the nations to grapes that God will squash in His winepress. He will tread down the peoples (63:3, 6). Elsewhere, however, the prophet presented the nations favorably. The second chapter of the book describes the nations gathering to Zion to learn about God (vss. 2-3). At that time, there will no longer be battle or war, for God will be their Judge (vs. 4). In the book's concluding verses, Isaiah described all nations and languages gathering to see God's glory (66:18). He will send people to distant lands and islands to proclaim His glory among the nations (vs. 19).

If even individual books exhibit such variation in their treatment of the nations, how can Christians adopt a biblical perspective on the matter? The key is finding them along God's redemptive history. The theological story arc that Scripture contains provides coherence and continuity to the nations.

After the Fall, humanity descended into wickedness at an accelerating rate. In the first eleven chapters of Genesis, human sin took the global stage, and whole nations epitomized the fallen state (cf. 11:1-9). But God had a plan. In the next chapter, He called Abraham and his family, promising He would bless the nations through them (12:1-3). The nations stood against God, but He desired to redeem them. As Israel's history unfolded, various nations and empires opposed God's people and His plan for the world. God poured out His wrath against them. However, even the worst of nations was not doomed without warning and opportunities to repent. As God explained to Jeremiah at the potter's shop, He will always restore wicked nations that turn to Him (Jer. 18:7-8). That is what Jonah witnessed in Nineveh (Jonah 3:6-10).

Ultimately, God's promise to Abraham finds fulfillment in Jesus. Through Him and the church, the nations are blessed. After Christianity spread throughout Jerusalem and Judea, it expanded to other regions, growing until it reached the known world. In the final chapter of the Bible, John saw the River of Life flowing through the New Jerusalem. Along it grew the Tree of Life with therapeutic leaves. Those leaves are for the healing of the nations (Rev. 22:2). That is the culmination of God's promise to Abraham and His mission of redemption. God will restore creation, and He will welcome the redeemed nations to gather in a new garden, where leaves for their healing will grow in abundance.

—Andrew Rudolf

Guiding the Superintendent

What are the top things needed to run a successful government? What causes some governments to lose or lack them? Today's text compares the rule of God with the rule of the nations, highlighting that He possesses all the wisdom and strength needed to rule the world.

DEVOTIONAL OUTLINE

1. The incomparable Lord (Isa. 40:12-14). Even as Judah endured conquest under powerful nations, Isaiah depicted the Lord's strength as incomparably greater than any nation. The seas that hindered Assyria's and Babylon's imperial expansion fit "in the hollow his hand" (vs. 12).

The passage after Isaiah 40:12-17 addressed the inefficacy of idols (vss. 18-20), and for ancient people, idols were closely associated with the nations that worshipped those idols. When a nation prevailed over another, the people involved assumed the victor's gods to be stronger than the defeated people's gods (cf. 36:18-20). That also explains why the pained people of Judah needed to hear about the incomparability of the Lord.

First, Isaiah declared the incomparable sovereignty of the Lord (40:12). Assyria's and Babylon's affliction of Judah was not proof of God's weakness. Instead, in His wisdom God uses wicked nations like Assyria and Babylon for His purposes and then discards them in judgment when His purposes are completed (cf. Hab. 1:6; 2:6-8).

Next, Isaiah declared the incomparable wisdom of the Lord (Isa. 40:13-14). The Lord possesses within Himself the wisdom to govern the world's affairs justly. The rhetorical questions in Isaiah verses 12-14 imply that the listeners were doubting these truths about the Lord's sovereignty and wisdom. The audience was grieving (vs. 1), weary (vss. 28-31), and saying, "My way is hid from the Lord, and my judgment is passed over from my God" (vs. 27). Judah needed to reaffirm the all-powerful, all-wise nature of the one true God.

2. The insignificant nations (Isa. 40:15-17). Missions-minded participants may wonder why Isaiah considered the nations "as nothing" (vs. 17) when other passages express the Lord's love for all nations (cf. Gen. 12:3; Matt. 28:19-20). Isaiah 40:15-17 considers the nations insignificant in a specific sense: as arbiters of the destiny of God's people. Although circumstances made the nations look like the ultimate determiners of the future, the Lord allowed them no input into His people's future (vs. 14).

The Lord rules the nations with the ease of carrying "a bucket" containing a single "drop" or hoisting "small dust" to a scale (vs. 15). Since the nations are "nothing" compared to the Lord (vs. 17), He can and will use them to move world history along His planned course for His glory and the good of His people.

So glorious is the Lord that Lebanon, renowned for its magnificent cedar trees (cf. Ps. 29:5), did not have enough forests to give an offering worthy of Him (Isa. 40:16).

CHILDREN'S CORNER

In the home, children benefit when their parents are stable in their relationship with God and with each other. That makes children feel safe. But even children who experience less-than-ideal home situations have the benefit of the stabilizing power of the matchless God of the universe.

—Matthew Swale

EDITORIAL

(Continued from page 3)

This sort of knowledge is far beyond our comprehension.

The fact that God knows everything should be greatly comforting for us for many reasons. He is never surprised by unexpected circumstances. He is never caught off guard and unsure of what is best. He always has a plan and knows how things will work out (cf. Isa. 46:10).

When God first saved us, He knew all the ways that we would fail. He knew that Peter would deny Him (Matt. 26:31-35). He knew that Adam and Eve would sin before He created them, and He already had a plan to send Jesus to die (Eph. 1:3-4; Rev. 13:8). We can never sin so badly that God will say, "What? If I had known that *this* was coming, I would not have saved you." He already knew how we would fail and sin when He saved us. If we are willing to truly repent, we can be confident that we have not crossed some line that God did not foresee, and He will always forgive us.

Additionally, given how often people (particularly teenagers) complain that "nobody understands me," the fact that God perfectly knows our hearts and understands us should be comforting. He knows all the difficult circumstances we have endured, and He knows all the pain that we feel. This is not the cold, impersonal knowledge of a distant observer either. Because Jesus became fully and truly human, He has personal, experiential knowledge of human emotions and suffering (Heb. 2:17-18; 4:14-16). He has both the big picture of everything that happens in history and the firsthand experience of a participant.

God's omniscience is also comforting because we know that our prayers do not inform God of what we need (cf. Matt. 6:31-33). God is not left scrambling to respond and deal with surprises. He already knows all our needs, but He delights to answer our requests. Prayer is not how He learns about our problems. It is how we come to Him as His children. The fact that He already knows our needs does not mean that we need not pray! God responds to our prayers (Jas. 4:2), and we should come to Him with anything, big or small (Phil. 4:6).

God knows everything that has happened in the past, everything going on in the present, and everything that will happen in the future. He knows about massive world events, as well as what we think and feel. Jesus has both the overall view of history and the personal perspective of someone who has experienced the joys and tears of life. God is all-knowing, and this is a great comfort.

In the beginning, God created everything by simply speaking (Gen. 1). He upholds everything that currently exists (Heb. 1:3). All the might of all the nations on earth are like nothing compared to Him, and no one can oppose Him (Dan. 4:35; Isa. 43:13). His might is insurmountable.

God has demonstrated His unparalleled power in countless ways. Creating everything with a word was a staggering display of power but only the beginning of what we see in Scripture. God flooded the earth as judgment upon sin (Gen. 7). He sent powerful plagues upon Egypt, bringing one of the most powerful nations on earth and all their gods to their knees (Ex. 12:12). He caused the Red Sea to part for the people of Israel so that they could cross (14:10-22). Imagine walking upon the bed of a sea, with hundreds of feet of water standing in a wall on either side of you!

Jesus displayed this same power over creation when He instantly calmed a violent storm with a command (Mark 4:35-41) and when He completely and permanently cured people of diseases that had plagued them for years (Luke 13:16). Not only that, but He raised the dead (John 11:43-44)!

While He was on earth, Jesus healed many people by merely touching them. So great was His power that He could heal from a distance, without even seeing the person (Luke 7:1-10)! In addition to being able to heal people, God can impart wisdom as no one else can (1 Cor. 2:6-16). He can send us unexpected and undeserved blessings. In fact, every good gift is from God (Jas. 1:17)!

There are opposing forces, of course. Not everyone peacefully submits to God's rule. But when men sought to establish their own kingdom and build a tower so high it reached heaven, God *came down* to see their tower (Gen. 11:5-7) because it was so small and pitiful. Then He confused their languages in a display of His might. When demons oppose God, they fare no better. Jesus cast a legion of demons out of a man easily (Mark 5:1-20), and they know that their time is short (Matt. 8:29; Rev. 12:12) and that they are doomed to the abyss (Luke 8:31; Rev. 20:7-10). Even the most powerful and vicious of God's foes are powerless before Him.

In light of God's infinite power over everything, we must conclude that truly no one is like Him and that He is completely unmatched (cf. Isa. 40). But that sometimes leads to questions. If God is so powerful, why do we see evil? Further, impertinent questioners often ask questions such as "Can God create a rock so big He cannot lift it?"

God can do anything that He wishes (Ps. 115:3). Another way to put that would be to say that He can do anything *consistent with His character.* Although subtle, this qualifier is an important guard against cheeky questioners who ask why God cannot lie (Titus 1:2; Heb. 6:18) if nothing is impossible for Him (Mark 10:27; Luke 1:37) or whether He can create a rock too big for Him to lift. God cannot lie because He is truth, and no lie comes from Him (cf. John 14:6; 1 John 2:21). It would be contrary to His nature to lie. He cannot create a rock so big He cannot lift it because it would go against His nature as the infinite and all-powerful God.

But if God is all-powerful and good, why do we see evil? This is one of the great questions that people have wrestled with down through history. We must acknowledge that God does not avoid this question: He says that natural disasters come from Him (Lam. 3:37-38; Amos 3:6). God does not shift the blame for our difficulties to some outside cause that is beyond His control. He could instantly stop the evil that we see in the world now, but He allows it without causing it (cf. Jas. 1:13-14).

Although He uses the troubles of this world for good (Gen. 50:20; Rom. 8:28), we do not fully understand this. Different theologians have emphasized different answers to this question, but one answer that we must completely reject is that God is not all-powerful. The Lord claims full sovereignty, even though we may not fully understand how that can be.

God is powerful over big things like creation and the plans of the nations (Ps. 33:6-11). God laughs when the nations rage and could dash them to pieces in a moment (2:1-12). The king's heart is in the Lord's hand, and He can turn it however He wishes. When kings, dictators, or presidents make baffling decisions that defy explanation, it may be that the Lord is working to prevent some great tragedy that we could not foresee. Who knows how history would have been different if Napoleon or Hitler had not tried to invade Russia? When unexpected events or weather change world events, that is also the Lord. Who knows how history would have been different if Cortes had not been preceded by an eclipse in Mexico in 1519, which the Aztecs interpreted as a heavenly sign?

The Lord is also in control of small things like sparrows and the hairs of our head (Matt. 10:29-31). He cares about our personal lives, not just the grand movements of history. He is in control of seemingly random events (Prov. 16:33) and parking spots. He even orchestrates events that impact us that we do not even know about! An annoying red light might prevent us from being in the wrong place at the wrong time several moments later when a drunk driver runs a red light several blocks away. We do not realize God has protected us, because we are a safe distance away and never even see him.

God is all-powerful. He created all things and upholds everything. He can bless His people beyond what we can even imagine. He rules over all creation, powerful nations, and the tiniest details of our lives. Therefore, we need not fear our circumstances.

TOPICS FOR NEXT QUARTER

December 7

The Glory of the Lord
Exodus 33:12-23

December 14

God's Glory in the Tabernacle
Exodus 40:1-11, 34-38

December 21

God's Glory in the Coming Christ (Christmas)
Isaiah 9:1-7

December 28

No One Is like God
Isaiah 40:21-31

January 4

Jesus Cleanses God's House
John 2:13-17

January 11

Worshipping God in His Sanctuary
1 Chronicles 16:23-33

January 18

Isaiah's Glimpse of God's Throne
Isaiah 6:1-13

January 25

God's Dwelling on High
Psalm 113:1-9

February 1

Solomon's Dedication Prayer
1 Kings 8:22-30

February 8

Holy as I Am Holy
Leviticus 19:1-4, 9-18

February 15

Holy Conduct
1 Peter 1:14-17

February 22

Run toward Holiness
Hebrews 12:1-17

PARAGRAPHS ON PLACES AND PEOPLE

EGYPT

God sent Joseph to Egypt to save many lives, though this was not obvious for years (cf. Gen. 50:20). In Egypt, the family of Jacob grew tremendously (Ex. 1:6-9). The pharaoh treated Israel terribly, and God used Moses and powerful plagues to deliver Israel.

Throughout the Old Testament, God issued many warnings against going back to Egypt. Returning to Egypt became a symbol of turning away from God and looking instead for earthly help (cf. Isa. 30:1-5). When the Babylonian army came against Judah, some of the people fled to Egypt. They even forced the prophet Jeremiah to come with them, despite his warnings (cf. Jer. 43:5-7). However, this did not bring them the safety they desired.

Despite the themes connecting Egypt and judgment, Isaiah shockingly prophesied that one day Israel, Egypt, and Assyria would all be God's people (Isa. 19:23-24).

JACOB'S WELL

Jesus met the Samaritan woman in John 4 at Jacob's well. Where was this? Although Genesis records Abraham and Isaac digging wells (Gen. 21:22-34; 26:18-33), there is no record of Jacob digging a well.

Some speculate that it was the well where Jacob met Rachel and Leah (cf. Gen. 29). Tour guides are happy to show you the presumed location of Jacob's well in modern-day Nablus, forty-nine miles from Jerusalem, but that location is also not certain. The living water Jesus gives is more important than the location of Jacob's well.

NATHANAEL

Before his first encounter with Jesus, Nathanael, also known as Bartholomew (cf. Matt. 10:3; Acts 1:13), showed some prejudice, wondering if anything good could come out of Nazareth (John 1:46). But he was curious enough to follow Philip and meet Jesus. He was quick to believe Jesus was the Son of God and King of Israel (vss. 43-51). He was also by the sea when Jesus restored Peter (21:2), but Scripture says little else.

Early church tradition reports that Nathanael traveled widely after Jesus' ascension, reaching as far as India according to Eusebius and Jerome. He is also said to have later traveled to Eastern Europe, and he was likely martyred in Armenia, Romania, or Azerbaijan. (There are conflicting accounts.)

BARNABAS

A Levite from Cyprus, Joseph, better known as Barnabas, sold a field and laid the money at the apostles' feet (Acts 4:36). This was only the beginning of his service to Christ's church. The Lord used him mightily, and he was the one who brought Paul to Antioch, one of the early centers of Christianity, after Paul's conversion (11:22-30).

Later, he traveled with Paul as a missionary for some time (13:2—14:28). However, the duo separated over the issue of whether to take John Mark with them on a missionary journey, since he had deserted them previously (15:36-41). Years later, Paul acknowledged that Mark was useful (2 Tim. 4:11), so Barnabas apparently discipled Mark effectively. Although not perfect (cf. Gal. 2:13), Barnabas was a godly, influential leader in the early church.

—Tom Greene

Daily Bible Readings for Home Study and Worship

(Readings are for the week previous to the lesson topics.)

1. September 7. In the Beginning

M—God Made Everything. Ps. 8:1-9.
T—God Controls Creation. Job 38:12-21.
W—Clothed in Majesty. Ps. 104:1-9.
T—The Source of All Life. Ps. 104:24-30.
F—New Creation Coming. Isa. 42:5-9.
S—New Creation in Christ. 2 Cor. 4:1-7.
S—Creation of Heaven and Earth. Gen. 1:1-13.

2. September 14. Before All Things

M—God's Firstborn. Ps. 89:19-29.
T—God's Dwelling Place. 1 Kgs. 8:12-19, 27.
W—A Better Dwelling Place. Hag. 1:7-8; 2:1-9.
T—God Dwelt among Us. John 1:14-18.
F—King of All Things. Heb. 2:5-10.
S—God Dwells in His Church. Eph. 2:11-22.
S—The Purpose of All Creation. Col. 1:15-23.

3. September 21. In Heaven and Earth

M—Foretelling Israel's Fall. Deut. 31:24-29.
T—False Hope. Jer. 23:9-15.
W—False Prophets. Ezek. 13:1-9.
T—False Peace. Ezek. 13:10-16.
F—Hope for a Sinful People. Isa. 57:15-21.
S—The Nearness of God. Acts 17:24-31.
S—God Fills Heaven and Earth. Jer. 23:18-24.

4. September 28. Nothing Is Hidden from God

M—Kept by God. Ps. 121:1-8.
T—Overwhelmed by God's Presence. Job 42:1-6.
W—Exposed to God's Sight. Heb. 4:11-16.
T—God's Watchfulness. Ps. 33:13-22.
F—God Knows Our Needs. Matt. 6:5-8.
S—Praising God's Wisdom. Rom. 11:33-36.
S—God Is Everywhere. Ps. 139:1-16.

5. October 5. God Warns Pharaoh through Dreams

M—The Source of All Knowledge. Dan. 2:17-24.
T—Revealer of Mysteries. Dan. 2:25-30.
W—The Providence of God. Gen. 50:15-21.
T—Interpreting Two Dreams. Gen. 40:1-15.
F—Joseph Forgotten. Gen. 40:16-23.
S—Pharaoh's Dream. Gen. 41:14-24.
S—God's Purpose Unfolds. Gen. 41:25-36.

6. October 12. God Sees Our Hearts

M—Caring for the Poor. Deut. 15:1-11.
T—Judgment on Presumption. Lev. 10:1-11.
W—Judgment on Greed. Josh. 7:10-26.
T—Judgment on Irreverence. 1 Chr. 13:5-12; 15:11-13.
F—Judgment and Deliverance. Ps. 34:11-22.
S—Principles for Giving. 2 Cor. 8:1-15.
S—Fear the Lord. Acts 4:32—5:11.

7. October 19. God Sees Nathanael

M—Jesus Knows All People. John 2:23-25.
T—Jesus Is the Son of God. Matt. 16:13-20.
W—Heaven Opened to Jacob. Gen. 28:10-17.
T—Heaven Opened to Jesus. Matt. 3:13-17.
F—The Glory of the Son of Man. Luke 9:26-36.
S—Finding the Messiah. John 1:35-42.
S—Son of God and Son of Man. John 1:43-51.

8. October 26. God Sees the Samaritan Woman

M—Water for Israel. Ex. 17:1-7.
T—Sustained in the Wilderness. Neh. 9:15-21.
W—Wells of Salvation. Isa. 12:1-6.
T—The Fountain of Living Water. Jer. 2:9-13.
F—Jesus Gives the Holy Spirit. John 7:37-39.
S—Comforted by God's Knowledge. Ps. 56:8-11.
S—Jesus Gives Living Water. John 4:5-19, 28-29.

9. November 2. Power to Impart Wisdom

M—Wisdom before Creation. Prov. 8:12, 22-31.
T—Unexpected Deliverance. Isa. 63:15—64:4.
W—What the Spirit Reveals. Eph. 1:15-21.
T—Born of the Spirit. John 3:1-8.
F—We Have the Truth. 1 John 2:18-27.
S—Christ Is Our Wisdom. 1 Cor. 1:18-31.
S—The Spirit Gives Us Wisdom. 1 Cor. 2:6-16.

10. November 9. Parting the Red Sea

M—God's Steadfast Love. Ps. 136:1-16.
T—Lord of Heaven and Earth. Josh. 2:8-11.
W—No Other Savior. Isa. 43:1-13.
T—Making a Way. Isa. 43:16-21.
F—Delivered through Water. Ps. 18:13-19.
S—Wait for God's Salvation. Ex. 5:15—6:1.
S—God's Power to Save. Ex. 14:10-22.

11. November 16. Jesus Calms a Storm

M—God Is Sovereign over Creation. Ps. 135:1-7.
T—God Calms the Sea. Jonah 1:4-16.
W—God Stills a Storm. Ps. 107:23-32.
T—Paul in a Storm. Acts 27:13-26.
F—God Preserves Paul. Acts 27:27-44.
S—We Will Not Fear. Ps. 46:1-11.
S—The Power of Jesus' Words. Mark 4:35-41.

12. November 23. Jesus Casts Out Legion

M—Jesus' Authority over Demons. Mark 1:21-28.
T—Demons Recognize Jesus. Mark 3:7-12.
W—Binding Satan. Mark 3:22-27.
T—Defeating Satan. Rev. 20:1-10.
F—A Sinner's Reaction to Jesus. Luke 5:1-11.
S—Declaring What God Has Done. Ps. 145:4-12.
S—Freeing a Captive from Satan. Mark 5:1-20.

13. November 30. Who Is like God?

M—Tremble before the Messiah. Ps. 2:1-12.
T—God's Mighty Works. Ps. 89:5-18.
W—The Song of Moses. Ex. 15:1-18.
T—The Futility of Idols. Jer. 10:1-10.
F—God Governs the Earth. Jer. 10:11-25.
S—All Nations Will Worship God. Rev. 15:2-4.
S—The Greatness of God. Isa. 40:12-17.

REVIEW

What have you learned this quarter?

Can you answer these questions?

God Is "All" That

UNIT 1: God Is Always Present

September 7

In the Beginning

1. What was the first action God performed in Genesis 1?
2. What did God do to the earth so that it was no longer without form and void?
3. What is significant about the Spirit of God moving over the face of the waters?
4. In Genesis 1, what always immediately followed God seeing something?
5. How did days 1, 2, and 3 of Creation relate to days 4, 5, and 6?

September 14

Before All Things

1. How does Christ's identity as the "image of the invisible God" affect humanity (Col. 1:15)?
2. What are the "thrones," "dominions," "principalities," and "powers" Christ created (vs. 16)?
3. How does Christ's resurrection relate to His identity as the Head of the church?
4. What does the wedding imagery in verse 22 tell us about the goal of Christ's reconciliation?
5. What must believers do to ensure their faith is "grounded and settled" (vs. 23)?

September 21

In Heaven and Earth

1. What did Jeremiah say was wrong with the false prophets?
2. What did Jeremiah understand about Israel's future that none of the false prophets did?
3. What was the "whirlwind" Jeremiah prophesied about (Jer. 23:19)?
4. What misconception about His presence did God address in verse 23?
5. What was the false prophets' fatal flaw?

September 28

Nothing Is Hidden from God

1. How did David describe God's knowledge of him?
2. What did David say to anyone trying to escape God?
3. What is one reason that every human life is precious?
4. When did David say God began caring for him?

UNIT 2: God Is All-Knowing

October 5

God Warns Pharaoh through Dreams

1. Why were dreams important to ancient Egyptians?
2. What did the fourteen cows and fourteen ears of wheat in Pharaoh's dream represent?
3. What did the doubling of Pharaoh's dream signify?
4. How did deliverance from the famine impact the larger redemptive story of Scripture?

October 12

God Sees Our Hearts

1. Why did the early church demonstrate extraordinary care for one another?
2. What societal benefits occurred because of the church's mindset?

3. What was the issue that caused Ananias and Sapphira's gift to be rejected?
4. What happened as a result of Ananias's judgment?

October 19

God Sees Nathanael

1. What was Philip's immediate reaction to Jesus' call?
2. How did Philip respond to Nathanael's skepticism?
3. What convinced Nathanael of Jesus' identity?
4. What did it mean that Nathanael would see angels ascending and descending on Jesus?

October 26

God Sees the Samaritan Woman

1. How was Jesus' meeting with the Samaritan woman significant for the early church?
2. Why was it unusual that Jesus spoke with the Samaritan woman?
3. What was special about the water that Jesus offered to the Samaritan woman?
4. What was the woman's conclusion when Jesus described details of her personal life?

UNIT 3: God Is All-Powerful

November 2

Power to Impart Wisdom

1. Why did the Corinthians not recognize the wisdom of Paul's message about the cross?
2. What is the purpose of our experience of the Holy Spirit?
3. What does it mean to "know the things that are freely given to us of God" (1 Cor. 2:12)?
4. What was the content of Paul's "spiritual" message (vs. 13)?

November 9

Parting the Red Sea

1. How did the Israelites respond when they saw the Egyptians pursuing them?
2. How did Moses respond to the Israelites' fear?
3. Why did God let the Egyptians follow the Israelites into the divided sea?
4. What two previous acts of God were echoed in the parting of the Red Sea?

November 16

Jesus Calms a Storm

1. Why were the disciples caught in the storm?
2. What did Jesus falling asleep demonstrate?
3. What did Jesus' calming of the storm demonstrate?
4. What is the main point of this story?

November 23

Jesus Casts Out Legion

1. Why could the demon-possessed man not be restrained previously?
2. What was unusual about Jesus casting out these demons?
3. Why *might* the demons have driven the pigs into the sea?
4. Why *might* Jesus have allowed the demons to drive the pigs into the sea?

November 30

Who Is like God?

1. How does Isaiah imitate Genesis 1?
2. Why did Isaiah use language from a familiar Babylonian prayer?
3. How does Israel's history magnify God's might over the nations?
4. Which resources of Lebanon fell short before God?